The Grammar of Time

Kreuzer offers guidance to scholars looking to comparative historical analysis (CHA) for the tools to analyze macro-historical questions. Like history, CHA uses the past to formulate research questions, describe social transformations, and generate inductive insights. Like social science, CHA compares those patterns to explicate generalizable and testable theories. It operates in two different worlds – one constantly changing and full of cultural particularities, another static and full of orderly uniformities. CHA draws attention to the ontological constructions of these worlds; how scholars background historical and geographic particularities to create a social reality orderly enough for theorizing, while others foreground those particularities to re-complexify it and generate new inductive insights. CHA engages in ontological triage, dialogue between exploration and confirmation, and conversation on how to translate test results into genuine answers. This book is supplemented by online materials that include a glossary, diagnostic quizzes, advanced exercises, and annotated bibliography.

Marcus Kreuzer is Professor of Political Science at Villanova University. His research builds a bridge between the worlds of history and social science methodology. His earlier research focused on the nineteenth-century origins of modern democracy and the role party systems played in the consolidation of interwar and post-communist democracies. His subsequent work on comparative historical methodology has won several best paper awards from the American Political Science Association. He also regularly teaches CHA at various methods schools.

Methods for Social Inquiry

Editors

Colin Elman, Syracuse University
Diana Kapiszewski, Georgetown University
James Mahoney, Northwestern University

The *Methods for Social Inquiry* series comprises compact texts offering practical instructions for qualitative and multi-method research. Each book is accompanied by pedagogical data and exercises.

The books in the series offer clear, straightforward, and concrete guidance for teaching and using methods. While grounded in their relevant prescriptive logics, the books focus on the "how-to" of the methods they discuss – the practical tasks that must be undertaken to effectively employ them. The books should be useful for instruction at both advanced undergraduate and graduate levels.

The books are tightly integrated with digital content and online enhancements through the Qualitative Data Repository (QDR). QDR is a new NSF-funded repository housing digital data used in qualitative and multi-method social inquiry. The pedagogical data (and related documentation) that accompany the books in the series will be housed in QDR.

Books in the series
Oana, Ioana-Elena, Schneider, Carsten Q. and Thomann, Eva, *Qualitative Comparative Analysis Using R: A Beginner's Guide*
Cyr, Jennifer, *Focus Groups for the Social Science Researcher*

The Grammar of Time

A Toolbox for Comparative Historical Analysis

Marcus Kreuzer

Villanova University

CAMBRIDGE
UNIVERSITY PRESS

CAMBRIDGE
UNIVERSITY PRESS

Shaftesbury Road, Cambridge CB2 8EA, United Kingdom

One Liberty Plaza, 20th Floor, New York, NY 10006, USA

477 Williamstown Road, Port Melbourne, VIC 3207, Australia

314–321, 3rd Floor, Plot 3, Splendor Forum, Jasola District Centre, New Delhi – 110025, India

103 Penang Road, #05–06/07, Visioncrest Commercial, Singapore 238467

Cambridge University Press is part of Cambridge University Press & Assessment, a department of the University of Cambridge.

We share the University's mission to contribute to society through the pursuit of education, learning and research at the highest international levels of excellence.

www.cambridge.org
Information on this title: www.cambridge.org/highereducation/isbn/9781108483780

DOI: 10.1017/9781108652728

First published 2023

A catalogue record for this publication is available from the British Library.

Library of Congress Cataloging-in-Publication Data
Names: Kreuzer, Marcus, 1964– author.
Title: The grammar of time : a toolbox for comparative historical analysis / Marcus Kreuzer, Villanova University, Pennsylvania.
Description: Cambridge, United Kingdom ; New York, NY : Cambridge University Press, [2023] | Series: Methods for social inquiry | Includes bibliographical references and index.
Identifiers: LCCN 2022049029 (print) | LCCN 2022049030 (ebook) | ISBN 9781108483780 (hardback) | ISBN 9781108718233 (paperback) | ISBN 9781108652728 (epub)
Subjects: LCSH: Social sciences–Research–Methodology. | Event history analysis. | Time–Sociological aspects.
Classification: LCC H61 .K676 2023 (print) | LCC H61 (ebook) | DDC 300.72–dc23/eng/ 20221013
LC record available at https://lccn.loc.gov/2022049029
LC ebook record available at https://lccn.loc.gov/2022049030

ISBN 978-1-108-48378-0 Hardback
ISBN 978-1-108-71823-3 Paperback

Additional resources for this at www.cambridge.org/kreuzer

Contents

Figures

Tables

Acknowledgments

Writing this book was a humbling experience, as it made me realize how much I depended on others to help me articulate my thoughts. My thanks are therefore numerous.

Several books – exploring the outer perimeters of social science methodology – helped me situate comparative historical analysis (CHA). Stephen Kern's *Culture of Time and Space, 1880–1919* (1983) and *Cultural History of Causality* (2004) discuss the historical construction of time, space, and causality – three building blocks of CHA – thus offering a counterpoint to their otherwise often reified treatment in standard textbooks. Howard Becker's *Tricks of the Trade* (1998) and *Telling about Society* (2007), Andrew Abbott's *Methods of Discovery* (2004) and *Digital Paper* (2016), Stuart Firestein's *Ignorance* (2012) and *Failure* (2015), and Giovanni Sartori's writings (1970) on conceptualization explore the messier and more exploratory aspects of social inquiry. They recognized that sleuthing is required to discover new evidence, that closely parsing texts helps develop clearer concepts, and that a dose of adventurism is indispensable to escape from the cul-de-sacs into which research invariable lures scholars. Most importantly, they celebrate those messier elements of social inquiry as being essential to engage with the real world. They stand for a more pragmatic, less math-centered, maybe even older, but increasingly marginalized understanding of social science that has, thank God, survived and flourishes in CHA.

Turning the broad inspiration these books provided into practical research advice required integrating insights from far-flung literatures and navigating a messy terminological terrain. Not surprisingly, my drafts took many wrong turns, were too snarky in tone, and would never have progressed were it not for the kindness, generosity, and thoughtfulness of many colleagues. I would like to thank Amel Ahmed, Pablo Andrade, Janice Bially-Matter, Sarah Busch, Ali Cirone, Tasha Fairfield, Michael Findley, Marc Gallichio, Laura Garcia, Jakob Gerner Hariri, Kendra Koivu, Alan Jacobs, Jeffrey Johnson, Jan Klenke, Erik Kuhonta, Leontin Loeber, Tomila Lankina, Per Lindgard, Johannes Lindvall, Jørgen Møller, David Nickerson, Craig Parsons, Mark Pollack, Carsten Schneider, Jason Seawright, Deborah Seligsohn, Svend-Erik Skaaning, Emily and David Skarbek, Hillel Soifer, Paul Steege, Antonio Tavares, and Sean Yom for their helpful comments. My research assistant Raymond Horchos provided helpful feedback for the exercises. I also am grateful to Lund University, the University of Gothenburg, Aarhus University, Temple University, and Cornell University, as well as to the George Mason University's Mercatus Center for inviting me to present chapters. Finally, special thanks go to Christine Trampusch, Florian Fastenrath, and the Cologne Center for Comparative Politics for hosting me to teach a CHA course to their graduate students.

Particularly heartful thanks go to Colin Elman, Diana Kapiszewski, John Gerring, and James Mahoney for noticing my fondness for all things historical, inviting me to write this book, and letting me test-run its ideas at the Institute for Qualitative and Multi-Method Research IQMR Authors' Weekend. You are as tough in the seminar room as you are kind-hearted over drinks at Lemon Grass; nobody offers more constructive feedback. Manuela Tecusan from Cambridge University Press did a superb job copy-editing the manuscript. I am grateful to Stathis Kalyvas for inviting me to present at Oxford, and also for our long-standing conversations about how to insert history more effectively into social science. I would like to thank Jennifer Dixon, Gerry Munck, Richard Bensel, Steven Wilson, and Jason Wittenberg for their thoughtful comments on several drafts of these chapters. Robert DeFina is the most widely read social scientist whom I know; he helped me work through the complexities of Bayesian process in a jointly authored paper (still unpublished). Jennifer Dixon deserves an additional shout-out for sending interesting readings that added innumerable nuances. I will forever be indebted to so many bookish and generous colleagues. A bittersweet thank you goes to Mark Zacher, who passed away in 2014. He hired me as an undergraduate research assistant and, over pitchers of beer in the faculty club at the University of British Columbia, he brought me out of my shell and set me on a path of continuous fulfillment. My biggest thank you goes to my IQMR and European Consortium for Political Research (ECPR) students, who patiently read earlier drafts and whose feedback improved them immeasurably.

At Villanova University, I am grateful to Dean Adele Lindenmeyr for giving me research leave that allowed me to finish a draft before my impending chair responsibilities kicked in; to Emily Carson, Director of the Faculty Writing Program, for her insightful feedback on the penultimate draft; and to the university's Augustinian heritage, which values interdisciplinarity and supports a community in which complex ideas have time to mature and are sheltered from our "publish or perish" culture. Working at an institution with traditions strong enough to withstand the present-day neoliberal, bibliometric pressures has been a privilege.

Outside academia, John O'Rourke has tried to make sense of this "book thing" of mine by comparing it to a legal brief, the closest equivalent his private sector mind could conjure up. This less than perfect analogy might explain why he remained puzzled over its slow completion. But he nevertheless cheered me on, as if writing were the same as one of our long, grinding tennis rallies. And, as it turns out, over many stretches it is. Daisy and Copper kept me safe from squirrels, rabbits, and any other wildlife that threatened to distract me from my writing as I sat in our backyard. My parents and my brother supported me, as always, from afar. Finally, my most profound thanks go to my family, Pam, Lucas, and Julia, who got excited when the writing progressed and were supportive when I struggled. Each contributed in their own idiosyncratic ways. Pam's genealogical forays made me appreciate the indispensability of sleuthing skills to penetrating the past. Julia's discussion about complex adaptive environmental systems let me realize the parallels between *her* natural history and *my* human history. Lucas allowed me to test-run my ideas on his honors thesis on the deindustrialization of rural Ohio and became my editor-in-chief. But, most importantly, Pam, Lucas, and Julia redirected my attention to things outside my narrow professional world. For all of this, I am grateful every day to have you as my loving family.

Reprint Permission

Introduction
How to Study a Disorderly World in an Orderly Fashion

It is easy to get results, but difficult to get answers.

(Aschwande 2015)

These are tumultuous times, yet again: a failed insurrection in the world's oldest democracy, a pandemic costing lives and disrupting global supply chains, an ascending China altering geopolitical dynamics, and global warming threatening our very planet. What makes understanding our present so challenging is its constantly changing and hence historical nature. And it has not slowed down much since Karl Marx and Friedrich Engels – describing nineteenth-century capitalism – wrote in their *Communist Manifesto*: "all fixed, fast-frozen relations . . . are swept away; all new formed ones become antiquated before they can ossify. All solid melts into air."[1] History transforms not only our world but also our research agendas. History thus requires close attention.

This book offers social scientists who work with comparative historical analysis (CHA) guidance on how to leverage the methodological riches of history. Like historians, CHA scholars use the past to formulate research questions, describe complex social processes, and generate new inductive insights. And, like social scientists, they compare those patterns to formulate generalizable and testable theories. CHA builds a bridge between the fascinating but disorderly world of history – which historians explore – and the slightly blander but more orderly world of methodology – which social scientists construct to test hypotheses. And CHA builds this bridge between exploration and testing to translate results into answers.

CHA's dual emphasis on exploring and testing reflects its problem-driven nature and resulting commitment to put questions before methods. It creates an intellectually vibrant community, united by the belief that the noise chronicled by daily headlines is more readily understood when placed in a longer-term historical context. It shares the conviction that history, despite its noisiness, is just as knowledge-generating as the rigors of math. Yet this community lacks a synthesis of the different ways its members leverage history's methodological riches. Several factors contribute to this gap.

[1] Marx and Engels (1986), 83.

With devotees in sociology, political science, economics, and history, CHA is spoken in different vernaculars that frequently require translation for us to realize that, for example, an exogeneous shock in economics, a critical juncture in political science, an event in sociology, and discontinuity in history all refer to the same thing – a moment of historical change. CHA also engages in the ontological triage necessary to facilitate the conversation between history and social science, between exploration and testing. This triage involves aligning methods, which prefer an orderly, stationary, and more math-friendly world, with history, which is disorderly and full of moving objects, and thus requires more interpretivist sensibilities. Understanding the methodological implications of using history ultimately necessitates explicating a grammar of time.

The grammar analogy is meant to highlight several features of CHA. Grammars analyze cultural phenomena – language – that emerged independently of one another in different places. The same goes for CHA. It established itself in different disciplines independent of one another and therefore subsumes different traditions that are distinct without necessarily being unique. Grammars also incorporate time to capture change. The conjugation of verbs differentiates degrees of the past and their relationship to the present and the future. And the past perfect tense even makes the past come alive by identifying activities that were *ongoing in* the past rather than having just *occurred in* the past. Grammars also consider geography, since their rules vary with each language. And etymology, a cognate discipline of grammar, recognizes that language itself is a changing and hence historical phenomenon. Finally, learning grammars is peculiar because it involves understanding more systematically what we already mastered intuitively. It requires paying attention to the scaffold of language, which neither is particularly elegant nor serves many uses after we have learned a language.

Readers may wonder why they should learn a semi-orderly grammar of time when they could invest in more highly valued statistical skills. To those readers I can only reply, "just bear with me," as you will be introduced to a research tradition that has thrived for almost two centuries, has produced numerous classics, and complements existing methodologies. CHA pays particular attention to the pre-testing stage of the research process: this stage involves description, conceptualization, formulating questions, and theorizing, which produce test-worthy hypotheses. The function the pre-testing stage plays in social inquiry has been discounted in recent years, as attention has shifted to ever more complex causal inference strategies. CHA offers a corrective to this trend by ensuring that our ability to produce answers keeps up with our capacity to generate results.

To readers who are still skeptical of CHA's methodological contributions, let me preview the three central ones presented in this book. First, CHA uses distinct exploratory tools and leverages history for inductive insights. It employs what historians call *historical thinking* to figure out what is going on, look for interesting patterns, formulate new research questions, and update existing foreknowledge. Second, CHA is very attentive to *time* and employs a distinct temporal vocabulary, which is essential for studying the unfolding of historical processes. Third, CHA embraces a *heterodox conception of methodology* that configures the exploratory and confirmatory stages of the research process into distinct strands.

I.1 Historical Thinking

There are numerous everyday reasons to be interested in history. Historians tell good and insightful stories. Their work appeals to our curiosity as to where our families, communities, nations came from, what obstacles they overcame, and how their past shaped their present. Historians offer a second, more polished draft of history, which clarifies the first one, typically still very noisy, written by journalists and contextualizing our rapidly changing world.

But there are also methodological reasons to be interested in history; and it is on these methodological offerings that the book focuses. CHA treats the *past as a domain of discovery* and uses the inductive insight that the past offers to update theories. It treats theories as frozen distillations of past historical experiences and historiographical insights. They function like probability distributions, which assume that history repeats itself and that yesterday's distributions provide inferential guidance for explaining tomorrow's events. Theories thus have a stationary, frozen quality that limits their capacity to address new historical phenomena. History protects theories from their potential obsolescence by unfreezing the past and looking at social reality in its full – but only partially explored – disorderliness. History offers social scientists what the telescope offers astronomers: an instrument for us to look outward from where we stand and discover new things that the myopia of our naked theoretical eye misses. It allowed, for example, international relations scholars to realize that their realist bipolar models became increasingly anachronistic after the end of the Cold War.

CHA leverages the exploratory potential of the past through *historical thinking* (Wineburg 2001). Historical thinking uses the past to ascertain whether the latest headline is something unprecedently new, whether it is a mutation that rhymes with earlier events, or whether it is something that repeats itself, and, if so, for how long. It uses the past to enter an ontological universe where history – backgrounded and frozen by theories and methods – comes alive and can be explored. It leverages dates to compare the past with the present, to look for patterns, generate new questions, or update older ones, by now potentially obsolete. Historical thinking also pays attention to geography by probing whether a phenomenon is exceptional and geographically bounded or universal and uniform across geography.

CHA borrows the historical and geographic sensibilities of historical thinking to build a bridge between a constantly changing, inescapably historical world and a largely static, history-free methodological apparatus employed to study it. It realizes that building this bridge requires attention to the ontological assumptions embedded in theories and methods that scholars bring to a research question, and also to the ontological properties of the phenomenon under study. *Different methods permit answering different questions, and different questions require different methods.* The proper alignment of questions and methods necessitates close attention to ontological matters. CHA is mindful of such matters because it starts from the default assumption that God assigned all the easy research questions to physicists (Berstein et al. 2000), thus allowing them to translate their orderly and historyless world into elegant mathematical theorems without having to worry about any ontological translation problems. CHA, however, does not fret about having drawn the short straw when God assigned research topics, but instead delights in exploring this disorderly world in much of its complexity, even if this means engaging in ontological triage. CHA makes such exploration an integral part of the research process, because studying a constantly changing world requires continuously updating your research questions.

I.2 Temporal Vocabulary

Thinking historically invariably requires paying attention to time. And understanding time is necessary for analyzing phenomena that move through time and thereby become qualitatively transformed by it. CHA's attention to time is arguably its most distinguishing but also its most complicating feature. It is complicating because time is elusive, frequently banished behind ceteris paribus assumptions, and thus becomes too frozen to be explored. CHA confronts these challenges by using a precise temporal vocabulary to navigate the complexities of an unfrozen history and leveraging data visualizations to discern temporal patterns more readily. It thus taps into a long-standing tradition, exemplified by Charles Minard's 1869 graph of Napoleon's ill-fated 1812 Russian campaign (see Figure I.1). This deservedly famous graph offers a helpful initial survey of CHA's temporal vocabulary, on which the three opening chapters elaborate. Readers, particularly those unfamiliar with historical thinking, will thus require a bit of patience to develop their temporal literacy.

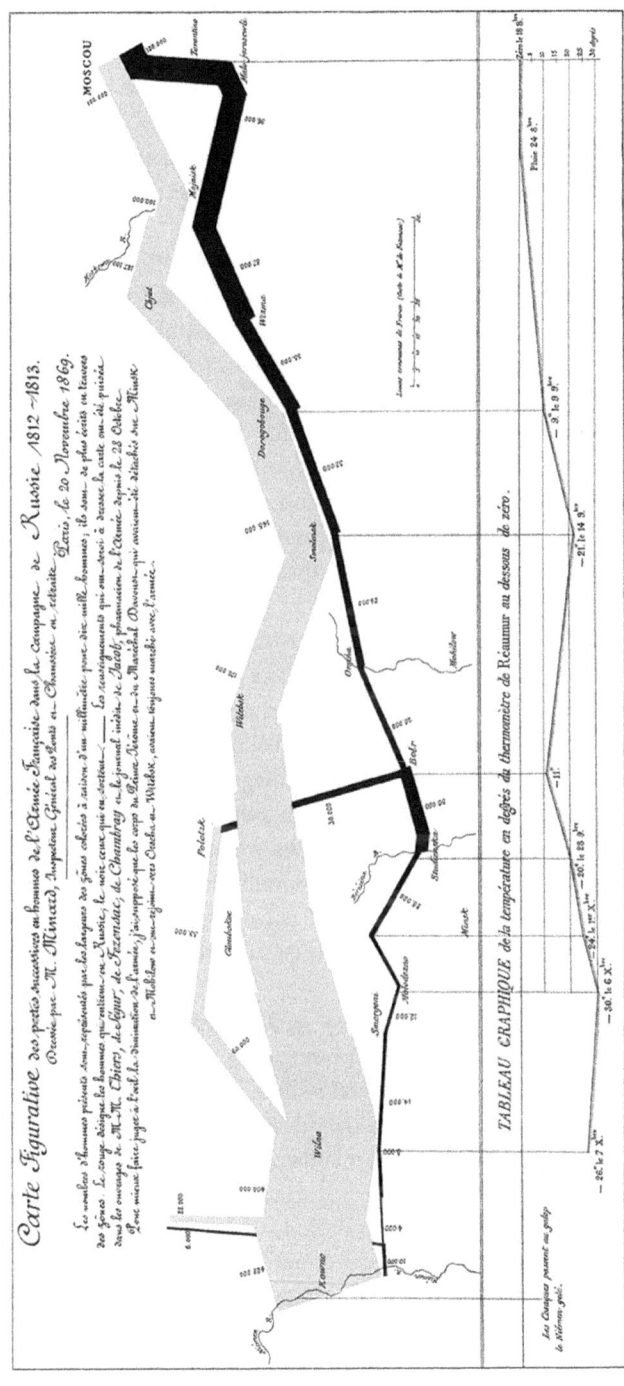

Figure I.1 Carte figurative des pertes successives en hommes de l'armée française dans la Campagne de Russie 1812–13 (comparées à celle d'Hannibal durant la 2ème Guerre Punique) / Minard. Régnier & Dourdet by Minard, Charles-Joseph (1781–1870). Fonction indéterminée – 1869. National Library of France, France.

At the height of his power, Napoleon assembled 685,000 soldiers, the largest army to have been mobilized up to that point in history, to march eastward, land a decisive blow on Russia, and cement France's hegemony in Europe. The campaign proved disastrous: within a year, 500,000 of these soldiers had perished, Napoleon had abdicated his throne and remained exiled on the island of Elba, and France had lost its military dominance. Napoleon's Russian campaign is one of those historical turning points that CHA loves to study.

CHA draws on *historical time* to analyze such key moments. Historical time is closely linked to two fundamental questions that CHA shares with historians: on what dates did an event or series of events occur, and what patterns do they form? To identify patterns, CHA asks a series of follow-up questions. How much or how little continuity is there between events in a set? What events are linked to discontinuities? Do events converge across different geographic units of analysis? And what notion of causality is appropriate for explaining historical transformations? The common denominator of these questions is the effort to explicate patterns from moving objects, to describe how the past differs from the present, and thereby to understand the most elusive of social phenomena: change.

Historians typically answer such questions with thick narratives – highly contextualized accounts retracing causal processes across multiple events – while CHA scholars are more theoretical and use data visualizations whenever possible. Minard, while not a card-carrying CHA scholar himself, provides such a visualization. He uses a so-called Sankey diagram, a sideway funnel, to track the shrinking size of the French army. This diagram is plotted against several events, indicated by the names of towns where military action took place, that connect the past – the wide brown mouth of funnel indicating the start of the campaign – with the present – the narrow black tail indicating its end. Arrayed in this way, the events create a quasi-chronology that replaces the dates of a traditional timeline.

This timeline highlights three qualities of historical time. First, it is anchored in dates that order events chronologically and thereby construct the historical process by connecting the past with the present. Second, Minard lumps the events into two broad phases: the advance, indicated by the brown segment of the funnel; and the retreat, symbolized by the black segment. Such truncations of historical processes, what historians call periodizations, make the past more legible by breaking it into periods of continuity, in which the past stays unchanged, and periods of discontinuity, in which the past qualitatively changes. These two phases are relevant because they convey information about Napoleon's changing military fortunes. Those fortunes become even clearer if we extend the time horizon beyond what Minard's graph shows. We can frontend it with France's military power before the campaign and bookend it with the loss of France's hegemony after. Third, historical time views changes through time as irreversible because history does not repeat itself, even though it might, as Mark Twain pointed out, rhyme on occasion. France's military hegemony on the continent was gone for good after Napoleon's defeat, which marked a historical and permanent qualitative transformation.

Historical time focuses on the qualitative breaks that help us understand how the past is different from the present. It is less adept at capturing the five elements that mark the rhythms at which historical time unfolds: tempo, duration, timing, sequences, and stages. These elements make up *physical time* because they have context-independent and clock-like temporal characteristics that give them a material or physical-like quality. Historical and physical time complement each other. Historical time does not always unfold in a linear fashion but quickens its pace, stops for a while altogether, begins at a different starting point, changes the order of events, or is more disciplined and sticks to a specific sequence. Physical time draws attention to these rhythmic, non-linear qualities of historical time and, as Chapter 7 discusses, to complex non-linear causal dynamics.

Minard's graph captures the rhythmic, physical time elements of Napoleon's ill-fated campaign in several ways. The Sankey diagram tracks the dwindling size of his army as well as the slow tempo with which Napoleon lost his soldiers. This slowness reflects Russia's scorched earth strategy, through which its army avoided large-scale military encounters with the French that typically produce a fast but intermittent rise in death tolls. Russians deprived the French army of potential resupplies by burning harvests and towns, and thus contributed to a slower death by starvation. And if you zoom in closely enough, you see that the death rate accelerated whenever the French army crossed a river; thus you identify drowning as another, quicker source of death. Minard's graph captures the intent of extending the duration of the military campaign so as to lure Napoleon deep into Russia, to make escaping its unforgiving winters more difficult. Minard also adds at the bottom a regular line graph for the temperature. It captures the weather element of Russia's military strategy and highlights how the sequencing – another element of physical time – of the onset of winter and of the decision to withdraw played a significant role in Napoleon's defeat.

Minard's diagram hopefully provides a first glimpse at the centrality that unfreezing historical time assumes in exploring history, that visualizations acquire in interpreting historical patterns, and that unfreezing physical time earns in analyzing temporally complex, non-linear processes.

I.3 Varieties of Comparative Historical Analysis

CHA has a distinct origin story, as it was invented in different disciplines that were independent of one another while sharing an elective affinity, in that they all employed historical thinking and paid close attention to historical and physical time. CHA cannot be traced to a sole founder, a singular notion of causality, or a formalized set of testing techniques. Instead, it owes its origins to different disciplines that analyzed the ever-changing world and required a more heterodox tool set than the one employed by frequentist, set theoretic, or experimental methods. Theda Skocpol and Margaret Somers (1980) first recognized this heterodoxy when they identified CHA's three strands: eventful, longue durée, and macro-causal analysis.[2] Each offers distinct solutions for how to configure historical and physical time, as well as description and explanation. Subsequent chapters elaborate on these strands; for now, they are summarized in Table I.1.

Eventful analysis is the most exploratory and descriptive strand of CHA. It pays particular attention to a thick version of historical time, unfreezes the past to figure out what precisely is going on, and identifies historical continuities and discontinuities. Physical time plays a more marginal role. Its causal inference strategies are a bit more difficult to pin down. It employs what several scholars call "historical explanations," which increasingly have been influenced by path dependency. Historical explanations are particularly well suited for explaining historical change. They recognize that change itself is too fluid to be easily explained and thus needs to be analytically differentiated into periods of discontinuity and periods of continuity. They explain discontinuities through a distinct set of analytical steps whose goal is to illuminate the generative process that produced a particular discontinuity. Similarly, historical explanations view continuity as something that needs to be explained rather than to be assumed, and explains it by looking for the increasing return mechanisms that reproduce a particular set of events.

Long durée analysis uses time series data and visualization tools to explore broader and longer-term, slower-moving patterns of change. It employs a refined vocabulary for differentiating among different trends that, just like Minard's graph, are particularly well suited for capturing elements of physical time. Longue durée analysis is the least developed strand in CHA and thus

---

[2] I relabel here Skocpol and Somers' original typology. I kept their macro-causal analysis label, but renamed parallel demonstration of theory 'longue durée analysis' and the contrast-oriented analysis 'eventful analysis'. This relabeling serves to better capture the temporal assumptions of the three approaches. It is also meant to reflect the evolution of CHA since Skocpol and Somers' original typology and its growing attention to time (for this evolution, see Kreuzer forthcoming).

Table I.1 Varieties of comparative historical analysis

Assumptions About	Eventful Analysis	Longue Durée Analysis	Macro-Causal Analysis
Historical Time	Very central and thick. History very unfrozen. Focus on describing (dis) continuities.	Central. History slightly frozen. Focus on describing historical trends.	Less important. History partially frozen. Focus on understanding historical boundary conditions
Physical Time	Limited importance.	Important. Served to differentiate the rhythms of trends.	Important. Used as an explanatory factor.
Description vs. Explaining	Thick descriptive. Employs historical explanations, path dependency.	Thin descriptive, data visualization. No clear explanatory frame.	Description confined to updating theories. Focus on causal process tracing.
Example	Skocpol *Protecting Mother and Soldiers* (1995)	Skocpol *Diminished Democracy* (2013)	Skocpol *States and Social Revolutions* (1979)

CHA employs three distinct strands that can be differentiated according to the notions of time they employ and how they balance exploration and explanation. The examples point out that Skocpol uses all three strands across her different projects, thus underscoring CHA's commitment to align methods with questions.

lacks a well-established causal inference strategy. It is most widely used by economic historians, demographers, and environmental historians. At times, longue durée analysis favors evolutionary explanations or draws on complexity theory. CHA scholars view such theories skeptically, because they are difficult to distinguish from ahistorical functionalist explanations.

Macro-causal analysis, in turn, is the most established strand in CHA. It unfreezes physical time to foreground the causal effects of tempo, duration, timing, and sequencing. It points out that these causal effects are non-linear and require close attention to causal processes themselves – processes that are backgrounded by more traditional, linear notions of causality. Macro-causal analysis employs theorizing to update existing explanations and thereby constructs stronger empirical tests. It explains cross-sectional variations by developing historically bounded and theoretically grounded explanations that pay close attention to physical time. Macro-causal analysis uses causal process tracing as its primary form of causal inference strategy. Unlike historical explanations, which are favored by eventful analysis, causal process tracing assumes a more orderly world that resembles conventional hypothesis testing.

Part I explores the temporal foundations of CHA. It invites readers to put on an ontological veil of ignorance that allows them to explore social reality more fully. It uses historical thinking as a make-belief to show how history, largely freed from theories and methodological concerns, engages with social reality in a more inductive and exploratory fashion. It then explicates two key elements of historical thinking – historical and physical time – and shows how they serve as key pillars of CHA. Part II discusses the more workman-like elements of historical thinking that help scholars go out into history and explore it. It shows how to use eventful, longue durée and macro-causal analysis for such exploratory purposes. Part III discusses the causal inference strategies employed by the respective strands.

Let me conclude with a brief reading note for the different audiences this book tries to reach. The book makes a scholarly contribution by trying to translate the various CHA vernaculars into a more systematic grammar. This is a work of methodological anthropology that loosely observes CHA research practices, labels them, and brings them in conversation with broader methodological discussions. Seasoned CHA scholars should be able to follow my analysis, even though they might disagree with some of it. But the book also addresses CHA novices who might be familiar with only one vernacular, may have read just a few CHA classics, or may be grappling with a historical project that they cannot shoehorn into existing methods. For such novices, the book will require patience, particularly Part I, which deals with the complexities of ontology and time. These newcomers will find their patience rewarded in the final two sections, which are more application-based. For readers still struggling with, or with little background in, qualitative methods, the book provides a companion webpage that includes diagnostic tests, a glossary, an annotated bibliography contextualizing each chapter, and application exercises. I sincerely hope that the book is accessible to these different audiences, so that they come to appreciate CHA's comparative advantage in the study of macro-historical phenomena and its methodological ecumenism, which is capable of renewing conversations with existing, more orthodox methodologies and ultimately of linking up with a two-century-old research tradition that demonstrates history's enduring contributions to social inquiry.

Part I

The Temporal Foundations of Comparative Historical Analysis

> If one explores on foot – and at present comparative history does exactly that a great deal of the time – the details are what one learns first. Their meaning and relationships emerge only gradually. There can be long periods when the investigator feels lost in an underbrush of facts, inhabited by specialists engaged in savage disputes about whether the underbrush is a pine forest or a tropical jungle. He is unlikely to emerge from such encounters without scratches and bruises.
>
> (Barrington Moore 1966, xi)

Let me start our discussion about the temporal foundations of comparative historical analysis (CHA) with an admittedly odd date and even odder subject matter: John Cage's 1952 composition "Four Minutes and Thirty-Three Seconds," or "4:33" for short. Cage was an avant-garde American composer who pushed his audiences to reflect on how they listened and thought about music. "4:33" is his most famous composition. Its première in 1952 had many of the trappings of a traditional classical concert: a pianist dressed in tuxedo walks on stage in a concert hall, settles down in front of a grand piano, and unfurls his music sheets. After that point Cage starts toying with his audience: the pianist reaches for a stopwatch perched on the grand, closes the keyboard cover, starts the stopwatch, and intently inspects the music sheet. After a minute or so, he pauses the stopwatch, opens the keyboard cover, and takes a short break. He then repeats the same steps for the next two movements, bows before the audience, and leaves the stage. The audience just experienced a 4:33-long performance without hearing anything that it would have construed as music in the traditional sense. Not surprisingly, the responses ranged from befuddlement to outrage. Listeners missed Cage's intent of using the piano's silence to make other sounds audible. What ostensibly seemed like silence to the audience was intended by Cage to draw attention to the clap of the closing keyboard cover, the click of the stopwatch, the hissing of the ventilation system, and whatever other noise could be heard in the auditorium.[1]

---

[1] This example was inspired by Louis Menand's (2021) discussion of John Cage's "4:33." The details of the performance are based on William Marx's December 15, 2010 concert in the McCallum Theatre, Palm Desert, CA.

My fear is that introducing the reader to CHA's hidden methodological contributions might come off like Cage initial performance of "4:33," intentionally bewildering the reader by eschewing traditional methodological topics such as case selection, measurement error, research design, or other technicalities related to causal inference. CHA has something to say about causal inference, but those contributions are not what makes it distinct or interesting. CHA is unique because it highlights the importance of exploration and history in social inquiry, and thus operates under broader ontological assumptions than variance-based methods. To appreciates its exploratory contribution requires temporarily silencing considerations about causal inference, because such considerations rest on ontological assumptions that background history and thus mask its role in the exploratory process. This opening section therefore follows Cage's lead. Where he imposed an acoustic veil of silence so that listeners could explore new sounds, this section asks readers to put on an *ontological veil of ignorance* that manifests itself in the historian's longstanding impatience with theory and methodology. The veil backgrounds the ontological assumptions about history, geography, and causality that social scientists use in order to create a social reality orderly enough to allow them to test hypotheses. This opening section discusses how this veil, just like Cage's silence, draws our attention to the complexities that historians explore. Reading this section will, alas, take longer than 4:33. But the extra time it demands will provide a solid understanding of CHA's temporal foundations and give readers an initial sense of what makes CHA unique and exciting. And, for those concerned that causal inference is taking the back seat, rest assured, regular programming resumes in Part III.

If CHA were to have a John Cage, Barrington Moore would be an excellent stand-in. He asked scholars to ignore the silence that methodology imposed on social reality so that they could better hear history. His epigram expresses a scorn for methods that would not pass mustard today, and rightly so. But it serves as a useful reminder that our present preoccupation with causal inference frequently overshoots the target and makes it difficult to see the contributions that history makes to social inquiry (D. Smith 1984). In Moore's case, his *Social Origins of Dictatorship and Democracy* (Moore 1966) uses history to unmask the linear, teleological, and Western-centric attributes of modernization theory, which was more helpful in generating testable hypotheses than in providing valid answers to the various political developments of countries. It thus became a landmark because it not only revived CHA in the late 1960s but also drew attention to the methodological implications of history.

Moore particularly emphasized the exploratory potential of history. As a Maine native, he loved the outdoors, which might explain why he chose a wilderness analogy to express his fondness for discovering new ideas. He advocated a particularly adventurous form of exploration – bushwhacking – that insists on leaving marked trails, heading for the underbrush, and being ready for unexpected discoveries. To the frustration of his students, Moore limited his bushwhacking advice to the imperative "read a lot and look for interesting patters" (personal communication to Skocpol). Fortunately CHA has come a long way since Moore's Spartan advice.

This first part explicates CHA's temporal foundation and its emphasis on ontological transparency. Chapter 1 elaborates on the key features of historical thinking – the more technical term for Moore's bushwhacking. Historical thinking unfreezes history and geography, so that CHA can explore what is going on and identify new patterns, unexplained by existing theories (Przeworski 2019, 133). Chapter 2 refines this general account of historical thinking. It shows that historians do not have a monopoly on historical thinking. It pushes back against the widely held notion that history and geography are dichotomous entities that scholars either freeze or unfreeze. It demonstrates that CHA treats history as a plurality and employs four notions of historical time: cyclical, bounded, serial, and eventful. Each notion pays differing kinds of attention to historical dates, explores distinct patterns, and stipulates different causal mechanisms. Chapter 2 also identifies the limits of this historical ecumenism. It discusses at what point history becomes so solidly frozen that it ceases to be historical in any meaningful sense and devolves into what I will call *historical tourism*.

Finally, Chapter 3 pays close attention to the vocabulary that CHA employs to describe the rhythms in which historical processes unfold. CHA recognizes that historical processes involve dynamics that operate independently of dates and are not linked to the qualitative changes that historical time tracks. These dynamics are marked by context-independent rhythms that CHA analyzes with the help of a second, physical notion of time. This physical time pays attention to tempo, duration, timing, sequencing, and stages. It further shows how the three strands of CHA – eventful, longue durée, and macro-causal analysis – combine historical and physical time in ways specific to each.

Taken together, these three opening chapters lay the foundations that are necessary to fully understand CHA's exploratory tools, discussed in Part II, and its causal inference strategies, covered in Part III. These chapters will be the most abstract ones, and thus may prove challenging for CHA novices. Hopefully Part II, with its more applied focus, will clarify what Part I leaves unexplained.

1 Historical Thinking
Stop Talking about Testing for Once!

> For the most part, we do not first see and then define, we define first and then see.
>
> (Lippmann 1922, 81)

> A good enough answer to an important question – important both substantially in the field and the real world – is more valuable than a definite answer to a trivial question.
>
> (Skocpol 2019, 15)

We have an intuitive sense of what makes headlines historical, thus suggesting that something is new, yet to be explored, and eventually to be explained. The failed insurrection on January 6, 2021 that sought to block the certification of President-elect Biden was an immediate candidate for being declared historical. Its unprecedented nature was instantly apparent, even though its long-term implications remain unclear. Such moments are not everyday occurrences, but they nevertheless are common enough to shape our lives in profound ways. We still live in the shadows of the Cold War, 9/11, and the 2008 financial meltdown. Such crises raise more questions than they can answer. And finding answers is further complicated by the fact that each crisis is entangled with slower-moving, quieter, less visible technological, demographic, ideational, and cultural changes. Nothing stands still, since our world is continuously remade while remaining linked to the past.

Ever since history emerged as a discipline in the early nineteenth century, historians have specialized in analyzing the modern, constantly changing world by employing what they call *historical thinking*. This chapter explicates the elements of historical thinking because comparative historical analysis (CHA) draws on it to bring this changing world in conversation with the more static world of methodology and theory. Historical thinking provides an inductive window on social reality, so that the latter can be analyzed independently of the geographic and historical strictures that methodology and theory impose on it (Abbott 2004; Wineburg 2001). CHA draws on historical thinking to describe social reality, as Lippman's epigram suggests, before we define it in terms of the pre-existing concepts that we use to explain it. Such descriptions are crucial because, as the sociologist Stanley Lieberson points out,

A question cannot be approached until a more fundamental base of know-ledge exists. It would as if one tried to build a locomotive before the wheel was discovered. ... It is valuable to recognize this possibility, because when one does see an issue raised in the sociological literature as empirically undoable, it is usually with respect to the quality of the data or the statistical issues, and so on. *Rarely is an empirical question viewed as premature simply because underlying knowledge is not yet available before the specific problem can be approached.* (Lieberson 1985, 9, italics added)

Being unconstrained by theoretical or methodological priors, historical thinking plays a vital role in discovering the wheels necessary to build the locomotive or, in our case, in translating results into answers. It serves as a crucial complement to our often overly narrow methodological preoccupation with testing. We are exhorted to test and retest without first carefully describ-ing what is being tested. Historical thinking enables the exploration necessary to produce a testworthy hypothesis. It ultimately supplements rather than substitutes causal inferences.

The broad contributions of historical thinking are, then, clear enough: explore and describe *before* you explain and test. Translating these goals into practical research advice is more challenging because neither historians nor standard textbooks provide much guidance. Both treat exploration and description as a serendipitous activity. For historians, they are part of a tacit craft and, in standard methodology textbooks, they belong to the pre-methodological domain of discovery (Gerring 2012b, 26–36).

This chapter starts to fill this gap by using James Morone' s delightful *The Republic of Wrath: How American Politicians Turned Tribal from George Washington to Donald Trump* (2020) to explicate the elements of historical thinking. As the title suggests, Morone follows the standard historiographical practice of placing contemporary issues in a broad context and then starts looking for patterns. He finds patterns that highlight the importance of cultural conflicts in the rise of populism but are overlooked by the prevailing economic theories, which focus on globalization and deindustrialization (2020, 4–5). He links those patterns to periodic renegotiations over race, immigra-tion, and gender – and ultimately over who gets to partake in American democracy. Morone's work exemplifies the type of political history that has been marginalized in history departments but continues to thrive in American political development (APD) – a charter member of CHA. I treat Morone as exemplifying a kind of work of card-carrying historians that highlights five interrelated elements of historical thinking: the unfreezing of history and geography for the sake of opening new terrains for exploration; the use of comparisons to turn those explorations into new discoveries; capitalizing on those discoveries; the formulation of new research questions; and the use of abduction to update theories. As will become clear, the common denominator of these five elements is to describe, undescribe, and redescribe – and thereby update – the existing foreknowledge. Let me start with the most fundamental step in this exploration process: the unfreezing of history and geography.

1.1 Unfreezing History and Geography

Any representation of social reality involves choices. Photographers, for example, use different lenses to capture wide angles or zoom in on an object, and they select shutter speeds and apertures to capture motion properly. They take artistic license in how they represent space and time (Kern 1983). Social scientists use theories rather than cameras. They make ontological choices and, to represent time and space, calibrate history and geography rather than lenses, apertures, and shutter speeds. They take ontological license, which is more constrained than the photographer's artistic license, because they follow the dictates of transparency and replicability. And by being more constrained, social scientists leave their readers less latitude in reading a theory than a viewer has in interpreting a photograph (Becker 2007, 1–29). But, just as photography aficionados, who understand the mechanics of photography, appreciate an image more fully, so social scientists, who are ontologically literate, can better grasp how theories and methods construct social phenomena. And, as will become apparent, this plea for ontological transparency is one of my book's most frequently recurring themes.

How, then, can we make the ontological choices that are embedded in theories and methods more transparent? Historians offer an excellent starting point because they prefer to travel light when they head for the archives. They are mindful of the constraints that too much theory and methodology impose on their sleuthing instincts. Historians engage in a delicate ontological calibration process by constructing and deconstructing, or by freezing and unfreezing, the self, social identities, geography, and, above all, the past. The specific calibration formulae define the different modes of history. Cultural history unfreezes the self to explore its plasticity, social history unfreezes collective identities to understand their construction, and global history unfreezes geography to investigate its colonial lineage (Hunt 2014, 78–118). These unfreezings thus all serve – as the historian put it – to problematize our existing understanding and discover new insights.

CHA follows in the footsteps of history but confines its unfreezing to historical and geographical assumptions so that it can explore what remains hidden behind ceteris paribus parameters of variance-based analysis (VBA). The ontological license that CHA takes can be viewed as the equivalent in

Google maps of switching from the default view to the satellite, or even to street view, in order to foreground new geographic details. Unfreezing history, in turn, involves downloading Google Earth and using the time slider to compare present-day with earlier satellite images and to explore what changed.

Being skeptical of theories, historians treat them as *coagulated history* that slows, thins, and finally freezes the flow of history. Historians are leery of transforming historical objects, whose motion is marked by dates, into dateless and hence static snapshots. They are uncomfortable treating chronologically discreet events as occurring simultaneously. Historians emphasize instead that those events jointly form a process that can be understood only by paying attention to dates (Kreuzer 2019, 126). This attention to dates unfreezes history by drawing attention to chronological contexts and to the change that occurs across them. Historians use dates to demonstrate that the past does *not* repeat itself (i.e. is not frozen), that it is not just prior to the present but also qualitatively *different* from it (Schiffman 2011, 2). This attention to dates makes history flow again, quickens its pace, and re-embeds events in specific contexts. In short, historians like a more unfrozen, more liquid conceptualization of the past. To CHA, such unfreezing of history is attractive because it treats the past as something to be explored. This unfrozen history can provide new insights into what is happening outside theories and into how this outside might have changed since a theory was first articulated. It invites scholars to use the past to first undescribe and then redescribe existing theories.

Put more technically, unfreezing history amounts to taking ontological license with the statistical assumption of *conditional independence*. This assumption freezes history by stipulating that the value of any measurement is independent from earlier measurements. The speed of a train, for example, is unaffected by the speed of an earlier train. This independence allows treating each measurement as a single snapshot, without having to understand the larger historical process in which it is embedded. It permits ignoring dates and the past to understand the present. Ignoring dates is less problematic when we compare trains than when we compare context-specific human events (P. Hall 2003; Hanson and Kopstein 2005; Sewell 1996).

Historians are skeptical also about theories' ambition to generalize; and they treat theories as a *universalized geography* that standardizes, homogenizes, and ultimately freezes geographic particularities. This freezing of geography translates spatially contextualized objects into locationless and hence homogeneous observations. It constructs contiguity by assuming that geographically distal locations are in the same vicinity and thus are uniform (Gaddis 2002, 20–5; Kreuzer 2019, 126–8). Historical thinking challenges the assumption that theories are geography-free or placeless and that they reflect a world so uniform that zip codes do not matter. It unfreezes geography so that theories can travel to different locations and explore how universal or exceptional they actually are. This unfreezing opens geography to exploration. Put more technically again, unfreezing geography takes ontological license with the statistical assumption of *unit homogeneity*. This assumption freezes geography by stipulating that the units of analysis used to gather evidence are, despite their geographic differences, sufficiently uniform for us to be able to infer, from aggregate causal effects that have been observed across all cases, the workings of uniform causal mechanisms that are present in each case (P. Hall 2003; Hanson and Kopstein 2005; Sewell 1996).

To Morone, historical thinking is so much a second nature that he never talks about unfreezing history or geography. His "unfreezing" is nevertheless evident in several ways. He uses the past, and regional differences, to explore populism. He employs proper names rather than concepts, organizes his chapters chronologically rather than theoretically, favors narratives over parsimonious theories, and uses the word "testing" only four times and never in conjunction with hypothesis.

1.2 Comparisons: Turning Explorations into Discoveries

While unfreezing geography and history constitutes the first step in historical thinking, comparisons guide the explorations of this newly unfrozen temporal and geographic terrain. We compare, for example, when traveling. Alexis de Tocqueville visited the United States to study the prison, but ended up exploring the complex interplay between politics and culture by comparing American democracy with postrevolutionary France. We compare when we look at data across cells on a spreadsheet, when we juxtapose photographic images, or when we interpret graphs. In all these instances, comparing involves looking for patterns and producing descriptions of what is going on or redescriptions what theories have already described (Becker 2007, 32–53). *Comparing is central to translating exploration into discoveries.* The historian Raymond Grew writes:

> [the] initial stage of truly original research is focused curiosity that comes with asking a fresh question. And comparison is probably their most important source, suggesting for example, that what looks like change may be continuity or that things seemingly unrelated may be connected. To look at other cases is to see other outcomes. By considering them, the historian wins some freedom from the *tyranny of what happened* and develops that awareness of alternatives . . . that underlies some of the most provocative historical questions. (Grew 1980, 769; italics added)

"Tyranny of what happened," what a fabulous phrase to underscore how comparisons help us escape established ways of viewing phenomena and invite us to explore and make new discoveries.

But how are we to compare? The literature has produced few insights until recent contributions began treating comparison as a plurality (Boswell, Corbett, and Rhodes 2019; Schaffer 2021; E. Simmons and Smith 2021). These contributions shifted the standard notion of comparison, which is embedded in terms such as "comparative politics" or "comparative methods." This notion links comparing to controlling by juxtaposing cases that have been carefully selected from a known universe (Lijphart 1971; Ragin 1987). Comparing holds constant potential confounders to make it possible to estimate the strength of theorized causal effects. It accomplishes this control function by freezing history and geography – that is, by invoking parameters or parsing reality into endogenous and exogenous factors. This notion of comparison as controlling overlooks four other types of comparison that serve to discover and describe patterns: *cross-sectional* comparisons explore *variations* in degrees across space; *serial* comparisons explore *trends*, that is, variations in degrees across space and time; *contextual* comparisons explore *varieties*, that is, differences in kind across space; and *historical* comparisons explore *transformations*, that is, differences in kind across time and, to a lesser extent, in space. As Table 1.1 shows, these four kinds of comparison are defined by their respective freezing of history and geography. The grey cells identify the three kinds that are the most exploratory and the most closely associated with historical thinking. They are contrasted with cross-sectional comparison, which freezes history and geography and thus has a more limited exploratory potential.

Cross-sectional comparisons have the limited exploratory purpose of identifying variations in degree. Morone, for example, could have compared the US populist movements to movements in other democracies in order to explore *variations* in their electoral strength or membership sizes. Such cross-sectional comparisons would freeze geography by limiting the analysis to a single, ex ante, theoretically defined dimension. It would freeze history by limiting comparisons to a single chronological snapshot. The resulting discoveries are thin, as they leave us in the dark about trends in the populists' strength over time, varieties of populism, or their transformations.

Serial comparisons are a longitudinal extension of the static snapshots that cross-sectional comparisons uncover. They typically use time series or panel data to explore trends across space and time. They freeze geography by assuming cases to be uniform enough to be compared through variables. They unfreeze history by anchoring measurements in specific dates that permit exploring trends across time. The observations within a given trend

Table 1.1 Types of comparisons

		Geography	
		Frozen (Thin)	Unfrozen (Thick)
	Frozen (Thin) (Single or multiple moments without dates)	**I. Cross-Sectional** → exploring geographic or within-case *variations*. Differences in degree. Units of analysis are homogeneous and independent (e.g., variations in populists' electoral strength).	**II. Contextual** → Identifying geographic *varieties* across cases. Differences in kind. Units of analysis are heterogeneous and independent (e.g., varieties of populists, right-wing, left-wing).
History	**Unfrozen (Thick)** (Multiple moments with specific date)	**III. Serial** → exploring historical and geographic *trends* across time, either within single or within multiple cases. Units of analysis are homogeneous and interdependent (e.g., longitudinal trends in populists' electoral strength).	**IV. Historical** → exploring *transformations* across time, patterns of continuities and discontinuities. Units of analysis are heterogeneous and interdependent (e.g., how contemporary populists are different from interwar fascists).

The function of comparing depends on the ontological assumptions it employs. Historical, contextual, and serial comparisons unfreeze either history or geography, or both. The gray cells indicate shared exploratory function. Cross-sectional comparisons freeze history and geography and thus have a more limited exploratory potential.

are interdependent, allowing past values to influence subsequent ones. This interdependence gives serial comparisons their historical quality. Morone, for example, could have used serial comparisons by tracking the electoral ebbing and flowing of populist candidates in US history. I elaborate more fully on serial comparisons in the next chapter, and particularly in the chapter on longue durée analysis.

Contextual comparisons are interested in similarities and differences in order to discover varieties – phenomena that are similar enough to be related but are qualitatively different enough to constitute distinct types (Locke and

Thelen 1995; Schaffer 2021). In paying attention to differences, contextual comparisons serve as a corrective to the *overgeneralizations* to which cross-sectional comparisons are prone as a result of treating all cases as uniform. They serve, to borrow from Kenneth Burke, to "bring out the thisness of that and the thatness of this" (Burke, quoted in Schaffer 2021, 48). Morone uses contextual comparisons sparingly because he focuses on the national patterns of a single country. Still, he employs them to capture the regional variations in the lead-up to the Civil War. He points out that different regions had very distinct preferences on the issues of immigration and slavery and that those differences deeply divided the parties. In the 1840s and 1850s, the Northeast was opposed to slavery and deeply divided over immigration; the Midwest was indifferent to immigration but opposed to extending slavery to the new Western states; the West Coast was concerned about the status of Native Americans, Chinese people, and Mexicans; and the South was hell-bend on maintaining the status quo of slavery and extending it westward. Morone (2020, 95–126) uses these geographic differences to explain first the displacement of the old Whig Party in 1854, by the anti-immigration Know-Nothings, and then the newly formed Republican Party, as well as the growing North–South tension that led to the Civil War. In subsequent chapters he demonstrates how these regional variations, while still important after the Civil War, gradually diminished as the federal government assumed a more prominent role in national politics. Contextual comparisons serve a second, less frequently discussed purpose. Attention to similarities provides a corrective against historians' propensity to *undergeneralize* as a result of assuming that each case is unique (Kreuzer 2003, 2019, 126). It constitutes a safeguard against the tyranny of where something happened, to adapt Grew's words. For example, claims that populist outbursts are unique to US democracy could be countered by pointing to similar patterns in France and Germany.

Historical comparisons serve to help us discover qualitative transformations over time (W. Steinmetz, Simon, and Postoutenko 2021). Morone uses them to explore populist outbursts across US history and to assess whether they were marked by continuities or discontinuities. To capture transformations, he pays close attention to dates, compares events, and looks for two types of patterns.

- *Discontinuity patterns.* Historical comparisons explore how qualitatively different an event is from prior, related events, or whether it is unprecedented. They ask whether an event is something entirely new, marking a major discontinuity; a mutation of something of that occurred at an earlier point in time; or a carbon copy, suggesting the lack of any discontinuity. They pinpoint the moment of change.

- *Continuity patterns.* If events repeat themselves, historical comparisons explore for how long they endure and what mechanisms reproduce them.

Morone employs historical comparisons so naturally that he does not even talk about using them. He compares populist outbursts to look for patterns of attempted or actual racial emancipation and of the democratic backsliding they provoked. The first outburst in the early 1800s involved a backlash against domestic slave uprisings and fear of "contagion" vis-à-vis Haiti's successful slave revolt. The Jacksonian era, from the 1840s to the 1860s, saw the first mass parties advancing their goals by mobilizing racial anxieties, manipulating electoral rules, and increasingly fighting for the extension of slavery to new states. The populist episodes from the antebellum era were followed by the Jim Crow reversals of the political reforms that had passed in the 1880s, the Prairie populism of the 1890s, the slowly simmering white resentment against postwar advances in blacks' civil rights, and the more recent Tea Party and white nationalist backlash against the growing social prominence of non-white groups and the election of the first black president. These historical comparisons point both to discontinuities and continuities. Contemporary voter suppression laws, for example, are different from those enacted during the Jim Crow era, even as disenfranchisement efforts continue. This dark pattern challenges the exceptionalist account of America as the world's oldest and most stable democracy and raises questions as to how its democratic backsliding compares to the behavior of other democracies. Morone's historical comparisons show that, while history does not repeat itself, it often rhymes. They help us escape the tyranny of Trump's endless tweets and figure out more clearly what was unprecedented about this presidency and what it shared with the presidencies of earlier periods (Przeworski 2019, 133).

1.3 Formulating New Research Questions

The comparativist ability to discover four types of patterns – variations, trends, varieties, and transformations – typically occurs in the context of already described patterns. The differences between the old and the new patterns invites rethinking the former's descriptive validity and ultimately asking new questions – the next step in historical thinking. But historical thinking generates new questions also by offering first-time descriptions of previously undescribed phenomena – and not just by undescribing and redescribing existing patterns. Historical thinking recognizes that posing questions is an integral, but also labor-intensive element of the research process. And historians are not alone in making this point. The neuroscientist Stuart Firestein (2015, 65) explains: 'the popular conception seems to be that scientists solve problems. They get answers to questions. . . . I do not think that this is true at all. Finding problems – good problems, relevant problems, important problems – that is what good scientists do." This insight is doubly true when it comes to CHA, which analyzes the constantly changing world and thus engages in questions that constantly risk becoming obsolete (Gerring 2012b, 37–57).

Morone uses the pattern of populist outbursts and democratic backsliding to raise a series of questions. He opens his book by asking: "Is there anything new in our screaming political division? Do they endanger the Republic . . .? Or should we all take a deep breath as American politics runs through just another rowdy stretch?" (Morone 2020, 1). These questions, stated so plainly and elegantly, were far from self-evident when Morone started this project (357). They became so only after he waded through two centuries of US history to explicate those patterns. Morone's reliance on historical thinking to formulate new research questions is central to CHA and its commitment to problem-driven research. To appreciate the depth of this commitment, I would like to zoom out briefly from Morone's work and place it in CHA's broader thematic genealogy.

Since the late nineteenth century, CHA has explored four key macro-historical themes: the expansion of capitalism, the transformation of political regimes, the formation of nation states, and the transformation of war. It also began analyzing changing gender and racial identities, the advent of transnational phenomena, and, with Covid 19, pandemics. Figure 1.1 summarizes CHA's thematic evolution. It underscores the incredible continuity of CHA, as it reformulated the original questions in the light of changing historical circumstances and each of these reformulations gave rise to new subliteratures that adapted the original question. Like a family tree, these topics share a common but continuously evolving lineage. The diagram in this figure is partially based on excellent intellectual histories by Abrams (1982), Adams, Clemens, and Orloff (2005a), Møller (2016), and Skocpol (1984).

The rise of capitalism and the never-ending encroachment of markets on non-economic domains of life have formed the most central theme of the four macro-historical themes in CHA. This theme informs the work of economics sociologists, economics historians, labor historians, historical institutionalists, and comparative political economists. Next to capitalism, the advent of modern liberal democracies and of their autocratic alternatives is the most significant CHA topic. This second theme – the transformation of political regimes – has been studied in the literatures on democratization, history of political thought, fascism, totalitarianism, and democratic

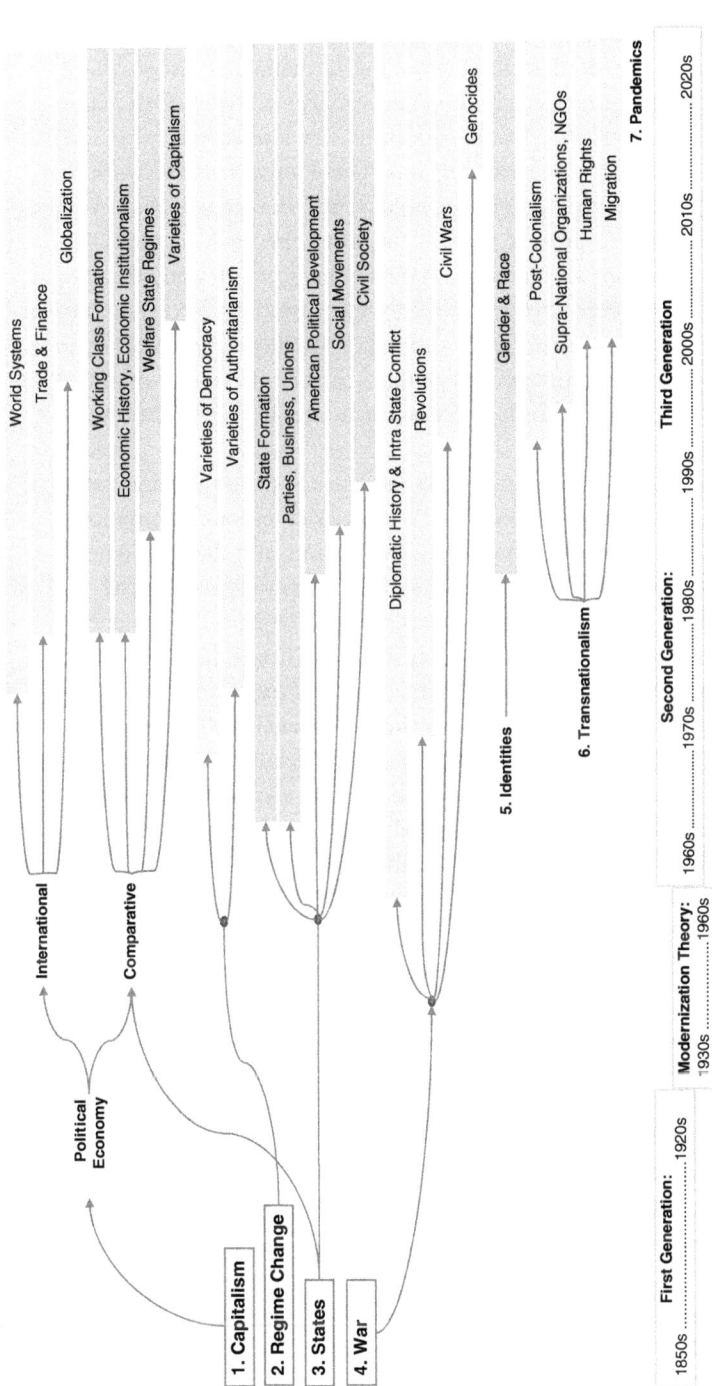

Figure 1.1 CHA's genealogy

This figure illustrates the thematic genealogy of CHA research from the late nineteenth century (left side) to the present (right side). It illustrates, after a hiatus in CHA research between 1940 and 1960, both the continuity of the four original themes (on the left of the figure) and their evolution into more specialized literatures. The bottom right of the graph identifies three topics (identities, transnationalism, pandemics) on which CHA has focused more recently.

backsliding. The modern nation state has fascinated CHA as well, because its structure is so closely intertwined with the advent of capitalism and democracy. This is the third major theme: the formation of nation states. Here scholars analyze the growing bureaucratic capacity of the modern nation state, its efforts to establish a national identity, its interactions with civil society, and the expansion of social programs. These topics inspired work on state formation, nationalism, political sociology, and the welfare state. War and conflict – or how to prevent them – constitute the final original CHA theme. Military historians and international relations scholars study the ebbs and flows of war and peace between states, while historians of revolutions, protests, or civil wars analyze domestic turmoil or stability. Scholars examine how technology, military strategy, geopolitics, balance of power, or international norms affect the outbreak or containment of war or produce revolutions and civil unrest.

In the 1980s younger scholars added two new themes: the transformation of racial, gender, and sexual identities and the analysis of various transnational phenomena related to the diffusion of ideas, migration, and the proliferation of transnational actors and organizations. These themes first entered the political arena during the 1960s, when new cultural movements drew attention to women, LGBTQ, racial, ethnic, and colonial issues. These cultural issues did not fit comfortably in the more material and structural framework of the first and second generation of scholars. They were also analytically difficult to integrate in the prevailing conceptualization of modernity as an entity that consisted of a set of coherent categories such as class, secularism, rationality, or bureaucratic domination. Such conceptualizations left little room for non-material and more fluid categories like gender, ethnicity, or more informal social practices (Adams, Clemens, and Orloff 2005b, 13). Thus the new literatures on gender and race identities, transnationalism and post-colonialism have begun to fill in more fully the cultural and ideational gaps in the older CHA works. And the COVID-19 pandemic, a macro-historical event if there ever was one, will introduce epidemiological and public health questions to CHA. Clearly CHA does not just study historical objects in motion but is itself a historical discipline in motion.

Parenthetically, I should point out that CHA's thematic updating stopped only once, between the 1940s and the 1960s, when the United States' postwar hegemony gave the appearance that history had ended. Modernization theorists were confident that they had sufficiently cracked history's DNA to retire historical thinking altogether. The Vietnam War, student protests, civil rights struggle, women's liberation, and above all decolonialization made it clear that history had merely taken a time out in a few American universities, while marching on in the real world. History returned so forcefully in the

1960s that it did not fit the tidy, linear historical trajectory stipulated by modernization theory. CHA was back in business, formulating new research questions.

1.4 Abduction and Updating Theories

Historical thinking does not end with the formulation of good questions but eventually drifts into conjectures about possible answers. The discovery of variations, trends, varieties, and transformations, the undescribing or redescribing of existing patterns, and the formulation of new research questions invariably generate clues for possible answers. Exploration and explanation rarely are analytically as distinct as they are presented in certain textbooks. Instead, they are intertwined and involve a back-and-forth that reflects historiographical, Bayesian, or abductive sensitivities. I prefer the term *abduction*, coined by the nineteenth-century philosopher Charles S. Pierce, who used it to underscore that explaining involves a complex interplay between new inductive insights and the received scholarly consensus (Swedberg 2014; Yom 2015). Abduction involves using new descriptive insights to update existing theories, as well as withdrawing theoretical elements that have been misdescribed or that the march of history has made obsolete. Abduction resists the old and tired division of research into a domain of discovery – misleadingly characterized as involving barefoot empiricism – and a domain of confirmation – focused on the deductive testing of hypotheses. It implies an open-ended understanding of knowledge production, not limited to methods that narrowly emphasize falsification. The very term "falsification" implies what Jeffrey Checkel (2014, 31) slyly called the "gladiatorial style of hypothesis testing," which starkly differentiates between old and new theories and prefers outcomes where "one theory slays all the others." Falsification leaves far less room for updating theoretical insights than the term abduction which emphasizes a dialogue between testing and exploration.

Morone clearly has no gladiatorial aspirations as he obliquely differentiates his cultural from his economic explanations without ever pitting them against each other. And yet, on closer inspection, he makes various theoretical contributions that go well beyond highlighting the cultural dynamics driving US populism. We find his most significant contributions in the answers he provides to the opening question of whether Trump is "just another rowdy stretch" in American politics. Morone ultimately concludes that Trump is quite different, indeed. In the past, race, immigration, economic dislocation, and gender rarely ever took center stage *simultaneously*, nor did such divisions align perfectly along party lines. Before the 1960s, southern and northern

Democrats and Republicans held distinct positions particularly on race and immigration. The resulting intraparty divisions moderated the interparty conflicts because internal party factions would align with their ideological peers from the other party. This cooperation across parties thus moderated the divisiveness of issues (Morone 2020, 21–2). However, since the 1960s, intraparty conflicts receded as a result of the northward migration of African Americans, the white backlash against civil rights, the Conservatives' response to gender equality, and the arrival of a growing number of non-Caucasian immigrants. By now, those former intraparty divisions have morphed into the strict interparty conflicts that fuel our present-day polarization; and the polarization is further aggravated by unprecedented economic inequalities (265–335). Cultural and economic conflicts reinforce each other like never before. And the government's ability to address such inequalities has been curtailed by global markets, which give bond rating agencies, global investors, and the International Monetary Fund more say in public policies than ever before. Looking back in time, Morone sees a bleak future.

Furthermore, Morone's analysis also contributes to debates within election literature. These debates pivot on the importance of economic decline – outsourcing of manufacturing jobs and the resulting geographic income inequalities – in relation to status anxiety, mostly in white males. Scholars find that this anxiety is driven less by declining income and more by the upward mobility of blacks, by immigrants, by the browning of America, by backlash against Obama's presidency, and by the United States' declining global standing. Morone's historical findings corroborate the status anxiety thesis in distinct ways. He shows that those anxieties and voter repression are part of a long-standing pattern – one that, alas, seems more threatening now than ever before.

My discussion so far concentrated on the centrality of historical thinking to CHA and demonstrated that the former has more structure than is generally acknowledged. Let me conclude by emphasizing that historical thinking is central not just to CHA but constitutes an inescapable element of every social science method that requires attention to VBA just as much as CHA does.

1.5 The Inescapability of Historical Thinking

Historical thinking is inescapable in two ways. First, disciplines closely linked to the natural sciences and whose experimental orientation suggests a history-less analysis typically are in dialogue with subfields that employ historical thinking. Pharma companies used randomized control trials to test new Covid vaccines while simultaneously tracking the virus' mutations. Recent cancer treatments became more effective after the discovery of the mutation in cancer genes that revealed these genes' previously overlooked heterogeneity. This insight lead doctors to abandon uniform treatments in favor of more individualized ones. Thus genetic mutations are the medical equivalent of historical change, as they also involve qualitative transformations. In psychology, psychometricians are in dialogue with developmental and social psychologists who pay attention to historical changes and cultural variations in human cognitive abilities (Gladwell 2007; Mukherjee 2016). Admittedly, the elements of change over time are far less pronounced in those disciplines, and this lessens their reliance on historical thinking. But those qualitative changes remain an ever-present confounding factor that, when acknowledged, produced significant scientific advances.

Second, historical thinking does not surface just in the natural sciences but is also embedded in variance-based methods, thus changing the question from one about whether it is employed to one about when it is employed, and how transparently. VBA's use of historical thinking is difficult to detect because it is masked by unfamiliar vocabularies. We face again the dilemma of too many vernaculars and not enough grammar. Let me therefore explicate the uses of historical thinking in VBA and, to a lesser degree, even in CHA. Once the inescapability of historical thinking established, I use it as a conceptual anchor for mapping the broader intellectual terrain in which CHA operates and that the book's subsequent chapters discuss.

VBA – allegedly the methodological nemesis of CHA – engages in historical thinking that is easily overlooked because it occurs *after* test results have been generated. It appears in the language of robustness checks, locating confounders, identifying causal bias, or assessing internal and external validity. As subsequent chapters will clarify, these post-testing activities involve historical thinking in the sense that they assess the confounding effects of history and geography that were frozen in the first place by stipulating that all other things are assumed to be equal. Discussions about external validity, for example, assess the historical boundary conditions of test results and thereby draw on historical thinking. Natural experiments, in turn, stipulate historical discontinuities that are so abrupt as to justify as-if randomization. They stipulate historical discontinuities so unfrozen that, again, all other things can be assumed to be equal. However, natural experiments require historical thinking in order to empirically corroborate this unfrozeness before we can declare that a discontinuity qualifies as a natural experiment (Kocher and Monteiro 2016).

Discerning such historical thinking is complicated by the fact that VBA employs a different vocabulary. We already discussed how VBA uses the technical terms "conditional independence" and "unit homogeneity" as equivalent with freezing history and geography respectively. Statistics acknowledges history by referring to events that do not repeat themselves or that are not reversible – thereby constituting the very essence of unfrozen history – as being out of sample. Analogously, historians, who identify continuities, look for sufficiently stable and recurring events that could be said to be "in the sample." Economists, in turn, distinguish between endogenous factors, which explain variations in otherwise uniform and qualitatively unchanging variables, and exogeneous factors, which are external to existing explanations and still need to be explored. Endogeneity corresponds to a history so frozen that the present has no past or future. Exogeneity, in turn, refers to the unfrozen, disorderly world outside the theory that needs to be navigated through historical thinking. Economists claim that this disorderly world can be ignored as long as it does not produce so-called exogeneous shock (Samman 2019, 29–31). These shocks correspond to what non-economists refer to as history. Economists use "shock" as a synonym for history, without reflecting on its devious ontological obfuscation, which has understandably irritated historians (Gaddis 2002). The term marginalizes history not only by rhetorically othering it – that is, by treating it as something foreign or invasive, which requires walls or parameters to keep it out – but also by pathologizing it: a "shock" in the medical sense is something threatening, undesirable.

Leaving aside the historians' understandable irritation, historical thinking is masked not just in VBA but also in CHA. We discussed so far CHA's historical thinking in terms of unfreezing history and geography in relation to VBA, thus implying a social reality so fully unfrozen that it becomes liquid. However, CHA also freezes history and geography in relation to regular historians. Unlike historians, CHA uses theories to reduce the noise of social reality. In doing so, it realizes that the only noise reduction strategy available is to freeze history and geography. It concurs with Gary King, Robert Keohane and Sidney Verba (1994, 43) on the point that "the difference between the amount of complexity in the world and that in the thickest description is still vastly larger than the difference between the thickest of descriptions and the most abstract quantitative or formal analysis." However, CHA's historical thinking takes place at a different stage in the research process from that of VBA's historical thinking. CHA freezes geography and history after historical thinking adequately described a phenomenon, updated the theories, formulated the research question – in short, it freezes history and geography only after historical thinking generated tentative answers worthy enough of being tested. It also avoids dichotomizing the world into endogenous and exogeneous domains and thereby pathologizing historical thinking.

Ultimately VBA and CHA share historical thinking as a potential topic of conversation, but face the challenge of lacking the vocabulary to engage in a productive dialogue – a challenge that puts one in mind of George Bernard Shaw's famous quip "Britain and the US are divided by a common language." The next two chapters therefore introduce CHA's temporal vocabulary, which is necessary for such a dialogue. Historical thinking owes this potential for cross-methodological dialogue by virtue of being inescapable. Every method needs to make social reality more orderly by freezing history and geography *to some degree*, because without ontological simplifications it would be impossible to describe and explain.

Let me conclude with a map designed to guide through this dialogue. Figure 1.2 leverages the inescapability of historical thinking. If both VBA and CHA freeze history and geography to make social reality more orderly, then they differ in the degree of their freezing. It therefore stands to reason that freezing history and geography can provide the coordinates to map CHA's intellectual terrain. Figure 1.2 anchors the space along the diagonal axis, defined at one end by statistical thinking and at the other end by historical thinking. The two modes of thinking serve as ideal types, defined

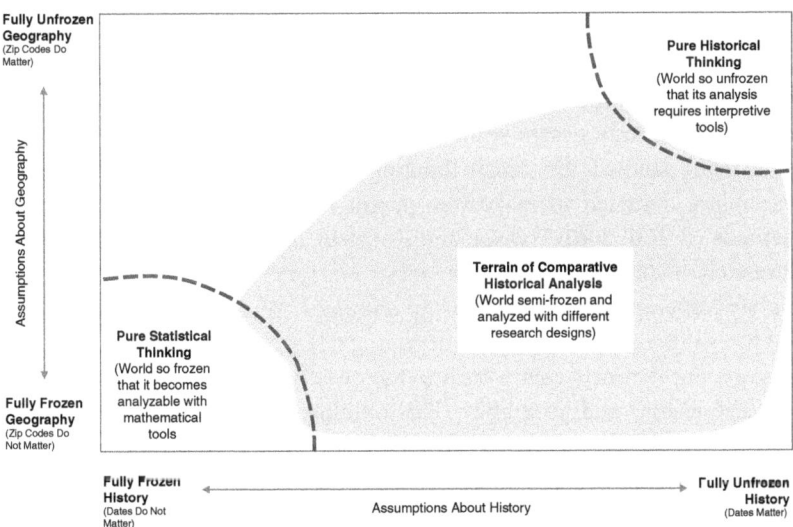

Figure 1.2 Ontological map
Modes of social inquiry rest on distinct ontological assumptions about how much to freeze history and geography and thereby pay attention to temporal and spatial particularities. Historical and statistical thinking represent two ideal typical modes of social inquiry that make diametrically opposing ontological assumptions. CHA builds a bridge between these two modes of analysis and thus occupies the large terrain between them.

by either fully freezing or unfreezing history and geography. The horizontal axis treats history along a continuum that benchmarks its freezing against how much scholars ignore historical dates and qualitative changes over time. Chapter 2 will refine this crucial axis further. The vertical axis conceptualizes geography along a continuum that calibrates spatial freezing against how much scholars ignore zip codes and qualitative differences across space. CHA touches the outer boundaries of pure statistical and historical thinking, but mostly covers the vast terrain in between. It does not extend to the upper left-hand corner, where history is too frozen for CHA.

The terrain is meant to convey the vastness of CHA's intellectual territory and its liminal position between statistical and historical thinking. It differs from these two prototypical modes of thinking by refusing to define itself in terms of strict ex ante ontological precedents. It departs from statistical thinking by rejecting the assumptions of unit homogeneity and conditional independence, which freeze history and geography too much. And it deviates from pure historical thinking by being skeptical about the belief that each case is exceptional and that history neither repeats itself nor even rhymes. CHA thus becomes the Goldilocks' method, in which social reality is neither too solid nor too liquid, but has just the right ontological viscosity. CHA fills this liminal space between statistical and historical thinking with what I will call *ontological triage*, the complex process of aligning the ontological presuppositions of a research design with the ontological properties of the phenomenon being studied. Historical thinking assists this triage by providing a vocabulary designed to make transparent the ontological assumptions of methods (P. Hall 2003; Hanson and Kopstein 2005). This ontological triage ultimately involves a conversation about *what sort of history and geography are most appropriate for what sort of questions*. Within CHA, this dialogue produces different answers, thus depriving CHA of a single causal inference strategy, but it always comes back to the question of how much to freeze or unfreeze history and geography. This ontological triage is the corollary of CHA's precept to place *questions before methods*, thus always requesting aligning the latter with the former. Subsequent chapters will elaborate on this alignment process.

The vastness of CHA's ontological terrain and of the ontological triage it necessitates raises the question of why, unlike statistical and historical thinking, CHA does not hunker down in the southeast corner, dig a protective ontological moat, and offer less heterodox methodological advice. The answer, of course, is that CHA is problem-driven, and thus grapples with macro-historical questions that are stubbornly disrespectful of the narrower ontological boundaries drawn by VBA and by historians. And this problem-driven nature also explains why it emerged in different disciplines that are independent of one other, which translates into an origins story that is very different from that of VBA – a point to which I will return in the conclusion.

Now that we identified the broad contours of CHA's territory, let me pivot and introduce the temporal vocabulary necessary to explore it more systematically.

Exercises

Notes on exercises:

Students initially push back when having to learn regular grammar because it appears to teach them merely something they already think they have intuitively mastered. They eventually relent when realizing that understanding grammar makes them more conscious thinkers, as Sartori put it. Learning to think historically and to master CHA's temporal vocabulary is likely to go through a similar process, from initial recalcitrance to eventual appreciation. The following exercises are meant to facilitate this learning process. Each chapter offers three to four exercises. The first two are typically more rudimentary, using material from the book or readily accessible everyday examples. The third and fourth exercises, particularly in the later chapters, are more involved and require applying the content to scholarly articles. To facilitate connecting the content of the chapters with those readings, the exercises provide questions that are at times detailed. These are meant to encourage close analytical reading – one of CHA's hallmarks – and get the conversation going. So students should treat them as prompts rather than as a rigorous checklist. Instructors are encouraged to use these questions and apply them to works or examples that are closer to their area of expertise. Finally, I used several of the readings or examples across several chapters, in order to economize the students' preparation time.

1.1. Theda Skocpol is the grande dame of CHA and the conversation with her student Eric Schickler touches on broad themes on which this book elaborates (see Skocpol 2019). How has her biography shaped her scholarship, and particularly the subject she studies? What parallels are there with your biography and scholarship? What role does historical thinking play in her research? (Note: she does not use this term.) Where would you place her various works on CHA's genealogy (Figure 1.1)? Where would you place her on the ontological map (Figure 1.2)? How does she think about methodology? How does her thinking differ from yours?

1.2. Earl Cook's serial graph in Chapter 6 (Figure 6.4) offers a sweeping history of human energy consumption. The paragraph preceding the graph explains it. Identify the ways in which this graph freezes particularly history but also geography. What sort of comparisons does it use? Where would you place this graph on the ontological map (Figure 1.2)? Here are some pointers for the more hidden elements of time and geography. (i) The time scale shortens across the six periods. What are the implications of this for freezing time? (ii) Do you detect a geographic dimension in the four categories of energy consumption that make up the bar graph? How do they vary in their freezing of geography?

1.3. In his influential book *What Is History?* the historian E. H. Carr introduced an example about a hypothetical car accident, to illustrate how our ontological assumptions determine the way we construct causal arguments (Carr 1961, 136–40). Subsequently this example was widely adopted by other historians[1] The example is rudimentary enough to be used without extensive background reading. I will therefore return to it repeatedly in the coming chapters.

Here is a slightly modified version of this story. I added two labels: antecedents serve to identify potential causal factors and consequents to designate the outcome to be explained.

Mr. Jones, who is returning after midnight$_{\text{antecedent 1}}$ from a party$_{\text{antecedent 2}}$ where he had had several drinks$_{\text{antecedent 3}}$ and driving a car$_{\text{antecedent 4}}$ with defective brakes$_{\text{antecedent 5}}$, knocked down and killed Mr. Robinson$_{\text{consequent 1}}$ at a blind corner$_{\text{antecedent 6}}$. Mr. Robinson had left home; he was on his way to buy cigarettes$_{\text{antecedent 7}}$ and was about to cross the street$_{\text{antecedent 8}}$, lit by the light of the full moon$_{\text{antecedent 9}}$ when he was hit $_{\text{consequent 1}}$.

Assess the causes by evaluating the story from two different ontological perspectives:

Step 1: *Look at the story without historical thinking*, that is, like a VBA-trained social scientist, freezing history and geography. Answer the following questions. First, which of the nine antecedents would you deem to be the causally most and the causally least important? Either ordinally rank them or lump them into groups according to their shared causal relevance. Second, identify the criteria you used in you ranking. What makes some factors more causally relevant and others less so? For example, do you privilege human agency over circumstances, or vice

---

[1] For the popularity of Carr's example, see Appleby, Hunt, and Jacob 2011, 304; Evans 1997, 112–14; Gaddis 2002, 93–4.

versa? Would you agree with Carr that Mr. Robinson's smoking is immaterial to explaining his death? Third, depending on which factors you deem to be more important, what would this story be a case of? In other words, what larger population of similar cases do you have in mind when making causal inferences in this particular case? Is this a case of bad street lighting, smoking, etc.? Fourth, formulate a brief theory that could explain the fact pattern laid out by Carr. Fifth, what would be a possible alternative theory?

Step 2: Look at the story with historical thinking. Add the following clause to the end of the story "... when he was hit, on Sunday September 3, 1939, in Lerwick, Scotland." What additional clues do these two pieces of information add to your analysis? What happened specifically on that date? Where is Lerwick? (Do a quick Google search.) Also, ask yourself what you know about the broader period in which the accident occurred. What relevant clues related to car accidents, cars, medicine etc. might this period provide? What are the broader geographic characteristics in Lerwick that might be relevant for explaining this accident? How might those characteristics impose historical and geographic boundary conditions on the theory you developed in Step 1? Don't get too hung up about the specifics of the date and location. If September 3, 1939 and Lerwick do not suggest any clues, pick your own date and location and see how they change your analysis.

2 Varieties of Historical Time
History Is Not a Dummy Variable

> A sense of time is not a simple thing. Time is something which people must painfully learn to think clearly about – something, indeed, which they must be taught. And there are many obstacles in the path of understanding it. It is difficult enough in this day and age for a person to imagine that there really was a past and that there will be a future.
>
> (Fischer 1970, 132)

In his classic *Historians' Fallacy*, David Hackett Fischer (1970) makes clear that historical thinking is neither common nor natural. It runs up against a presentism bias deeply engrained in society that lets us discount the future, misremember the past, and reconstruct it by reading history backwards (Møller 2021). For example, we price corporations by their quarterly earnings, judge politicians by their latest poll numbers, and define happiness by the speed with which our desires are satisfied. And, as social scientists, we freeze history to make social reality orderly enough for our mathematical tools and thereby *methodologically construct distinct notions of history*. These constructions of history have been inadequately studied, as most scholars treat history as a dummy variable. This chapter fills this gap by thinking of history as a plural phenomenon. It draws on leads offered by comparative historical analysis (CHA) (Braudel 1980; Capoccia and Ziblatt 2010; Sewell 1996) as well as the literature on memory politics (Bernhard and Kubik 2014; Dixon 2018). Memory politics expands on George Orwell's (1961, 44) famous line in *1984*: "who controls the past controls the future: who controls the present controls the past." It studies the political construction of history by disentangling public debates over history textbooks, monuments, holidays, museums, or whatever other means are used to collectively remember the past. This political construction of the past has an ontological equivalent in the methodological construction of history.

Social scientists methodologically construct history through their ontological choices, just as cartographers construct maps by selecting different projections to graph three-dimensional geography and two-dimensional paper. These ontological choices are necessary to align research design – used to make causal inferences – with the question being answered. For example, using experiments to analyze the recurring populist surges in US history would be as inappropriate as using CHA to evaluate the effectiveness of a job training program. Waves of populism and outcomes of social programs have very different ontological qualities, and thus require research designs that rest on historical and geographic presuppositions appropriate to answer those questions. This alignment process involves *ontological triage* by asking either *how much history a method can handle* or *how much methodology a historical question can accommodate*. Answering these questions involves triage because there are no a priori rules for how to align methods and questions. Understanding the different methodological constructions of history can assist in this alignment process by making more transparent the historical presupposition on which different methods rest. Or to put it in Orwellian terms, who controls ontology controls methodology: who understands history controls ontology.

This chapter explicates four notions of history – cyclical, bounded, serial, and eventful – and discusses how they were constructed in light of different methodological exigencies. *Cyclical history* treats the past as solidly frozen and sees it as unfolding through a recurring pattern of rises and falls that preclude any qualitative changes. It plays only a marginal role in CHA, but is central to variance-based analysis (VBA). *Bounded history* partially thaws the past and carves out a single time block that remains frozen, but it acknowledges those frozen blocks to be qualitatively different from the blocks preceding and following them. It recognizes historical boundary conditions without being interested in how one period is different from another. *Serial history* further thaws the past, while also extending its time scale. It draws on notions of natural history, where change unfolds glacially and involves long-term secular trends. It plays an important role in time series and evolutionary arguments. Finally, *eventful history* entirely unfreezes history. It is the methodologically least constrained, least constructed, and embodies the historical thinking embraced by card-carrying historians. It pays close attention to dates and events and analyzes the unfolding of the past in terms of periods, in order to demarcate historical continuities and discontinuities.

The terms for these four histories periodically appear in some writings, but are not yet part of the standard CHA vocabulary. This chapter therefore conceptually differentiates them more systematically and labels them, so as to refine CHA's temporal vocabulary. However, CHA's historical pluralism has its own limits. I conclude the chapter by introducing *historical tourism* as an umbrella term designed to capture treatments of history that are either politically rather than methodologically constructed or so solidly frozen that they stop being historical even in the thinnest sense of the word.

2.1 William Playfair's Universal Commercial History Graph

Understanding history, let alone four different variants of it, is a challenging undertaking because the past is not something that we can readily visit; nor is it something we accurately remember. Data visualization mitigates this challenge of imagining history because it offers what the historians Daniel Rosenberg and Anthony Grafton (2010) aptly called a "cartography of time" that makes historical patterns more readily discernible. It therefore uses chronologies, periodizations, and time series line graphs to visualize time. These chart types provide the basis for more specialized visualizations – such as Gantt charts, heatmaps, Sankey charts, or rain cloud plots – or more complex composite graphs such as Minard's visualization of Napoleon's ill-fated Russian campaign of 1812 (Friendly and Wainer 2021). At various stages of this book, I draw on such graphs to make history more legible. Few individuals contributed more to visualizing historical processes than the Scottish polymath William Playfair. His 1805 Universal Commercial History graph (Figure 2.1) was not just the first line graph; it also remains to this day one of the most stunning historical data visualizations. This chapter uses this graph to illustrate the four notions of historical time.

Let me first introduce this chapter's colorful protagonist. Playfair (1759–1832) was born in Dundee, Scotland into a family of distinguished scholars who participated in the Scottish Enlightenment. He worked as an accountant, engineer, journalist, draftsman, investment broker, and speculator. His financial deals were shady enough to land him in prison. His adventurism took him to France, where he allegedly became involved in the storming of the Bastille. Having second thoughts about his revolutionary sympathies, he began to work as a British secret agent in a clandestine counterfeit operation that aimed to destabilize France's revolutionary government. Throughout all these exploits, Playfair developed an interest in political economy and in the visualization of economic data. He published several books that used beautiful charts to present such data. It is those books that established him as the pioneer of data visualization and the inventor of the pie chart, the line graph, and complex infographics. The Chart of Universal Commercial History arguably became his most famous graph and graced the cover of his 1805 book, *The Inquiry into the Permanent Causes of the Decline and Fall of Powerful and Wealthy Nations* (Friendly and Wainer 2021, 95–120; Sachs 2012). The graph itself provides a visual synopsis of the book's central question: How do nations, once they become prosperous, manage to sustain their prosperity? The graph ultimately illustrates the enormous exploratory and descriptive potential that data visualization has in identifying interesting

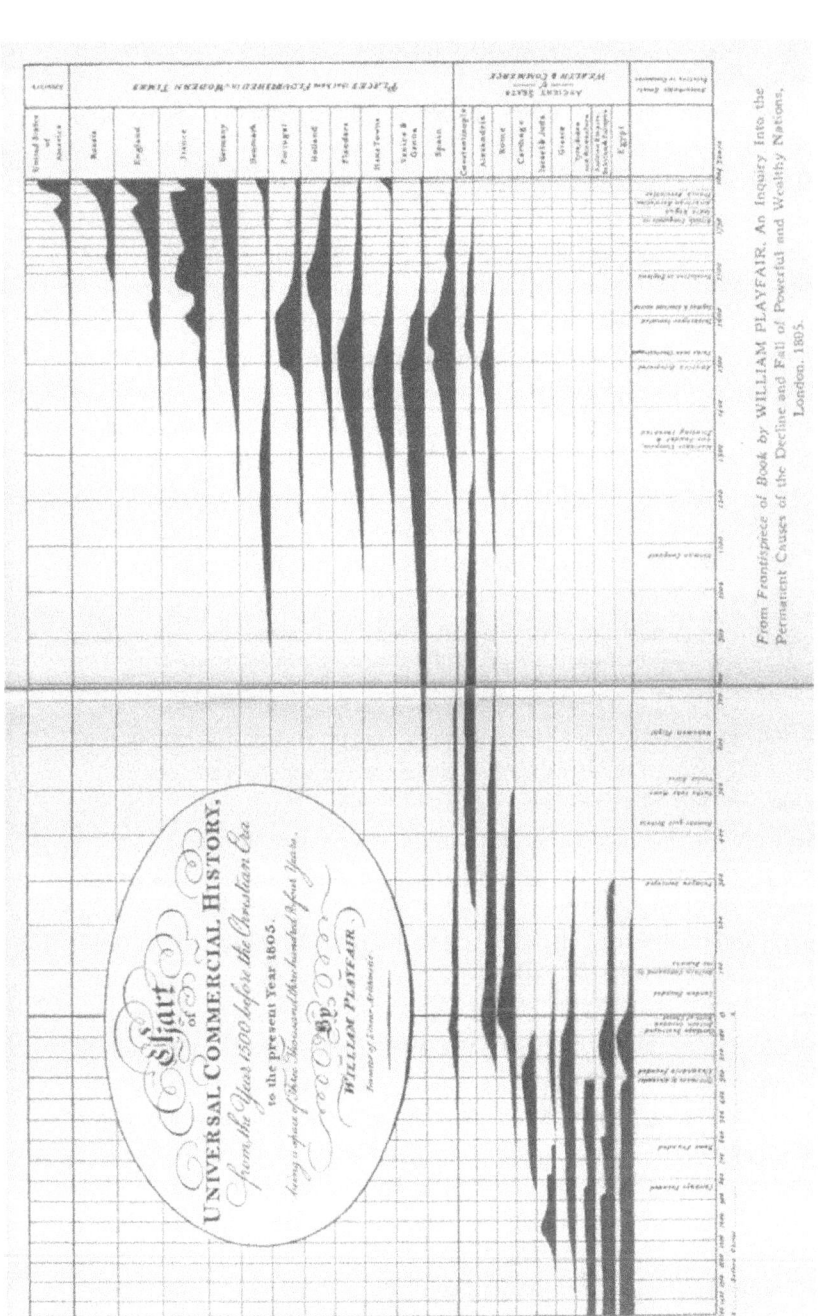

Figure 2.1 Playfair's Universal Commercial History graph

Playfair is one of the inventors of data visualization and this graph is his masterpiece. It is widely viewed as the first line graph and demonstrates the power of visualization to identify patterns and research questions. The bottom, illegible panel lists historical events. The graph points to three questions: What explains the rise and fall of economic fortunes of individual nations? What accounts for the economic slump between AD 500 and 1100? And what explains the geographic shift of prosperous nations from the Mediterranean to the North Atlantic? The graph employs four notions of historical time: cyclical, bounded, serial, and eventful.

patterns and formulating research questions. *Seeing historically stimulates thinking historically.*

To fully appreciate the graph's subtleties, let me first highlight its basic structure. The twenty-one-line charts constitute the graph's core. Playfair uses a particular line graph variant, known as cloud plots because they fill in the space below the line, creating cloud-like patterns. The horizontal timeline axis departs from the standard line graph in two ways. He inserts immediately above the timeline a chronology of important historical events to contextualize the otherwise eventless line graphs. He furthermore stacks multiple line graphs rather than anchoring them all in the same zero point. This stacking is crucial because it helps to compare the countries' economic fortunes. The stacked trendlines create a tacit meta-trendline. As the eyes move from the lower left to the upper right corner, the stacked trendlines reveal the geographic shift of prosperous nations from the Mediterranean to the North Atlantic. This shift would be less immediately visible if all the countries were plotted against a single vertical axis with a single zero point.

This stacking also allows Playfair to plot two separate dimensions on the vertical axis. The first dimension involves an indicator that tracks the economic fortunes of nations with each line graph. We will be polite and not probe too closely what indicator Playfair used to measure those fortunes. Asking for perfection in the very first line graph would be setting the bar unreasonably high. The second dimension uses the stacking to add time to the vertical axis as well. He does so by plotting Egypt as the first country to prosper, at the bottom, and the United States as the most recent one to do so, at the very top of the vertical axis. This allows Playfair to group the countries into three broader periods: antiquity, modern times, and, in a prophetic move, an American age. One stroke of genius in Playfair's graph, therefore, is to get time on both axes: this not only allows us to track the continuous unfolding of the trendlines but also gives us a thicker history by marking the discontinuities in those trends. It becomes apparent that countries rose and fell during antiquity, stagnated during the Middle Ages, began to rise and fall again from 1300 to 1700, and, since then, only rose, thus raising the question whether this time history would be different: Would the British Empire be everlasting, or would it suffer the same fate that its predecessors endured?

Graphs help us see historical patterns by drawing on and, as in the case of Playfair's Universal Commercial History, layering different conceptions of history. Understanding the construction of these different notions of history therefore is key to reading and ultimately also constructing such graphs.

2.2 Differentiating Four Types of Historical Time

The social critic Lewis Mumford observed that the clock "disassociated time from human events and helped create the belief in an independent world of mathematically measurable sequences" (quoted in N. Carr 2008, 84). In the most direct reading of this quotation, Mumford blames clocks for the fact that mathematics displaced historical analysis as the primary mode for studying human events. He further implies that, in creating an orderly world independent of the messiness of human events, clocks had the ontological capacity to produce a particular history-free social reality. This insight is key to understanding the methodological construction of different notions of history. Where clocks did away with history altogether, the four notions of history – cyclical, bounded, serial, and eventful – involve ontological choices that dissociate, and hence background, human events to varying degrees. I benchmark those ontological choices against three factors: the importance of dates and events, the type of comparison employed, and the attention given to qualitative changes. I use these three benchmarks, Playfair's graph, and contemporary CHA examples to differentiate the four notions of history.

2.2.1 Cyclical History: The Past as a Perennial Now

In writing *The Inquiry into the Permanent Causes*, Playfair was deeply influenced by Adam Smith's *Wealth of Nations* (1776), which discussed the general principles that structure market exchanges, and Edward Gibbon's *The History of the Decline and Fall of the Roman Empire* (1776), which uses the fate of the Roman Empire to explore the changing fortunes of nations. Smith's focus on transhistorical market principles and Gibbon's interest in recurring patterns of rise and fall of social systems lead both to employ a cyclical notion of history. This cyclical history reflected an older version of history, linked to the religious belief that key attributes of the past repeat themselves. The point of studying cyclical history was to learn universal moral lessons from earlier rises and falls; it was not to understand modernity by discovering how the present is different from the past (Eliade 1949; Toulmin and Goodfield 1965). This implies a notion of the past as a "perennial now" in which dates do not matter and, by consequence, where history, in the modern sense of involving qualitative and irreversible changes, does not matter either (Eliade 1949, 85).

The influence of Smith's and Gibbon's cyclical history is evident in the rising and falling trendlines of the twenty-one-line graphs and in Playfair's claim, suggested by the graph's title, of offering a "universal commercial history." Those graphs assume that economic fortunes rise and fall regardless of historical contexts and that they follow a transhistorical and hence universal pattern that allows us to compare ancient Egypt with the modern-day United States. The dates separating these two different periods or the specific events shaping them are irrelevant. In the line graphs, dates only matter by telling us that the rise and fall of Egypt occurred concurrently with Babylon and Greece and earlier than in the United Kingdom and United States. The dates serve to ordinally array the countries rather than linking their economic fortunes to specific historical contexts or events. In cyclical history, dates could just as easily be replaced by thinner time designators t_1, t_2, t_n used in a historyless analysis of time such as game theory. The delinking of countries' economic functions from their specific historical context permits cross-sectional comparisons, which are typically associated with contemporaneous geographic units of analysis used in VBA. But, since history repeats itself, it is possible to treat within-case, longitudinal variations as the equivalent of cross-sectional variations across multiple geographic units of analysis.

Cyclical history underpins experimental and frequentist methodologies because it creates a world orderly enough to meet the ontological prerequisites of statistics. Ironically enough, these advanced methodologies rest on a premodern, metaphysical notion of history. Cyclical history is also embedded in theories explaining phenomena that contain recurring, transhistorical causal mechanisms. It plays a central role in economics, where market dynamics recur across different historical contexts (Sewell 1996); in evolutionary psychology, where basic neurological processes transcend history (Henrich 2020); in demographics, where life-cycle effects capture recurring biological patterns; or in geography, where near constant, natural history–like processes shape short-term, more rapidly changing human history (Diamond 2017). The literature on business cycles and financial crises, for example, frequently employs cyclical history. Carmen Reinhart and Kenneth Rogoff's (2011) influential *This Time Is Different: Eight Centuries of Financial Folly* challenges the recurrent claim that the next financial crisis looming on the horizon will be different (i.e. will not materialize) because actors have learned from earlier ones, developed new tools to avert it or at least soften it. The two economists collected eight centuries of financial data to conclude that financial crises repeat themselves with disheartening regularity, which suggests that financial history follows a cyclical path.

However, cyclical history must be handled with utmost care because it freezes history to a degree where it barely matters. The notion of a past repeating itself suggests that contexts become so homogeneous that they can be ignored. Dates are no longer necessary to differentiate qualitative changes. Consequently, CHA views strictly cyclical history skeptically, unless it is embedded in the other, less frozen notions of history.

2.2.2 Bounded History: The Past as Frozen but Qualitatively Different Blocks of Time

Bounded history appears most frequently in discussions about historical boundary conditions that are invoked to qualify the external validity of test results. Such conditions stipulate that, within a given period, history is static enough for us to not confound causal inferences drawn from data collected within that period (Lieberman 2001). Scholars invoking such conditions recognize that history is frozen for some periods, but not so frozen that the past is never different from the present. Historical boundary conditions serve a methodological purpose, as the scholars invoking them are *not* interested – as regular historians would be – in the qualitative differences between two adjacent historical periods. In this sense, bounded history remains very thin: it serves as a quasi-control for potential confounders rather than as an analytical tool for studying historical changes.

Playfair employs a notion of bounded history to contextualize the cyclical notions implicit in the line graphs. This bounded notion appears on the vertical axis, where he lumps the twenty-one countries into three periods: ancient states, modern states, and America. Playfair's periodization acknowledges differences in these three historical contexts without exploring them further or looking for patterns of change. History still is largely eventless, and dates serve the limited purpose of marking the start and end points of the historical boundaries that truncate the past into static periods. The periods themselves are frozen and thus make inconsequential the three thousand years that separate Egypt and Alexandria within the ancient world period. The periods themselves therefore do not have any internal histories themselves other than being the "perennial nows" that define cyclical history.

The interchangeability between bounded history and historical boundary conditions underscores the former's methodological pedigree. Theda Skocpol employs a soft version of bounded history in her *State and Social Revolutions*. She treats the period between 1789 and 1949, during which the French, Russian, and Chinese revolutions occurred, as a largely frozen single period. She contends that the world capitalist economy and the permeability of national structures to external effects such as wars made this period uniform enough to permit bounded generalizations. She also uses bounded history to deploy both most similar and most different research designs and control for confounding effects (Skocpol 1979, 22, 39; for further discussion of her treatment of history, see Mahoney 1999; Sewell 1996).

On other occasions, scholars have used bounded history to identify boundary conditions that prior scholars overlooked. Kenneth Scheve and David Stasavage (2009), for example, challenge the widely accepted finding that redistributive social policies explain the reduction in income inequality on the grounds that this finding overlooks historical boundary conditions. They expand the existing data set from the post-1970s to the entire twentieth century and get a null finding (225–38). They also pay close attention to the timing of centralized wage bargaining, because existing theories identify it as the central causal factor in reducing income inequality. They check whether the timing of this change translates into a noticeable drop in income inequality. Here again, they do not find any correlation (238–45). Overall, their two null findings draw attention to historical boundary conditions that existing theories overlook. They, then, are not interested in thickening their historical analysis and explaining how the historical context, which bounds the external validity of findings, is qualitatively different from other periods.

2.2.3 Serial History: The Past as Fluid Trends

Serial history is linked to more structural, even natural, notions of history that the French Annales historians introduced to CHA. One of their most prominent members, Ferdinand Braudel, wrote that "some structures, because of their long life, become stable elements for an infinite number of generations: they get in the way of history, hinder its flow" (Braudel 1980, 31). Braudel associated such structures with long-term macro-economic, demographic, and even environmental processes that were more slow-moving than historical events, thus hindering but not blocking their flow. I will expand on the Annales historians' longue durée view of history in Chapter 6; here I limit myself to explicating the notion of serial history, which they introduced to CHA.

The term "serial" implies analyzing events that are recurrent enough to form a series but not recurrent enough to become cyclical. They recur because of statutory timing (e.g., elections, holidays, census dates, recording practices of statistical offices) or as a result of non-statutory factors linked to natural history (e.g., seasons, calendars, demographics). They are non-cyclical in that they form secular trends that help us understand how the past is related to the present. Their recurring nature makes it possible to compare and measure them. Serial history informs the work of economic historians and demographers, as well as any literature that can avail itself of time series data or other data capable of tracking long-term trends. For example, Thomas Piketty's *Capital in the Twenty-First Century* (2017) analyzes long-term inequality in the past two centuries in advanced industrialized countries, while Ian Morris' *Why the West Rules* (2011) uses measures such as energy consumption or urbanization rates to track the divergent social developments in the West and the rest of the world. It is a bit more difficult to detect serial history in Playfair. I pointed out that the rises and falls in his line graphs reflect cyclical history. However, if we shorten Playfair's multi-millennia time scale, those same line graphs also reveal century-long secular non-cyclical trends. Egypt, for example, experienced a short-term decline around AD 300 and then rebounded for the next two centuries.

Four characteristics define serial history. First, it looks at the past through a theoretical lens that determines ex ante which observations and occurrences are worthy of closer analysis and which ones constitute noise. This theoretical focus is linked to serial history's fondness for time series data, which require looking at the past through predefined analytical categories. Second, dates play an important role by linking measurement to a historical context, even though the exploration of these contexts is restricted to the attributes measured by a variable. Third, the measured events are interdependent enough to capture historical dynamics. For example, the electoral performance of a party in one election is conditional on that party's performance in the prior election; or the a country's Gross Domestic Product (GDP) in one decade is conditional on that country's prosperity in previous decades. Such interdependences are of course only partial. Prior events do not fully explain subsequent ones, because each subsequent event interacts with new contextual factors such as political scandals, economic crises, or new technologies and thus is also partially independent of the prior event. To return to Mark Twain's observation, this interdependence is not strong enough for the past to repeat itself, but strong enough to make it rhyme with the present. Fourth, serial history uses serial comparisons that anchor the events in specific historical contexts. But, unlike historical comparisons, serial comparisons limit the historical context to the attributes specified by the relevant variable. Playfair, for example, employs serial comparisons by applying a very abstract conception of national economy, namely as an economy that can be captured by a monetary metric by measuring the sum of all economic activities. This metric is context-independent, which makes economies comparable even though Egyptian economy from 1500 BC to 1 BC was qualitatively different from American economy in 1805. Serial history pays less attention to these qualitative differences and is thus thinner than eventful history.

2.2.4 Eventful History: The Past as an Alternation of Continuities and Discontinuities

With eventful history, we return full circle to the classical historical thinking deployed by card-carrying historians. I will therefore not reiterate its emphasis on dates, holistic treatment of events, and focus on continuities and discontinuities. Instead I will concentrate on its hidden presence in

Playfair's graph and discuss two further elements of eventful history: periodizations and directionality.

Eventful history is less immediately apparent in Playfair's graph, but it features in three subtle ways. First, the bottom panel offers a rudimentary version of eventful history. Playfair lists barely legible historical events such as the English, French, and American revolutions, either directly, to contextualize the economic trends, or obliquely, to hint at possible explanations. This eventful analysis is rudimentary because it does not employ historical comparisons to explicate patterns of recurrence across events. Second, the last five countries, starting with Germany, show only an economic upward trend and no sustained declines from 1700 onward. The graph therefore suggests that the economic fortunes of these cases might be qualitatively different from those of earlier ones, in that these countries are no longer subject to cyclical patterns. It looks as if Playfair anticipated, already in 1805, just how profoundly the technological breakthroughs of the Industrial Revolution would transform national economies. Third, the graph points to a long-term geographic pattern in which the centers of commercial prosperity shifted gradually from the Mediterranean to Northern Europe, after an overall decline during the Middle Ages. This pattern is the most historical one because it identifies clear continuities and discontinuities.

Eventful history's most defining characteristic is interest in reconnecting human events with time, particularly dates, in order to identify more intimately patterns of change and describe them in terms of continuities and discontinuities. This focus on qualitative changes becomes apparent in periodizations and discussions about the direction of history.

Eventful history uses *periodizations* to delineate continuities and discontinuities, to clarify how the past is different from the present, to pinpoint when those changes occurred, and to establish how long they endured. Periodization involves "identifying and naming coherent time intervals" and synchronizing the "temporal rhythms" of subjective human experience with the objective chronological order of calendars (Kosellek 2002, 110). A period is nothing but "the space between two markers that we place on the ticker tape of time to make history legible" (Lilla 2016, 133). Eventful history constructs such periods by lumping multiple contiguous events into chronological containers on the basis of the recurrence or non-recurrence of certain attributes across them. This focus on temporal *recurrence patterns* is different from the more standard focus on geographical *uniformity patterns*. Eventful analysis is interested in *chronological instead of spatial generalizations* (Kreuzer 2001, 10–11). In Playfair, it is the cross-sectional patterns of the stacked line graphs that provide the basis for the fourfold periodization into antiquity, Middle Ages, modernity, and, by 1805 standards, the still speculative American age.

As these vague guidelines suggest, there is no simple formula for truncating the past into periods that might explain why this important task has received little scholarly attention (Haydu 1998; Kersh 2005; J. S. Smith 1998). This lack of clear periodization criteria reflects in part how much eventful history unfreezes history. Periodization can be viewed as an effort to explore the degree of interdependence between the past and the present and to find points at which changes in degree amount to changes in kind. The hallmark of a period is a cluster of events that are sufficiently independent of prior events to become qualitatively different, and thus to deserve their own historical boundaries. Periodization involves a kind of temporal cartography that looks for *patterns of recurrence* or temporal generalizations.

Sometimes eventful history takes a more sweeping approach and looks beyond a few periods, to explore whether, if taken together, they follow a particular *direction*. In looking at such directionality, eventful history tries to disprove the tacit assumption – a kind of null hypothesis in historiography – that change brought about by discontinuities is too random to produce broader directional patterns in the long run. CHA and historians often remain skeptical about historical change having a direction, because this implies linearity, and even a telos that is suspiciously deterministic (Butterfield 1965; Sewell 1996). Nevertheless, historians discuss to what extent a country's history is exceptional; and, by doing so, they imply a distinct direction. American political development (APD) historians, for example, debate whether the liberal promise of its founders makes the United States exceptional and whether the country has expanded on this promise (Orren and Skowronek 2004). German historians regularly ponder on whether Germany's history converged with that of other European countries or it followed an exceptionalist *Sonderweg* that culminated in the Holocaust (Blackbourn and Eley 1984; Kreuzer 2003). Global historians, in turn, debate to what extent globalization can or cannot be equated with westernization, or whether it's making the world flatter (Conrad 2017). Eventful analysis thus employs different directionality templates to characterize the nature of long-term historical change.

Table 2.1 summarizes the key elements of the four types of history. As Part II will show, eventful, serial, and bounded history are closely associated with the different strands of CHA. The degree to which each strand freezes history is closely linked to distinct analytical imperatives that allow CHA to tailor its historical thinking to the research task at hand. Cyclical history freezes history to such a degree that it enjoys a rather ambiguous status in CHA. To explore this ambiguity, let me turn to historical tourism.

Table 2.1 Varieties of historical time

	Cyclical History	Bounded History	Serial History	Eventful History
Freezing of history	Solidly frozen. Very thin	Partially thawed. Thin	Fluid. Thick	Fully liquid. Very thick
Assumptions about the past	Is recurring and identical with the present.	Is different from present, but the differences are not further explored.	Is different from present and connected through secular trends.	Is different from present and connected through events.
Importance of dates	*Unimportant.* Context always the same. Contexts can be substituted with t_1, t_2, t_3.	*Marginally important.* Demarcates starting and end points of periods.	*Important.* Links measurements to a historical context.	*Central.* Helps analyze how earlier events shape later ones and delineate periods.
Importance of events	*Unimportant.* Is eventless	*Unimportant.* Is eventless because history is frozen within given period.	*Important.* Focuses on recurring, measurable, thin events.	*Central.* Focus on recurrence and non-recurrence of complex, thick events.
Importance of qualitative changes	*Unimportant.* Precludes qualitative changes. The past is constant and unchanging.	*Unimportant.* Periods are not compared to identify patterns of change.	*Important.* Secular trends track changes in degree.	*Central.* Identifies historical continuities and discontinuities and directionality of change.
Type of comparison	Cross-sectional	Contextual	Serial	Historical

CHA employs four types of historical time. They vary in the importance they assign to dates, events, qualitative change, and ultimately the frozenness of history. The grey cells identify three types of historical time most central to CHA. Cyclical time plays only a marginal role in CHA.

2.3 Historical Tourism: What Historical Time Is *Not*

CHA treats history as a plural, but its historical ecumenism has limits. It asks whether the construction of history becomes in some instances so static that it ceases to be historical at all. This question crops up often enough to warrant closer attention. And, not surprisingly, it is discussed under different labels, even though it deals with the same issue. I therefore coined the term *historical tourism* to describe these ahistorical uses of history. The tourism analogy expands the belief that to travel is to learn and links the degree of learning to the degree of adventurism that travelers bring to their journeys. Technically, visiting Paris to take selfies at the local Starbucks before the tour bus ships you off to the next gift shop constitutes traveling; but it forgoes cultural enrichments for the convenience of being able to order the same latte as back home – thus freezing geography – and skips the history lesson in order to appreciate a visited monument – thus freezing history. Analogously, traveling into the past can adopt those same non-exploratory, tourist-like qualities that deprive historical thinking of its potential to make discoveries. The historical tourist becomes the equivalent of the season-ticket holder in John Cage's concert hall, so firmly expecting classical music, preferably of the Mozart–Beethoven variety, as to be unable to hear any other sounds. Historical tourists are so beholden to ontological precedent, so unaware that history is constructed in a variety of ways, so unprepared to engage in ontological triage that they forsake the exploratory offerings of history. The telltale sign of the ontological obstinacy that defines historical tourists is their indifference of dates, which are so central to historical thinking.

Historians guard themselves against three forms of historical tourism: antiquarianism, teleology, and cyclical history. All three invoke prior philosophical claims that offer ex ante explanations for the unfolding of history that make it unnecessary to pay attention to events and the patterns they form. They engage in *mis-chronicling* which is the historical counterpart to mis-sampling. Events are mis-chronicled if relevant events are excluded, or their order is mis-arrayed. Such mis-chronicling frequently is politically motivated and thus involves historical tourism.

Historians use *antiquarianism* as a term of disparagement to categorize wannabe historians who cling to a virtuous notion of the past and contrast it with a less virtuous present. An antiquarian uses this past as a "sanctuary from the sordid [present] world which he neither accepts nor understands" (Fischer 1970, 140). In the American context, antiquarians include in their ranks nostalgia-filled Tea-Party members, MAGA supporters, Straussian political philosophers, constitutional originalists, and pretty much anybody untroubled by historical anachronisms. The historian Eric Foner (2017) points out that Civil War monuments were erected in the 1920s ostensibly to intimidate African Americans, even though its sponsors claimed that they served to commemorate war-time generals who had fought half a century ago. This is a clear example of mis-chronicling. The historian Jill Lepore points out that antiquarians share a set of assumptions about the relationship between the past and the present that is both broadly anti-intellectual, and quite specifically anti-historical, not least because it defies chronology, the logic of time. "To say that we are there or the Founding Fathers are here . . . is to subscribe to a set of assumptions about the relationship between the past and the present" that is anti-historical because it stipulates "a particular and quite narrowly defined past – 'the Founding' as ageless, sacred and to be worshipped." (Lepore 2011, 15–16)

Teleological explanations claim a heroic future to which history inescapably marches; and they treat all discontinuities as changes in moving toward this historical end state. Teleology reads history backwards and "abstracts things from their historical context and judges them apart from their context – estimating them and organizing the historical story by a system of direct reference to the present" (Butterfield 1965, 30). Such explanations closely resemble functional ones, minus the natural selection mechanisms. They abandon the analytical task of thinking about the ways in which history unfolds and, in doing so, transforms society. Finally, *cyclical explanations* hark back to ancient or Christian beliefs that the natural and the social world are guided by a single, mathematically ordered cosmos, which is eternal and thus free of a qualitatively different past. In such an ordered cosmos, there "could be no question of its having come into existence progressively" and of its being "continuously changing"; the universe must instead "have been created at one stroke, already complete in every essential feature, and with substantially its present form" (Toulmin and Goodfield 1965, 41). Despite the impossibility of any qualitative changes, time is not frozen and static, as cyclical explanations assume that history repeats itself in the same recurring cycles rather than "revealing patterns or having meaning" (Appleby, Hunt, and Jacob 2011, 57).

CHA scholars point to four potential forms of historical tourism: history as within-case variation, history as a randomization machine, historical persistence studies, and functional explanations. These forms of historical tourism also involve methodological constructions of the history. Unlike the constructions of bounded, serial, and eventful history, they do not freeze history, thus leaving traces of it, but misconstrue it so fundamentally as to deprive it of any exploratory purpose (Kalyvas and Fedorowycz 2022). For this reason they fall outside the purview of CHA.

In their landmark *Designing Social Inquiry*, King, Keohane, and Verba (1994) famously claimed that qualitative and quantitative scholars employ the same frequentist logic of causal inferences. They consequently recommended that their qualitative colleagues increase the number of their observations in a single case by using the history of the case to identify additional pieces of evidence. They asked in effect qualitative scholars to treat longitudinal, within-case observations as the same as cross-sectional observations linked to adding more cases (Tarrow 1995, 472). In making this assumption, they freeze history, render dates irrelevant to social inquiry, and end up treating the past as "a site for generating more data" (Pierson 2004, 5). More recently, social scientists have begun using history to find discontinuities or using natural experiments to identify quasi-randomizations in the data. They travel through history looking for military conflicts, plagues, natural disasters, boundary changes, or any random, God-like event. This new, strictly methodological interest in history has been part of the so-called inference revolution, imported from a largely historyless strand of economics (Diamond and Robinson 2011; Kocher and Monteiro 2016). Persistence arguments, currently popular among economists, share with antiquarianism a belief in extraordinarily enduring historical continuities. Their proponents forgo the reactionary nostalgia for a virtuous past by providing empirical support for this persistence. Consequently they do not automatically engage in historical tourism, but should nevertheless be assessed with a skeptical eye, given the extent to which they read history backwards, freeze intervening events, and teeter on the brink of historical determinism. Chapter 6 elaborates further the potential historical tourism of persistence arguments. (For a more differentiated treatment, see Wittenberg 2015.)

Functional explanations borrow from biology or neoclassical economics the idea of historical efficiency, according to which natural selection or "invisible hand" mechanisms choose at moments of discontinuity whatever available option is the most efficient (March and Olsen 1984, 737). Efficient is defined ex post, after history made its choices and thus revealed what was most efficient (Elster 1983). Such functionalism is particularly prominent in neoclassical equilibria assumptions, in which markets serve as discovery mechanisms that invariably allocate resources and pick new technologies on the basis of the greatest efficiency. Functionalist explanations are ahistorical because they read history backwards and explain change by considering the effects that produced it. They fail to explicate and empirically demonstrate the generative process and reduce all changes to a single, ahistorical natural selection mechanism. The economic historian Robert Gordon's monumental *The Rise and Fall of American Growth* is a sweeping broadside against neoclassical, functionalist models of economic change. Its analysis rejects the notion of historical efficiency and the pattern of the United States' gradual, linear, and continuous economic growth. Gordon points out here that "economic growth is neither steady nor continuous. There was no economic growth over eight centuries between the fall of the Roman Empire and the Middle Ages, and similarly economic growth over the 19th and 20th century in the US was much slower before and after the period between 1920 to 1970" (Gordon 2017, ix). He then explains those discontinuities in terms of the availability of different technologies and their respective capacity to generate different rates of growth.

Exercises

2.1. Identify the four types of historical time used in Playfair's Universal Commercial History (Figure 2.1) that the chapter discussed. Explain how Playfair translated those elements of historical time into graphical features. What particular insight does each notion of history provide? And how do they complement each other?

2.2. What notions of historical time does Earl Cook use in this graph? (see Figure 6.2). What criteria does he employ when changes in degrees of energy consumption (the trendline) become changes in kind (i.e. industrial, technological man)? In what way does Cook come close to engaging in historical tourism? And, if so, of what kind? The graph tracks changes in transportation in terms of degree of energy consumption. During the last two periods, the increase in energy consumption for transportation, tracked by the trendline, masks important qualitative changes in modes of transportation. What are these changes? How effectively are they captured by the increase in energy consumption?

2.3. The journalist Malcolm Gladwell has long explored historical and physical time, and hence will make several guest appearances in this book. In *Outliers*, he investigates the deeper historical roots of honor killings, common in Appalachia in earlier times (Gladwell 2008, 161–76). What notion of history does he apply in his analysis? What sort of pattern is he explaining – variations, varieties, trends, transformation? Given that honor killings are no longer as prominent as they were before the 1930s – the period Gladwell uses in his examples – to what notions of history would you look to understand this change? What factors might have contributed to the decline in honor killings? How do these factors differ from the ones proposed the historian (David Hackett Fischer) and two psychologists (Dov Cohen and Richard Nisbett) whom Gladwell cites? Thinking of the notion of history that these scholars employ, how similar is it to, or how different from, the notion that you used in elaborating your own explanatory factors? How close does Gladwell come to engage in historical tourism?

2.4. The historian Robert Paxton's *Five Stages of Fascism* walks readers through the challenges of defining fascism and employs historical thinking even though he does not formally use this term (Paxton 1998). How do the standard definitions of fascism freeze geography and history, and thus miss some of its key elements? What sort of comparisons does Paxton use to define fascism? In unfreezing history, does he end up just relying on eventful history? Or does he mix it with other notions of history? On what notions of history do his five stages rest? What do those five stages tell us about the nature of fascism? What notion of history is implicit in each individual stage? How likely are those five stages to repeat themselves outside the interwar period – for example to describe the dynamics of more contemporary right-wing political groups? If the answer is affirmative, to what notion of history would this point?

3 Physical Time
Capturing the Rhythms of History

> There are decades where nothing happens; and there are weeks where
> decades happen.
>
> (Lenin, attributed)

Chapter 2 demonstrated how comparative historical analysis (CHA) tames the
noisiness of historical events by constructing four notions of history. So
historical time definitely grounds CHA; but it does not exhaust CHA's temporal foundations, as it also pays close attention to physical time. Historical
and physical time make for admittedly odd ontological bedfellows. Historical
time is linked to the social, eventful world where dates matter, where history is
unfrozen, and where context is important. Physical time, by contrast, is
associated with the material world, where dates matter less, history shifts onto
the territory of slow-moving, more cyclical natural history, and where contexts
are more uniform and analytically less relevant.[1] Yet despite these differences
physical and historical time complement each other, as this and subsequent
chapters will show.

Physical time makes two contributions to CHA. First, it helps us see, just as
Lenin did, that the patterns created through the unfolding of historical time
are subject to rhythms that are defined by context-independent temporal
attributes. CHA identifies five such attributes: tempo, duration, timing,
sequencing, and stages. These elements shift our attention from *what changes*
to *how it changes* and the rhythms of change.[2] Physical time thus complements serial and eventful history by refining the analysis of qualitative
changes. Second, it makes a theoretical contribution insofar as its elements
produce causal effects that are overlooked in existing theories, with the linear
notions of causality they employ. Time challenges the linearity assumption

---

[1] This tension between the historical and the physical time surfaces periodically in CHA intramural debates, where champions of physical time advise their colleagues to drop historical time
on the grounds that it is too messy to produce generalizable insights (Gerring 2003; Pierson
2000b). Champions of historical time, in turn, excommunicate their colleagues for focusing too
much on physical time at the expense of historical time (Sewell 1996). Thankfully, most CHA
scholars ignore those intramural debates and heterodoxically combine historical and
physical time.

[2] Stefano Bartolini (1993) and Lynn Hunt (2008) have been most explicit in making the distinction between physical and historical time, even though they use different labels.

that history is efficient and unfolds in a fashion so incremental and continuous that the non-linear effects of tempo, duration, timing, and sequencing can be ignored (Abbott 1988; March and Olsen 1984).

This chapter therefore introduces physical time and discusses its complementarity with historical time. It concludes by showing that the three strands of CHA – eventful, longue durée, and macro-causal analysis – combine historical and physical time in three distinct ways. The discussion of how physical time unfreezes linear causality will be carried out in Chapter 7, which deals with macro-causal analysis.

3.1 Elements of Physical Time

Pandemics – a classic macro-historical phenomenon – illustrate the complex interplay between historical and physical time. They are historical in several ways. Each pandemic has a starting date and an end date that anchor it in a distinct historical context, so that no two pandemics are identical. Pandemics are also interdependent; for example, an earlier pandemic sometimes shapes the public health responses to a latter one. And each pandemic has its own epidemiological history, as viruses mutate from one strand to the next. These elements are historical because their analysis requires close attention to dates. However, outside these historical dimensions, pandemics also involve physical time dynamics that are independent of dates and historical context.

Figure 3.1 illustrates these elements of physical time. Its creator, the public health advocate Marian Olpinski, tellingly labeled it a "natural history," suggesting an analogy between immunization and other natural phenomena, for example the weather, geology, or evolution, where precise dates matter far less than in human history. The figure employs a multiline graph to track three processes: the course of the pandemic, vaccine coverage, and adverse events. It arrays those processes along a vaguely ordinal time metric, which uses the five maturation stages rather than a chronological timeline with concrete, experience-near dates. Disconnecting these processes from historical context permits observing the moving parts *within* a generic, context-independent, highly abstract pandemic. Figure 3.1 obliquely references history by including adverse events – the public health counterpart to the economists' exogeneous shocks. This residual category is open-ended and could cover historical elements such as virus mutations, the discovery of vaccines, or the capacity of healthcare systems. The figure assigns a low frequency to such adverse events, thus indicating how it freezes history in order to draw attention to a physical time that can be observed regardless of historical context. Let me discuss these five elements of physical time further.

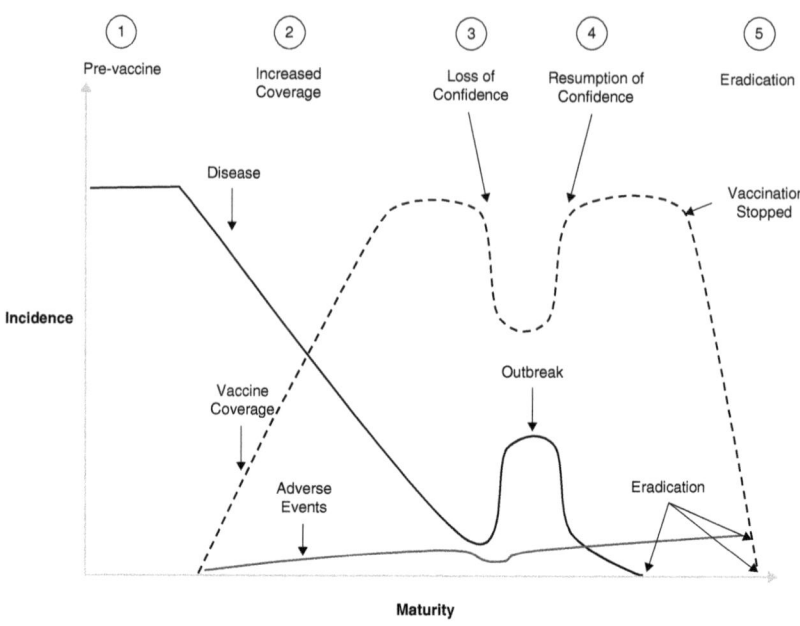

Figure 3.1 Natural history of an immunization program
This graph tracks the frequency of infections, vaccinations, and adverse events along an ordinal timeline. The resulting trendlines illustrate five elements of physical time: tempo/duration (changes in slope), timing (*early* start of vaccination by comparison with *late* infection outbreak), sequencing (do adverse events occur *before* or *after* vaccination starts), and stages (the five steps).
Source: M. Olpinski, cited in Gorman and Gorman 2016, 225.

Duration. Duration, together with tempo, is the most immediately measurable element of physical time because it is linked to clocks (Aminzade 1992, 460–2; Grzymala-Busse 2011, 1277–85). It measures the time elapsed between a starting and an end date and permits a *long and short* differentiation. In Figure 3.1 the duration of confidence loss varies across countries, depending on how effectively health officials communicate the vaccine's potential side effects. Duration not only affects the dynamics of an immunization program but also is central for understanding the spread of a pandemic. What made Covid-19 so treacherous was the seven-day time lag between exposure and the appearance of first symptoms. It is during this time window that asymptomatic infections take place that make Covid-19 so difficult to contain. The typical fourteen-day quarantine further recognizes that exposed individuals remain infectious for a fortnight (Christakis 2021, 47–74).

The political scientist Adam Przeworski (2019, 10–12) points out that understanding crises requires attention to duration. "Crises are situations that cannot last, in which something must be decided." Yet he points out that some crises endure, as the new scenario cannot replace the status quo even though the latter has become untenable. Other crises are shorter and become turning points, or what is called "critical junctures." The theorist Elizabeth Cohen (2018, 1–21), for example, investigates how political and legal procedures rely on duration to determine election or census intervals, citizenship eligibility, or sentencing guidelines. She shows how the measurable and hence seemingly impartial nature of duration legitimizes those procedures while also becoming a source of bias. The sociologist Karen Barkey (1996) points out that the Ottoman Empire limited the duration of local administrators' terms and randomized their reassignments. This dual measure was meant to preempt the development of local political networks that could challenge the central authority.

Tempo. The tempo measures the rate at which a particular phenomenon changes; thus the tempo allows for *slow–fast* or *acceleration* differentiations. The steep vaccination slope suggests a rapid vaccination rate, which is mirrored by an equally rapid decline in the infection rate. In a pandemic, this tempo is conditional on the transmissibility and severity of the virus, various attributes of the host (e.g., willingness to vaccinate, network of social interactions), and the environment (e.g., the season, capacity of healthcare system) (Christakis 2021, 47–74). The tempo also plays a role in many political phenomena. Stefano Bartolini (2000) compares the various tempi at which the franchise (i.e. the right to vote) was expanded across various countries. Ron Hassner (2007, 127–38) looks at the role that tempo and duration play in territorial disputes. He explains the different tempi at which countries entrench themselves in newly acquired territories in terms of the geographic constraints they faced and the symbolic significance of the territories in question. He then points out that in each case the tempo of this process affects the duration of the ensuing conflict with the country from which the territory was taken.

Sequencing has a distinct meaning in CHA. In ordinary language we talk about the sequence of days and nights, or the sequence of seasons, in other words we mean fixed and recurring patterns *within* a single case; or we talk about a sequence of events to reference a strictly chronological order. By contrast, CHA uses "sequence" in a comparative context, by juxtaposing two or more events *across* multiple cases so as to explore whether the order of those events varied. Sequencing pays attention to the temporal order of causal factors across cases and involves a *before–after differentiation*. It typically compares the fixed temporal order of causal factors stipulated by a theory with other possible and empirically observable temporal orderings. Sequences can deviate from the temporal order predicted by the theory by being fully reversed or by occurring simultaneously. Sequencing recognizes that the same causal factors, when unfolding in a different temporal order, produce different causal effects (Falleti and Mahoney 2015).

By contrast, pandemics involve multiple processes where we know from the outset that the sequence of their unfolding can have important consequences. The sequence between vaccine availability, pandemic outbreak, and virus mutation has significant implications. If a vaccine is available before or simultaneously with the spread of a pandemic, the outbreak can be contained much more quickly than in instances where it becomes available afterwards; or, if a vaccine is available before the virus mutates, this increases the chance of obtaining herd immunity before that vaccine loses its effectiveness. Tulia Falleti (2005) argues that the sequence of administrative, fiscal, and political decentralization determines the degree of autonomy of subnational units of government. Robert Dahl (1971) argues that democratizations in which limited elite contestation – permitted by rule of law, a free press, and freedom of association – preceded universal male suffrage were more stable than democratizations with the reverse sequence. He contends that the contest–inclusion sequence made it easier to develop norms of compromise because elite contestation involved smaller and more homogeneous groups of actors.

Timing. Timing compares the dates of singular, qualitatively equivalent events across multiple cases and makes an ordinal distinction between cases in which those events occur *early* and cases in which they occurred *late* vis-à-vis each other. Timing thus benchmarks the analysis against the first occurrence of a particular phenomenon, then differentiates later occurrences according to how proximate or distal to the first case they are in time. Timing is distinct from sequencing because it compares identical (or very similar) events across time rather than sets of distinct events.

This is also where we analyze to what extent the relative timing of events becomes causally consequential. For example, the later outbreak of a pandemic permits us to learn from the public health successes and failures of earlier outbreaks. Sociologists found that sentencing that takes place early in the day and later in the afternoon is more lenient than sentencing that takes place around mid-day. Similarly, when exams are timed early and late in the day, students perform better than when they are timed in midday. Sociologists explain these effects through timing: they claim that the timing of sentencing or exam taking interacts with the biological clocks of judges or students so as to produce these varied outcomes (Pink 2018). Alexander Gerschenkron (1962) discovered that the timing of industrialization profoundly affected its tempo, as late industrializers learned from their predecessors and used this knowledge to develop their economies more quickly. Various international relations scholars analyzed the timing effects of religious holidays. They found that such holidays reduce violence in civil conflicts, because actors are more likely to face normative disapproval for committing acts of violence on days that have been set aside for religious commemoration (Hassner 2011; Reese, Ruby, and Pape 2017).

Stages. Certain processes involve distinct stages that are relatively fixed across cases. In Figure 3.1, pandemics are marked by five distinct stages, which are in turn defined by different the configurations of rates of infection, vaccinations, and adverse events. Modernization theory identified stages of economic development marked by the interaction between technological, educational, and social processes. Demographers talk about life cycles in order to highlight various stages in recurring educational, professional, familial, and, alas, biological processes. They differentiate those stages from period effects, which involve specific historical experiences that affect all age groups (Duffy 2021, 1–15). Consequently life cycles serve as a reminder that stages should not be confused with periods, even though both truncate processes into fixed time units. Stages are distinct in that they identify context-independent patterns. The five stages in Figure 3.1 are repeated across pandemics regardless of the different dates, just as the stages of life remain remarkably similar regardless of the decade in which it occurs.

As Part II will clarify, CHA uses these five elements of physical time for descriptive purposes – to describe with more nuance the rhythms at which historical change unfolds – *and* for explanatory purposes – to unfreeze linear notions of causality and to pay closer attention to the non-linear effects of tempo, duration, timing, and sequencing.

3.2 Varieties of CHA

The time map in Figure 3.2 summarizes how CHA configures historical and physical time to define its three strands – eventful, longue durée, and macro-causal analysis – and how these strands differ from notions of time as analyzed in other literatures. The map refines the vertical axis of the ontological map introduced in Chapter 1 by adding the four elements of historical time discussed in Chapter 2. It replaces the freezing of geography with the freezing of physical time. It benchmarks this freezing against the number of elements of physical time that a work considers simultaneously. The dotted CHA boundary line differentiates between modes of inquiry according to how much they unfreeze physical and historical time. The space outside the boundary,

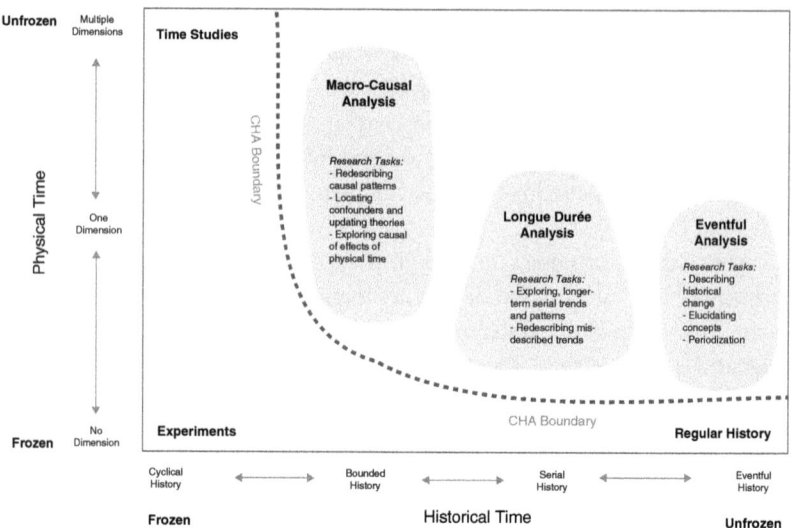

Figure 3.2 Time map

The time map situates CHA in terms of its treatments of historical and physical time. Physical time becomes more unfrozen the more of its five elements (tempo, duration, timing, sequencing, stages) are analyzed. Historical time becomes more unfrozen depending on which variants of history it employs. CHA differs from other approaches (indicated by the dotted line) in that it pays attention to both elements of time, even though its variants do so to different degrees.

running along the two axes, constitutes the CHA borderland, where scholars pay attention to either historical or physical time, but not to both. The territory inside the dotted line constitutes the domain of CHA, where the three strands combine historical and physical time in different ways.

Let me first discuss the borderland outside the CHA boundary.

Regular history, found in the lower right-hand corner, is the closest cousin of CHA, the one inspiring it to think historically and embrace eventful history. But it is one degree removed from CHA, because regular history pays little attention to physical time. *Experiments* employ frozen, cyclical history, which is thin and historyless. They take place in singular, snapshot-like moments of time, and thus are limited in exploring non-linear causal processes; these will be discussed further in Chapter 5, on macro-causal analysis. *Time studies* is a clunky umbrella term for literatures that study single or multiple elements of physical time, while ignoring thicker notions of historical time. Game theory, for example, employs a more unfrozen or thick treatment of physical time: it considers how actors' time horizons (i.e., duration) and choice sequences affect outcomes. The sociology of time employs time allocation studies to analyze how much time different demographic groups or employees devote to various tasks. The psychology of time looks at how the birth order influences children's psychological development, or how the timing of tasks affects their performance.

Let me preface the discussion of the three strands inside the dotted line with three observations. First, the three strands are not formalized approaches but lump together different literatures. They are defined by the notion of history they employ and by how much attention they pay to physical time. They also use distinct exploratory tools, on which I will elaborate in Part II. Second, the boundaries between the three strands are fluid, and many scholars configure the strands in a multitude of ways. They engage in what the French fondly refer to as bricolage – the typically self-taught skill designed to produce ingenious solutions to tricky home improvement-related projects. The bricoleur or bricoleuse – the person who masters the art of bricolage – is the antithesis of the architect who has the technical, engineering training; such a person starts from high-brow aesthetic visions and creates solutions that oftentimes are as bold as they are obtuse to the practical needs of the case. CHA is full of bricoleurs and bricoleuses defined by their heterodox problem-solving sensibilities and their willingness to combine historical and physical time. Skocpol and Somers were the first to realize that their activities can be lumped into three strands: eventful, longue durée, and macro-causal analysis.[3]

Eventful analysis is an umbrella term for literatures that explain patterns of historical change and are grounded in eventful history. It is deeply embedded in global history (Conrad 2017), diplomatic history (Elman and Elman 2001; Levy 1997; Trachtenberg 2006), global historical sociology (Go and Lawson 2017; Hobden and Hobson 2001), constructivist international relations theory (Finnemore and Sikkink 2001), American political development (Vallely, Mettler, and Lieberman 2018), historical institutionalism (Fioretos, Falleti, and Sheingate 2016), the history of the welfare state (Baldwin 1990; Hacker 2002; Pierson 1994), postcolonialism (Chakrabarty 2008; G. Steinmetz 2008), and race and gender studies (Adams, Clemens, and Orloff 2005a).

Eventful analysis is the most historical, most exploratory, and most interpretivist of the three strands. It frequently tackles little analyzed phenomena or older ones that have been transformed by recent historical changes. Its goal is to describe what is going on, to develop or update concepts, to understand the generative processes that bring about a particular phenomenon, and to analyze

---

[3] Skocpol and Somers (1980) used somewhat different labels. The provenance of these three strands is further discussed in Kreuzer (forthcoming).

a phenomenon's subsequent qualitative transformations (Abbott 1991; Sewell 1996; Zerubavel 2003)

Longue durée analysis was first pioneered by the French Annales historians in the 1930s, rests on serial history, and assumed a more prominent role in CHA from the 1990s on (Goldstone 2000; Møller 2016, 139–60). Economic history uses longue durée analysis to track how technological innovations transform capitalism. It made a short guest appearance in regular history as cliometrics. It informs neoclassical institutional theory that retraces the institutional foundations of modern-day capitalism (Acemoglu, Johnson, and Robinson 2001; North and Thomas 1976; Stasavage 2011). And it has been helpful to scholars who study long-term demographic trends or the impact of pandemics (Diamond 2017; Voigtlaender and Voth 2012), or explore why the West developed allegedly differently from the rest of the world (Goldstone 2000; Pomeranz 2001). Longue durée analysis studies how slow-moving, long-term demographic, economic, and environmental trends shape faster-moving, event-driven political history. It uses the thinner serial notion of history, time series data, and data visualizations. It thus can deploy more extensively elements of physical time to analyze the rhythms at which of the thinner serial history unfolds.

Macro-causal analysis is the oldest and most distinguished strand in CHA. It explores the broader implications of war, state formation, democratization, and in particular the varieties of capitalism. It uses the thin, bounded notion of history and articulates historically situated theories that explain cross-national variations. Macro-causal analysis thus builds heavily on the foreknowledge that eventful analysis in particular generated. It treats the past less as something to be compared to the present and more as a repository for the discovery of causal antecedents that existing theories overlooked. It uses such ignored causal antecedents to update existing theories and to assess the test-worthiness of hypotheses. It pays particular attention to the non-linear, causal effects of tempo, duration, timing, and sequencing.

With the temporal foundations in place, it is now possible to connect historical thinking to specific tools and research tasks. Part II turns readers' attention especially to these tools and elaborates on how they assist in exploring patterns, in describing and even visualizing them, and ultimately how they undescribe and redescribe existing theories to formulate new research questions.

Exercises

3.1. Identify the element of physical time in Earl Cook's graph (Figure 6.4). Where do you find tempo and duration? How would you characterize

Earl Cook's five periods? Are they historical periods employing historical time, or do they involve stages and thus are part of physical time? Are the types of energy consumptions sequences or stages? Contrast the insights you get from physical time (i.e. rhythms of change) with those you get from historical time (i.e. what changes, transformations).

3.2. Historical and physical time do not exhaust the notions of time used in the social sciences. This exercise is meant to alert you to these additional notions of time. Match these examples on the left with the temporal categories on the right. Do it in two steps. First, put on an ontological veil of ignorance, take the example at face value, and hold off on any potential complexities. Make your selections on the basis of what seems most likely given the available options. Second, lift your ontological veil ignorance and see whether temporal categories could be matched with different options, given different interpretations of the examples. For example, in step one, gender-based divisions of domestic work should be linked with sociological notions of time, because they provide the clearest example of sociological notions of time. However, now that you lifted your ontological veil of ignorance, you may change the geographic or historical context and reference instances where women are, or were, prohibited from working outside the house. Then, suddenly, the example involves political notions of time. Or it could be technological if the share of domestic work done by women has gone down over time as a result of washing machines and vacuum cleaners, which have made housework so simple that even men engage in it. You get the drift. Think historically, or even ethnographically, and see what other pairings are possible.

Description of Temporal Phenomena	Type of Time
1. Days and years linked to planetary rotations. Hours and minutes linked to mechanics of clocks	A. Time is technological
2. Past and future tenses of language. Religiously linked time notions (i.e. apocalypse)	B. Time is historical
3. Gender-based division of domestic work. Time horizons varying with educational levels.	C. Time is psychological
4. How social media shortens our time horizons	D. Time is biological
5. Body hormones, sleeping patterns	E. Time is cultural
6. The past is different from the present	F. Time is political
7. Conservatives value the past, progressives value the future	G. Time is sociological
8. Hindsight bias. Monday morning quarterbacking	H. Time is physical

3.3. E. H. Carr's story of a car accident (Exercise 1.3) does not include any elements of physical time. Reconstruct the story by adding elements of tempo, duration, sequencing, timing, or stages. Discuss how they might be relevant. What would be their specific causal effects? Try to find at least three of the five elements. (Note: not all elements of physical time might be relevant.) In what ways would those elements of physical time be context-independent, that is, invariant across different historical periods?

3.4. Physical time itself is something that has expanded its reach over the past two centuries, as Venessa Ogle's (2013) fascinating article illustrates. What are the conflicts that emerged in the efforts to expand uniform physical time (Ogle refers to it as clock time) to different parts of the globe? How has the expansion of physical time over time made it possible and even necessary to incorporate physical time as an analytical category in CHA? How has the same dynamic played out in the labor market, as discussed in E. P. Thompson's (1967) famous "Time, Work-Discipline, and Industrial Capitalism"?

Part II

How to Use History to Describe Patterns

> The failure to explain is caused by a failure to describe.
> (Benoit Mandelbrot, as cited in Hagstrom 2013, 85)

Part I discussed how comparative historical analysis (CHA) uses history to explore, describe and formulate research questions. It demonstrated – to reiterate Lieberson's analogy – that building a locomotive presupposes the discovery of the wheel – in other words description. Part II pivots to discussing the tools that CHA uses to explore and describe, tools that have received surprisingly little attention. Take the Great Migration between 1916 and 1970, when 6–7.5 million African Americans moved from the rural South to the North and the West. This was the largest peacetime movement of people within a country, and it immediately prompts the question: why did it happen? But properly answering this *why question* requires exploring first the *how question*; and we should do this by describing precisely who migrated, where-from, whereto, and when. Without detailed descriptions of how something happened, it is difficult to explain why it happened. No description, no answers.

CHA employs a wide range of exploratory strategies to answer "how" questions. It treats description not as a monolithic activity but as an activity that involves numerous tools, and these define eventful, longue durée, and macro-causal analysis. *Eventful analysis* is the most fundamental, interpretivist strand. It is grounded in eventful history, employs historical comparisons, and describes or re-redescribes the qualitative transformations that produce historical change. It also generates or updates concepts. *Longue durée analysis* uses those concepts to expand the geographic and historical scope of what is being explored. It employs serial history and serial comparisons, and describes and redescribes trends – that is, changes in degree across time and space. *Macro-causal analysis* employs bounded history, cross-sectional and contextual comparisons to describe and redescribe differences in degree (i.e., variations) or kind (i.e., varieties) across otherwise static units of analysis. It inspects those patterns for inductive clues in order to update theories, thus beginning to blur the boundary between description and explanation. Part II discusses more closely how these three strands deploy their tools to address specific research challenges. It pivots from what defines CHA to how to use it.

I illustrate these descriptive tools strands in two ways. I intersperse my general discussion of them with a wide range of examples drawn from across CHA. I also conclude each chapter with a more focused illustration drawn from the literature on the origins of proportional representation (PR). This literature explains a key episode in the first wave of democratization, between the 1880s and 1920s. It analyzes the role that the switch from first-past-the-post electoral systems to PR played in mediating broader class conflicts. As I wrote this book, the PR literature served as my go-to example; I revisited it endless times, as an incognito methodological anthropologist, to back-engineer the research process and to understand more intimately what scholars specifically do when thinking historically. I leverage this intimate knowledge to offer a deeper illustration of CHA's descriptive tools. Besides being familiar to me, the PR literature is also well suited because it addresses a single, straightforward macro-historical question, uses the same twelve cases, focuses on the same historical period, and employs all three strands of CHA. It holds everything constant except the uses of historical and physical time. This makes it easier to illustrate the distinct descriptive strategies used by eventful, serial, and macro-causal analysis. To make the PR literature more accessible, Chapter 4 offers a quick primer. Understanding the descriptive tools of CHA is not conditional upon knowing, or being particularly interested in, the PR literature. These sections can be skipped, but I still hope that they will be helpful. Newcomers to CHA may benefit from an additional opportunity to see how these descriptive tools are used. And CHA veterans would find here the space to retrace my ideas and to articulate more clearly any disagreements they might have.

4　A Primer on the Origins of Electoral Systems

> If you want to understand anything, observe its beginning and development.
> (Aristotle, as cited in Friendly and Wainer 2021, 10)

Each of the subsequent chapters concludes with examples drawn from the literature on the origins of proportional representation (PR), to illustrate the exploratory tools of comparative historical analysis (CHA). Most readers will be unfamiliar with this literature and therefore could benefit from a primer. Just to be clear, understanding the next chapters is *not* conditional on becoming an expert in PR literature. The chapters present CHA's tools *without* reference to this literature. Nevertheless, the literature is helpful for three reasons.

First, it offers a textbook example of knowledge accumulation where the more recent works translate the results of earlier works into more and more compelling answers. Second, the literature is methodologically pluralistic and involves a close dialogue between CHA and variance-based analysis (VBA). It thus illustrates the role that CHA's descriptive tools play in translating mere results into effective answers. Third, the adoption of PR leads to the kind of historical phenomena that typically interest CHA. PR literally needed the invention of a new voting technology, crafted on democratic institutions; and these, while not as new as PR itself, where still largely untried in most countries. The adoption of PR was historical in two ways. First it was historical in the trivial sense of having occurred in the past. Second, it was historical in a substantive sense of marking a major discontinuity: a qualitative change in how votes would be translated into seats. This PR primer follows Aristotle's insight that understanding the contributions of the PR requires retracing its origins and subsequent development.

4.1 The Genealogy of PR Literature

Electoral systems are one of the most studied elements of modern democracies. This is because they are enormously consequential. They determine how votes get translated into seats, how many parties end up winning seats, how the number of those parties affects the formation of governments and policy outcomes, and how those policy outcomes, in turn, influence overall political stability. The question of the historical origins of electoral systems – why between the 1880s and the 1920s some countries opted for PR while others, mostly Anglo-Saxon democracies, retained older, first-past-the-post systems – has received attention in 1968 in the form of a brief encyclopedia entry by Stein Rokkan (1968a) – another doyen of CHA – and began in earnest with the first systematic empirical analysis, made by Carles Boix thirty years later (Boix 1999).

Rokkan and Boix formulated an influential *left threat thesis*, which makes straightforward empirical claims. It places the adoption of PR as a brand-new electoral system in the broader context of how incumbent Conservatives across Europe tried to contain what they perceived to be the economic and political threats that emanated from the growing and politically ever more effectively organized working class. This threat became particularly acute in the wake of the expansion of the male franchise and the resulting growth of the working-class electorate. The right began considering PR in order to address an electoral coordination problem that emerged in situations where the electorate was fragmented into conservative rural and liberal urban camps. Such fragmentation carried the risk that the right would split its vote under the then existing single-member districts and would thus make it more likely for a united left to win a disproportionate seat share with just a plurality of the votes. Conservatives and Liberals had the hypothetical option of countering this kind of vote splitting by coordinating the withdrawals of candidates across districts and thereby pooling their votes around a single non-Socialist Party candidate. Or they could accomplish the same effect through gerrymandering. Both these options were logistically challenging and politically risky, particularly in instances where the divide between Conservatives and Liberals reflected long-standing rural–urban or clerical–anticlerical divides. PR therefore became the politically more feasible alternative because it did not require electoral coordination (e.g., strategic withdrawals) or institutional engineering (e.g., gerrymandering), and it did not split the vote of a divided right. Rokkan and Boix therefore contend that PR was adopted in circumstances where a divided right confronted a rapidly rising working class. The left threat thesis became the anchor theory around which the subsequent debate pivoted.

This debate is marked by two distinct characteristics. First, it is defined by a genuine knowledge cumulation where the more recent works employ better conceptualized and more valid measures, advance more refined theories, rely on larger datasets, and increasingly translate results into answers. Second, this knowledge cumulation is linked to the close dialogue between CHA and VBA, between historical and statistical thinking. This scholarly debate can be broken into five discreet research cycles, each marked by the prominence of different strands of CHA and variance-based explanations. Figure 4.1 chronicles these research cycles and shows to what extent individual contributions drew on the elements of CHA. Scholarly contributions were classified as eventful if they provided case studies with thick descriptions, as longue durée if the explored electoral system trends that extended beyond the 1880–1920 time window, as macro-causal if they developed new theoretical arguments, and as variance-based if they contained some multivariate analysis. The first two columns in Figure 4.1 sort the scholarly contributions chronologically, according to the decade of their publication, and then lump those decades into five broader research cycles.

This genealogy underscores three broad methodological patterns. First, the initial two cycles relied almost exclusively on eventful analysis and thus emphasized exploration over testing, as would be expected in early research cycles. Second, very few contributions during the third and fourth cycles employed only a variance-based research design; most of them combined it instead with elements of CHA. Strikingly, scholars in the fourth cycle renewed their eventful analysis to sort out theoretical impasses encountered in the third cycle. Third, the literature increasingly converged around an updated version of Rokkan's and Boix's original thesis of a threat coming from the left. This is a clear instance of knowledge cumulation. Figure 4.1 indicates this convergence by italicizing names of authors who elaborated on the original left threat thesis.

The remainder of this chapter gives a succinct overview of these five research cycles, in order to show the reader how the literature evolved. Then the subsequent chapters will demonstrate how the specific contributions of eventful, longue durée, and macro-causal analysis were used in the various research cycles.

The First and Second Research Cycles (the 1880s to the 1980s). The first research cycle, from the 1880s to the 1940s, encompasses contemporaneous accounts of PR adoption as well as normative debates on whether to choose first-past-the-post systems, which prioritize geographic representation, or PR systems, which favor group-based representation. The table does include those works under eventful analysis because they were uninterested in explaining the adoption of PR. The second cycle, from the 1950s to the 1980s, comprised historical case studies with thick descriptions – typically dissertations. These works employed more explicit historical thinking and produced a rudimentary understanding of the adoption of PR in individual countries. Rokkan's (1968a) formulation of the left threat thesis is the one exception. He used the patterns described in other works to give a first tentative explanation. The first two cycles constitute the prehistory of the left threat thesis.

The Third Research Cycle (the 1990s and the 2000s). Boix (1999) elaborated Rokkan's thesis and subjected it to the first empirical test. His article was then

Cycle	Period	Eventful Analysis	Longue Durée Analysis	Macro-Causal Analysis	Variance Based Analysis	Scholarly Works
First Cycle	1880s–1900s	✓	--	--	--	Journalist accounts, parliamentary proceedings
First Cycle	1910s–40s	✓	--	--	--	(Braunias 1932)
Second Cycle	1950s	✓	--	--	--	(Campbell 1965; Ziegler 1956)
Second Cycle	1960s	✓	--	--	--	(Butler 1963; Eckelberry 1964; Rokkan 1968a; Sternberger 1969; Törnudd 1968)
Second Cycle	1970s	✓	--	--	--	(Finer 1975)
Second Cycle	1980s	✓	--	--	--	(Carstairs 1980)
Second Cycle	1980s	✓	--	--	--	(Schanbacher 1982)
Third Cycle	1990s	--	✓	--	✓	(J. M. Colomer 1998)\
Third Cycle	1990s	--	--	--	✓	**(Boix 1999)**
Third Cycle	2000s	✓	--	--	✓	(Grofman and Lijphart 2002)
Third Cycle	2000s	--	--	--	✓	(J. Colomer 2004)
Third Cycle	2000s	--	--	✓	✓	(Blais 2005 et al.)
Third Cycle	2000s	--	--	✓	✓✓	(Alesina and Glaeser 2004)
Third Cycle	2000s	--	--	--	✓	(Penadés 2008)
Third Cycle	2000s	--	--	--	✓✓	(J. Colomer 2007)
Third Cycle	2000s	--	--	--	✓✓	(Calvo 2009)
Third Cycle	2000s	✓	✓	--	✓✓	(Andrews and Jackman 2005)
Third Cycle	2000s	--	--	--	✓✓	(J. Colomer 2005)
Third Cycle	2000s	✓	--	✓	✓✓	(Cusack, Iversen, and Soskice 2007)
Fourth Cycle	2010–14	✓	✓	--	--	(Cusack, Iversen, and Soskice 2010)
Fourth Cycle	2010–14	--	✓	--	--	(Lundell 2010)
Fourth Cycle	2010–14	✓	--	--	--	(Renwick 2010)
Fourth Cycle	2010–14	--	--	--	--	(Pilon 2013)
Fourth Cycle	2010–14	✓	--	✓	--	(Ahmed 2013)
Fourth Cycle	2010–14	✓	--	✓	--	(Barzachka 2014)
Fourth Cycle	2010–14	✓	--	✓	--	(Boix 2010)
Fourth Cycle	2010–14	✓	--	--	✓	(Kreuzer 2010)
Fourth Cycle	2010–14	✓	--	--	✓✓	(Leeman and Mares 2014)
Fourth Cycle	2010–14	✓	--	--	✓✓	(Schröder and Manow 2014)
Fourth Cycle	2015–19	✓	--	✓	--	(Santucci 2017)
Fourth Cycle	2015–19	✓	--	--	✓✓	(Iversen and Soskice 2019)
Fourth Cycle	2015–19	✓	--	--	✓✓	(Cox, Fiva, and Smith 2019)
Fourth Cycle	2015–19	✓	--	--	✓✓	(Walter and Emmenegger 2019)
Fourth Cycle	2015–19	✓	--	--	✓✓	(Emmenegger and Walter 2019)
Next	2020s	Unexplored				

Figure 4.1 A genealogy of PR literature

The knowledge accumulation around PR literature is a result of scholars' leveraging complementarities across the three CHA strands and their dialogue with VBA. This figure documents this dialogue and the five research cycles it produced.

replicated and challenged by seven alternative hypotheses (Alesina and Glaeser 2004; Andrews and Jackman 2005; Blais 2005; Calvo 2009; J. Colomer 2005, 2007; Cusack, Iversen, and Soskice 2007). Four more contributions *studied* other aspects of the origins of PR, without directly explaining its adoption (J. Colomer 2004; J. M. Colomer 1998; Grofman and Lijphart 2002; Penadés 2008). Boix and the authors of six out of the seven articles that challenged him used VBA. Some combined it with rudimentary macro-causal analysis, but none drew on eventful or longue durée analysis. In consequence, this cycle was characterized by the smallest knowledge cumulation, as seven articles advanced seven different theories and failed to replicate any of the earlier results. It was also marked by ad hoc testing of poorly specified and barely testworthy hypotheses. Those hypotheses were imported from other historical contexts and made thin conjectures, hardly using any historical thinking. Scholars were more interested in falsifying the findings of their competitors than in consulting case studies from the first two cycles or in engaging in their own eventful analysis. This cycle produced test results, which were theoretically insufficiently validated to count as full answers and which subsequent contributions consequently ignored.

The Fourth Research Cycle (2010 into the 2020s). The fourth cycle corrected the ad hoc testing and theory swapping of the third cycle and started producing answers. Three factors contributed to these advances. First, CHA works became more prominent during the fourth cycle. Amel Ahmed (2013), Dennis Pillon (2013), Nina Barzachka (2014), and Jack Santucci (2017) all published traditional CHA studies that were partly motivated by the shortcomings of the third research cycle. Second, variance-based studies shifted from analyzing cross-sectional national-level election outcomes to analyzing single-country district-level ones (Cox, Fiva, and Smith 2019; Emmenegger and Walter 2019; Leeman and Mares 2014; Schröder and Manow 2014; Walter and Emmenegger 2019). This turn dramatically increased the number of observations, because the number of electoral districts in each country was far greater than the number of countries that adopted PR. Focusing on a single case also allowed scholars to pay closer attention to the quality of the data and to the theoretical confounders (Pepinsky 2019). Third, more scholars incorporated eventful analysis. Boix (2010) and Cusack et al. (2010), who during the third cycle did just conventional hypothesis testing, now engaged in eventful and macro-causal analysis. On the whole, the better balance between heterodox and orthodox methodologies during the fourth cycle increased the level of confidence in research findings by making it possible to use richer contextual knowledge to identify confounders, to understand test anomalies better, to refine concepts, and to assess more clearly the internal validity of findings (Pepinsky 2019).

The Fifth Research Cycle (from the 2020s to the present). This fifth research cycle is just starting and will face the challenge of how to generalize the robust but country-specific explanations of the fourth cycle. This challenge requires better theorizing and falls mostly in the area of macro-causal analysis. Most fourth-generation studies remain vague as to whether their contributions are direct challenges or extensions of the left threat thesis, and thus they hand down numerous theoretical loose ends. Scholars will have to explore how to integrate those loose ends into the left threat thesis or into rival theories. They will also have to address problems of equifinality (same outcome explained by different causes) and multifinality (same factors explaining different outcomes).

Retracing these research cycles showed that the resulting knowledge accumulation, after the initial cul-de-sacs during the third cycle, owes a great deal to the improved dialogue between CHA and variance-based explanations.

Exercises

4.1. Section I claimed that historical thinking helps translate results into answers by generating new research questions. Select a dozen of articles from the literature in your research area and generate a genealogy like the one in Figure 4.1. Make sure that you select sources from across a wide time span. How did the research questions change? What role did historical thinking play? Can you detect research cycles? How did the mixture between the three CHA strands and VBA shift over time? How close was the dialogue between CHA and VBA? Can you detect any knowledge cumulation?

5 Eventful Analysis
Using Dates to Explore Patterns of (Dis)Continuities

> Concepts, like individuals, have their histories and are just as incapable of withstanding the ravages of time as individuals.
>
> (Kierkegaard, as cited in Brown 1976, 169)

Eventful analysis employs the most unfrozen and hence most exploratory version of comparative historical analysis (CHA). Its goal is to describe social reality, to figure out what is going on, and to leverage this understanding to potentially rewrite the description informing existing theories. It specializes in analyzing historical change or what is alternatively referred to as (dis-)continuities, transformations, exogeneous shocks, turning points, ruptures, or critical junctures. So the general contribution of eventful analysis is quite clear. What is less clear is the tools that eventful analysis employs to analyze change. This chapter discusses two such tools: historical description and conceptualization.

Eventful analysis generates *historical descriptions* that follow a specific protocol in order to compare the past with the present, explicate how much change has taken place, and describe the broader patterns of such change. Furthermore, eventful analysis constructs concepts designed to make such descriptions comparative. These conceptualizations involve identifying attributes that are shared across geography and that remain constant across time. As Kierkegaard's epigram that opens this chapter implies, concepts necessitate looking for new or changing attributes that older concepts do not capture and that require updating. This chapter elaborates on how historical description and conceptualization ultimately translate historical thinking into concrete research results.

5.1 Historical Description: What Is Going on and When Do Things Change?

Description is widely regarded as an unsystematic, pre-methodological, and structureless activity. The time-honored canard of "mere" description overlooks that description takes on distinct forms (e.g., thick description, ethnographic description, historical description, descriptive statistics, typologizing) and that even the thickest description is structured by a set of recurring tasks

(Gerring 2012a; Kreuzer 2019). Historical description is distinct from other forms in that it pays attention to dates and is interested in identifying the continuities and discontinuities that help us understand historical change. It is organized around six analytical tasks: fact gathering, chronicling, concatenation, periodizing, looking for intercurrence patterns, and rethinking research questions.

Fact Gathering. The starting point in any description is an undescribed, underdescribed, or misdescribed phenomenon, a test outlier, a theoretical anomaly, or something that is not understood and hence falls outside the descriptive coverage of existing theories. Historical description begins by identify a phenomenon requiring better description and provides an empirical check on the descriptions embedded in theories. It leverages historical thinking to bring existing theories into dialogue with the social reality, which they often represent as historyless and geographyless. Therefore the first step in historical description is fact gathering guided by investigative, journalistic-style questions (who, when, where, and how), which draw attention to the kind of evidence that will help clarify what is going on. These questions typically address the following points:

- Who are the principal actors? What resources (e.g., monetary, coercive, mobilizational, cultural) do they command? Have these actors and their resources changed over time, or do they vary across space?
- Are these actors single unitary actors, or are they collective actors who adopt decision-making rules or who are subject to factionalism? Has their organizational structure changed over time?
- How are these actors' choices shaped by those of others, which makes the choices interdependent? How stable over time or uniform across space have these strategic interactions been?
- What are actors' preferences? How stable are these preferences over time and how uniform across space?
- What sets of choices are available to actors if they intend to pursue those preferences? What determines those sets? How stable are they over time and how uniform across space?
- What are the motivational foundations of those choices? Are actors maximizing material self-interest? Are they motivated by ideas, group loyalties, or cognitive biases?
- What contextual factors (e.g., institutions, ideas, socioeconomic structures, broader environmental factors) shape these preferences and choices? How much agency do actors have in the formation of their preferences?
- To what extent do past choices constrain later choices, and through what mechanisms (e.g., increasing returns, legacies, sunken costs, network effects)?

- At what level or in what unit of analysis is a phenomenon studied (e.g., at the psychological level, at the individual level, at the group level, at the regional, national, international, or transnational level)? How stable are these units across time? How "portable" are they across space? How do phenomena interact across such units?

Given that gathering facts is largely not guided by theory, the resulting observations are inchoate and supply little more than the empirical raw material for the next stages of eventful analysis.

Chronicling. Chronicling imposes a preliminary temporal order on these initial observations by sorting them according to their chronology. It attaches dates to events, asks what event preceded or followed another event, and creates a simple timeline. Chronicling is a very elementary, mundane, clerk-like activity. It is nevertheless important for two reasons.

First, chronicles render history verifiable. The historian Richard Löwenthal (1986, 220–1) points out that "all history is knowable because it is datable. Without dates or permanent record to refer to, one can neither assess the duration of past events nor verify their order." Chronologies are what distinguishes scholarly history from oral histories, which in certain cultures pass on from one generation to the next. Collective oral histories also engage with the past, but do not anchor their analysis in dates. Löwenthal therefore concludes: "Where knowledge of the past is orally transmitted, for example, or where no records exist, the past is perceived entirely in terms of present accounts. Whatever changes may have occurred, continually reshaped narratives seek to make it appear that tradition has survived unaltered all along, no line divides the historical past from the present" (231). Scholarly oral histories differ from the popular oral histories that Löwenthal references here, because they convert oral accounts into recorded histories. This act of recording makes them more "fixed" and less readily reshaped by future generations.

Second, chronicling provides a simple, mechanical sorting device that supplies an easy to do activity during an early, exploratory, and hence more inchoate stage of research. It reduces historical noise by selecting, from a totality of historical occurrences or facts, the subset of potentially relevant events. The semantic distinction between occurrences or facts and events is meant to underscore that the latter constitute a purposively selected subset, which provides the evidentiary basis for later descriptions and periodizations (Abbott 1984; Abrams 1982, 191; Falleti and Mahoney 2015, 212–14).

In selecting events and arraying them chronologically, chronicling assumes a function analogous to that of sampling. Both make analysis more manageable by choosing a subset of observations – events picked out from everything that happened, or a sample from the entire population – and then figuring out what inferences can be drawn from this subset. But chronicling differs from statistical sampling. It involves temporal units of analysis, namely events, which are part not of a larger, homogeneous population but of an emergent, heterogeneous process. Furthermore, those events are not fixed by preexisting theories but are defined inductively, on the basis of their relevance to understanding a phenomenon. Minard, for example, designated as "events" those occurrences that were marked by a sizable number of deaths in battle. Morone selected as "events" all those broader historical episodes marked by populist backlashes against the efforts of marginalized groups to emancipate themselves politically. Chronicling and the selection of events follow the exploratory logic of historical thinking and involve "casing" – the construction of units of analysis[1] (Soss 2021). This makes chronicling different from sampling or case selection, which follow the testing logic of statistical thinking.

Concatenation. The principal goal of historical description is to make the very mechanical chronology more legible by rearranging events in ways that clarify precisely what was going on during a particular period (Gaddis 2002). Historians refer to this rearranging of events into patterns and narratives as *concatenation.* The term lacks a formal definition, but it broadly refers to fitting the events – identified during fact finding and chronicling – into the larger puzzle that allows identifying historical patterns or themes. It is the historiographical equivalent of topic modeling, the statistical technique used in sifting through vast amounts of text in order to identify topical patterns. Instead of algorithms, concatenation uses processes such as sleuthing through one event after another, sorting through the roles that actors played, and finding out what motivated them and how circumstances shaped them. It requires particularly close attention to what Nassim Taleb (2007, 100–20) aptly called silent evidence – pieces of evidence that previous descriptions overlooked, but that offer important new inductive insights. Concatenation involves making descriptive inferences necessary to figure out what is going o, to identify transformations and, ultimately, to find the points at which history and geography are sufficiently persistent or uniform to reveal patterns. It can

---

[1] Parenthetically, I should point out that the modern role of chronicling as part of the historical data-gathering process is quite distinct from the earlier one, before history became an academic discipline. Earlier on, chronicling served important political, economic, and religious functions. Genealogical chronicling legitimated claims to the throne and other hereditary privileges (Toulmin and Goodfield 1965); religious chronicling addressed eschatological questions about the apocalypse (Rosenberg and Grafton 2010, 44); and the chronicles in the farmer almanacs advised when to plant and harvest. The function of such chronicles, however, changed with the emergence of history as discipline in the late eighteenth and early nineteenth centuries. For historians, strict chronologies were too mechanical to allow identifying patterns of historical change, and thus they supplemented them with periodizations (Hunt 2008, 52; Rosenberg and Grafton 2010, 138).

be viewed as the inductive counterpart to the freezing of history and geography imposed on social reality by preexisting theories and methodologies. It translates individual transformations into broader, more structured patterns of historical change by looking for periods and intercurrences.

Periodizing. Chronicling and concatenation provide very granular, typically short descriptions of the events that mark historical transformations. Periodizing shifts the temporal unit of analysis from individual, temporally proximate events to clusters of temporally more dispersed events such as periods. In zooming out from events to periods, it becomes easier to explicate the longer-term recurrence patterns. Periodizing can be viewed as a macro version of historical description. It shifts analytical focus from happenings in a small set of short-term events to the larger question of whether events repeat themselves or mutate over a longer period of time. Periodization ultimately involves splitting events and them lumping them into broader event containers – periods. Here again, historical description ends up freezing history inductively in order to make it more legible.

There are no set rules for how to lump and split events into periods. Using years, decades, centuries, or other fixed calendrical units of time arguably yields the most rudimentary periodization scheme (J. S. Smith 1998). Operating with such units requires little historical foreknowledge from the reader, which explains why periodizations are often employed in high school history textbooks. But strictly chronological periodization schemes are limiting, because actual historical events unfold in more complex rhythms than the one fixed by the calendar. Thus eventful analysis splits events and regroups them into three types of periods, according to whether they recur across time: periods of strict *continuity* are periods during which events repeat themselves; periods of strict *discontinuity* are periods during which new events displace earlier ones; and *transitional periods* are periods during which new events are layered on top of existing ones and replace them only gradually. Ultimately the historical patterns captured by this tripartite periodization scheme is limiting, because it permits only categorical distinctions. As we will see, intercurrences and time series allow for the description of more nuanced patterns of change, continuous, and transitional.

Parenthetically, I should point out that qualitative changes are frequently confused with contextual, geographic differences. History and geography both draw attention to contextual particularities. History is interested in the recurrence or durability of those contextual particularities and in the pattern of change that their non-recurrence produces. Geography lacks this dynamic dimension and is interested instead in static, unchanging similarities and differences. History focuses on temporal heterogeneity and uses context to identify longitudinal transformations, while geography concentrates on geographic heterogeneity and uses context to spot cross-sectional varieties.

Intercurrence Patterns. Periodizations treat historical change in a categorical manner, which assumes a past that can be readily truncated into mutually exclusive chronological categories. This categorical treatment of the past often stipulates discreet turning points or big bang moments that have been criticized for exaggerating the degree of discontinuity (de Carvalho, Leira, and Hobson 2011). It consequently led some scholars to treat historical change in a more multilayered and continuous fashion. They view the unfolding of history less in chronologically discreet events and more as concurrently unfolding processes that interact. The sociologist Stuart Hall (1984, 112–14) usefully labels such concurrent processes as *multi-chronic*, to distinguish them from *mono-chronic*, strictly event-based analysis. American political development (APD) scholars coined the helpful term *intercurrences* to designate the interaction among multi-chronic processes (Orren and Skowronek 2004). Scholars shifting from mono-chronic to multi-chronic analysis therefore can be said to be looking not just for recurrence patterns but also for *intercurrence patterns*.

Working with different collaborators, Kathleen Thelen developed a typology of intercurrence patterns. She distinguishes between four types of change: displacement, layering, conversion, and drift.

The typology summarized in Table 5.1 was originally developed to analyze institutional change, but it can easily describe other intercurrence patterns. *Displacements* are similar to the wholesale and fast changes implicit in ruptures, critical junctures, or exogenous shocks. Displacements involve the replacement of existing institutions by new ones. The tempo of such

Table 5.1 Intercurrence patterns

	Displacement	Layering	Conversion	Drift
Removal of old rules	Yes	No	No	No
Neglect of old rules	–	No	Yes	No
Changed Impact/enactment of old rules	–	No	Yes	Yes
Introduction of new rules	Yes	Yes	No	No

Rather than lumping events together in periods, intercurrence patterns conceptualize historical change as involving multiple, concurrent, and interacting processes that produce different patterns. It produces a new typology around the interaction between three possible factors: old institutions, new institutions, and non-institutional bodies. *Source*: Mahoney and Thelen 2010, 16.

displacements may be slow or fast. The universal male franchise, for example, displaced the old *suffrage censitaire* in countries such as Finland or the Netherlands in a single reform step, while in other European countries this move was staggered: first came a gradual removal of tax, then landholding, and eventually gender requirements. The key feature of displacements is the active removal of an old status quo element and its replacement with a new functional equivalent that is qualitatively different. *Layering* alters the functioning of institutions by adding new rules on top of existing ones. With respect to voting, it involves introducing a secret ballot to enhance the franchise or adding arbitrary technical voter registration requirements to diminish it. Layering thus amounts to a discontinuity that is more incremental than displacements because it does not remove the procedures whose effects it tries to change. *Conversion* leaves the existing institutions unchanged but interprets them in a new light or implements them in new ways. Existing voter registration laws, for example, could be reinterpreted through new legal challenges, or the leverage of votes could be altered through gerrymandering. Conversions are politically attractive because they have a stealth-like quality that disguises their more partisan intent. Finally, *drift* alters the functioning of institutions by not changing them when they should be adapted to address changes in noninstitutional circumstances. Leaving electoral districts unchanged despite significant population shifts would result in malapportionment, which essentially means drift.

Reevaluating Research Questions. Taken together, the initial five steps of historical description – fact gathering, chronicling, concatenation, periodization, and intercurrence – will produce a sound description. Such a description is essential for reformulating research questions; and these reformulations, in turn, are relevant for studying macro-historical questions because, if indeed history does not repeat itself, then presumably neither do the research questions (Hunt 2014, 18). Suzanne Mettler and Rick Valelly (2018, 16) underscore this easily overlooked insight when pointing out that "a social science that implicitly or explicitly rests on shopworn, stale, or outdated understandings of the political past and its relationship to the present is not – to be blunt – a social science." Amen.

In reformulating research questions, historical descriptions get social inquiry to a place where it can pivot from description to explaining. The six elements of historical description provide a clear enough but also somewhat mechanical checklist. I therefore briefly draw on the proportional representation (PR) literature to illustrate how these elements combine to produce historical description. I then move on to discuss the second element of eventful analysis, conceptualization.

5.2 Application of Historical Description

The PR literature does not include a single article containing a full-scale historical description; and those article that do report only the final narrative but skip the intermediate steps between fact finding and formulating research questions. The backgrounding of these intermediate steps is understandable, given that they are of little interest to readers. I therefore constructed an example that foregrounds all the intermediate steps, so that we can follow them. I used a ten-page chapter on the origins of PR in Belgium, by the historian Alistair Carstairs (1980, 49–59), to illustrate the following steps of historical description.

1. identifying an undescribed, underdescribed, or potentially misdescribed phenomenon;
2. finding facts that contain new information to describe or redescribe a phenomenon;
3. organizing those facts chronologically and selecting the relevant events;
4. using those events to find evidence that is consistent with existing descriptions and distinguishing it from new, previously silent evidence that existing descriptions have overlooked; using concatenation to incorporate silent evidence and to update existing descriptions;
5. lumping together and splitting events into periods to identify continuities and discontinuities;
6. updating research questions in the light of the new understanding generated by historical descriptions.

Fact Gathering. Carstairs' chapter lacks a clear thesis and is so fact-filled that a general reader will feel disoriented by all the actors, proper names, occurrences, technical terms, and events. This disorientation is no different from what even an experienced scholar encounters when sleuthing through archives, reading parliamentary debates, or consulting contemporary newspaper accounts. It is helpful to remember that the thrill of discovery is not without its frustrations and requires perseverance and close reading. Carstairs' account supplies the information for potentially redescribing the left threat thesis first articulated by Rokkan and Boix. These two scholars provide a very stylized description, which is meant to illustrate their theory but also leaves many elements of the PR adoption process undescribed. For example, it does not describe actors' preferences, their organization, the timing of franchise expansion, or the strength of the left. Carstairs supplies information to describe those undescribed elements.

Chronicling. Chronicling is the first step toward making these inchoate facts of Carstairs' account less confusing. Below, 1 array Carstairs' forty-three facts chronologically, as a first step toward imposing some temporal order on them before determining which facts are relevant events. The forty-three facts contain two "mere facts" (nos. 8 and 9), that is, information irrelevant for understanding the left threat thesis. The fact that Wallonia industrialized before the Flanders and the fact that the Flemish bourgeoisie voted on the basis of economic rather than cultural concerns provide background information that, given our current foreknowledge, does not seem relevant for understanding the adoption of PR. This information therefore becomes noise, or what I earlier referred to as irrelevant facts or occurrences rather than relevant evidence or events. Of the remaining forty-one events, four – numbers 19, 26, 28, and 38 – will be readily understood because they relate to predictions made by the left threat thesis and thus give empirical support. This theoretical foreknowledge renders those events understandable and preempts the need for concatenation. However, readers will have difficulty understanding the remaining thirty-seven events, because there is no theoretical foreknowledge to help us make sense of them. These events consequently become silent evidence and, after being concatenated and periodized, will help redescribe Belgium's PR adoption in ways that is new and different by comparison with the descriptions implicit in left threat thesis. So far, then, the chronicling has foregrounded new, potentially relevant events that the existing left threat theory had backgrounded. It reflects eventful analysis' "desire to find new things that people have not seen before ... because we care very much about getting the answer to 'what happened' right" (Mettler and Valelly 2018, 15–17). Here are Carstairs' forty-three facts listed in the order in which they appear in his chapter:

1. 1830 to the 1960s: Constitution, division of power
2. 1830: Constitution revised with regard to electoral systems on two subsequent occasions in (1892 and 1919)
3. 1831: franchise very restrictive and based on single member districts
4. ca. 1870 to the 1920s: changing the electoral system required passing a constitutional amendment. This obstacle delayed electoral reforms and led to protest and violence by left
5. 1831: no demand for universal franchise
6. 1831: franchise favored rural catholic districts
7. 1848: reducing financial requirement for voting, slight expansion of electorate
8. ca. 1840–80: Wallonia industrialized earlier. Its bourgeois, more affluent class dominated the electorate
9. ca. 1840s to the 1880s: Wallon bourgeoisie voted on economics and not on culture

10. Industrialization led to demands for widening the franchise
11. 1830–99: electoral districts varied in number of seats, had block vote system, and required majority on first and plurality on second ballot. Increased left threat in urban districts
12. 1848–70: Liberals dominated
13. 1870–82: Liberals and Catholics alternated
14. 1882–1914: Catholics dominated
15. 1860: increasing demands for franchise expansion and PR
16. 1881: creation of the Belgian PR League, which had supporters among Catholics and Liberals
17. 1882: over-representation of Catholics-led Liberals and Socialists who demanded PR
18. ca. 1850– to the 1880s: means-tested franchise led to corruption and electoral manipulation
19. 1885: Socialists founded
20. ca. the 1880s: Socialists use protest and general strike to support franchise
21. ca. the 1880s: Socialist leader Vandervelde played a key role in adopting PR. Socialists otherwise divided over PR
22. ca. the 1880s: Catholic PR supported divided, varied on electoral strength in districts
23. Universal suffrage helped Catholics more than Liberals, given the large rural electorate
24. Catholics supported universal suffrage, but with plurality vote
25. Catholics opposed PR in the north, where their seats were more secure than in the south. In the south they supported PR
26. 1893: universal suffrage with plural vote passed. Electorate increased tenfold
27. After 1893 Liberal voters defected to Catholics because they were afraid of a Socialist majority
28. Socialist seat share increased significantly after 1893. Liberal votes share declined
29. ca. the 1890s: Catholics afraid of the growing left and declining Liberals
30. ca. the 1890s: Catholics afraid that existing electoral system might over-represent the left
31. ca. the 1890s: blocked vote system produced even more disproportionate outcomes than before franchise expansion
32. 1894 Catholic proposed a partial PR system but failed to win parliamentary majority because that system would have favored mostly Catholics
33. 1893–99: PR society started broad pro-PR campaign in response to disproportionality of blocked vote system
34. 1885–9: Liberals and Socialists formed electoral alliances in urban districts that awarded multiple seats

35. 1899, February: Catholic PR bill expanded, but only to urban multimember districts. Failed because of opposition from the left and from Liberals

36. Catholic vote weak in the districts that were industrial and had multiple seats

37. 1899: street protests and general strike over existing electoral system and plural vote

38. 1899, December: PR bill adopted (70 to 63 votes), most support coming from Catholics and Liberals. PR increased parliamentary strength of Liberals. Had support of PR Ligue. PR bill over-represented Catholics, under-represented Liberals and Socialists

39. the late 1890s: PR had strong popular support, played crucial role in PR adoption

40. 1900–10: Catholics favored female franchise. Street protest over plural vote that Socialists wanted abolished. Liberals wanted greater proportionality

41. 1919: introduced apparentement to increase proportionality

42. 1919: plural vote abolished, increased the left's seat share

43. 1921 female franchise introduced

Concatenation. Concatenation is the process of bringing silent evidence into dialogue with the existing foreknowledge and using inductive insights to update it. Let me provide a few examples of how the silent evidence of these thirty-seven events generates new descriptive insights. The failed PR reforms of 1894 (no. 32) and 1899 (no. 35) underscore that Belgium's PR adoption was not a singular event, as predicted by Boix, but was preceded by some overtly partisan electoral engineering. These failed reform attempts involved mixed electoral systems that were only partially of a PR character and that disproportionately favored Catholics. Belgium also had a peculiar block vote system, in which urban districts awarded multiple seats to whichever party won a plurality (nos. 11, 17, 30, 31, 34). The current left threat thesis ignores this kind of block vote system and assumes that the status quo systems involved either single-member first-past-the-post or double-ballot systems. It thus overlooks the supermajorities that the block vote system produced in urban districts. The left was growing in those urban districts and was going to benefit from these supermajorities far more than the right. This explains why it did not support PR (nos. 21, 38). Finally, the left was more interested in the franchise expansion – or, after 1893, in abolishing the multiple votes – than in electoral system reform. It also used extra-parliamentary protest and even general strikes to press for this demand (nos. 4, 20, 37). The left thus threatened the right not just electorally but also systemically, through extra-parliamentary protest as well as through the supermajorities that would eventually emerge as a result of the block vote system. Such new insights provide the building blocks not just for updating our descriptions but also for revising our concepts and theories. They explain why historical description is so fundamental to CHA.

Periodization. The goal of description is to identify patterns of historical change that clarify how the past differs from the present. It is by splitting recurring events from non-recurring events and by lumping them together in distinct periods that those patterns are constructed. Thus periodization schemes are not self-generating, unless decades or centuries are used. For example, the Belgian timeline from the 1830s to 1930s reveals no immediate pattern other than the PR adoption in 1899. The question therefore becomes whether the prehistory and post-history of this event could be further truncated. The post-history offers few periodization possibilities other than identifying a series of follow-up electoral reforms between 1899 and 1921. The prehistory is more promising and more relevant because it might generate new insights into the process leading up to the adoption of PR. This prehistory is marked by two periods: 1880–93 was characterized by growing reform demands; and 1893–9 was characterized by intense political engineering. The period from 1880 to 1893 was also marked by the creation of the PR Society, socialist demands for franchise expansion, a growing critique of vote-buying, which was common in small electoral districts, and voter intimidation without secret ballots. There was growing disenchantment with electoral malfeasance strategies that Liberal and Conservative incumbents used in order to contain the left threat. All this also signaled the growing realization of just how anachronistic the existing block vote system was – a practice that no longer exists in contemporary democracies. Parties thus began to look for alternatives such as PR (Carstairs 1980; Emmenegger and Walter 2019). As for the 1893–9 period, it marked a series of failed electoral system bills after the widening of the franchise in 1893. These bills were complex hybrids of single-member districts and PR elements. Neither bill gained parliamentary majorities; this was due to their overt partisan intent. Parliament approved a new law only in late 1899, after the government introduced a strict PR bill.

Together, these two periods illustrate that PR was not an instantly available and fully understood alternative to the existing system – certainly not in Belgium, the first country to adopt a national PR system. Instead, its adoption involved political mobilization, an increasing recognition of the anachronism and dysfunctionalities of the existing electoral institutions, and much learning from the failed reform attempts.

(Re)formulating the Research Question. The preceding description and periodization raise questions about the existing left threat thesis, which attributes the adoption of PR to the electoral strength of the left and the

fragmentation of the right. The historical description of the Belgian case identified the growing ideational acceptance of PR, the effects of the complex block vote system, and the role of extra-parliamentary mobilization in favor of electoral reforms as additional factors requiring future theoretical attention.

After this illustration of historical description, let me return to the more general discussion of eventful analysis and elaborate on its second key element – conceptualization.

5.3 Conceptualization: Making Descriptions Comparative

Conceptualizations translate everyday observations expressed in natural, ordinary language into standardized terminology and generalized concepts. Concepts differ from ordinary language by analytically identifying a set of core characteristics of a phenomenon and contrasting them with the dissimilar characteristics of a related but qualitatively different phenomenon (Sartori 1970; Schaffer 2021). Concepts establish a lexical and context-independent equivalence between a term and its empirical reference and, further, they clarify the term by differentiating it from its antonyms. They replace – as Adam Przeworski and Henry Teune (1970) memorably put it – "proper names with variables." Concepts ultimately serve to make observations sufficiently independent of history and geography to become comparable and measurable across time and space. Or, to put it plainly, concepts, just like theories, freeze history and geography.

Eventful analysis uses historical thinking to help view concepts as historical constructs, to revisit their genealogy, and, when necessary, to update them. It offers an interpretivist counterpoint to the often positivist and historyless treatment of concepts (Schaffer 2015, 5–20). It brings existing concepts into dialogue with the very phenomena from which they were abstracted in the first place and to which they now refer in a standardized, "experience-distant," context-independent terminology. Eventful analysis assists in the formation of concepts and in the elucidation of existing ones because it provides "experience-near," thick descriptive accounts from which broader concepts were extrapolated (Schaffer 2015, 5–8). This dialogue presupposes an iterative, inductive, and interpretive process whose structure is rarely discussed. (Two rare exceptions are Schaffer 2015; Becker 1998, 1–45.) Typically, this process capitalizes on historical thinking in six distinct ways:

- *grounding:* the selection of a specific historical context to identify a new concept or refine an existing one;

- *identifying or thickening the positive pole*: looking for *shared attributes* across phenomena and for synonymous linguistic terms that confirm those empirical similarities;
- *identifying or thickening the negative pole*: looking for *unshared, unique attributes* across phenomena and for antonymous linguistic terms that identify those differences;
- *assessing reliability*: looking for qualitative historical evidence to assess how reliably a concept translates qualitative evidence into quantitative data;
- *assessing content validity*: looking for *redundant or non-essential attributes* across phenomena;
- *assessing the temporal validity*: looking for *unstable attributes* that change as the phenomena change across historical time, and for etymological differences that confirm those changes;
- *assessing operationalism*: trying to establish to what extent variables are used without proper and prior conceptualization – that is, whether a variable is defined ex post vis-à-vis qualities or attributes of an already existing indicator or of a concept specified ex ante.

Eventful analysis helps elucidate the alignment between the linguistic concepts we use in comparing empirical phenomena and the empirical attributes of phenomena themselves. It does so by offering thick descriptive accounts that are mindful of historical changes.

Grounding. Howard Becker (1998, 109) wrote: "since concepts are a way to summarizing data, it is important that they be adapted to the data that they are going to summarize." He indirectly alludes to the importance of grounding concepts to establish whether they need to be modified. Grounding involves subjecting a concept to historical thinking by situating it in a rich empirical context, historically and geographically unfrozen, in order to elucidate whether it ignores essential attributes, includes irrelevant attributes, or contains outdated attributes (Schaffer 2015, 26–53). And, in the absence of established concepts, grounding phenomena in a small number of anchor cases serves as the first step to developing new concepts (Becker 1998). Eventful analysis is essential for grounding.

Identifying the Positive Pole. The shared elements of a concept constitute its positive pole. Eventful analysis evaluates it by asking whether the concept overlooks attributes that are observable in an empirical phenomenon, or whether it contains attributes that are not observable. This dialogue between concepts and context involves identifying substantive similarities – masked by ordinary language, which uses dissimilar descriptions in different geographic locations – and employing them to define a concept and to give it a more context-independent name or label – and, typically, also a more technical one. A concept is therefore a scholarly and linguistic construct that draws attention to empirical attributes that are common enough to be observed across space and stable enough to be observed across a certain time span. The Dutch American political scientist Arend Lijphart, for example, noted that various power-sharing practices used in Belgium, the Netherlands, Switzerland, and postwar Austria were known under different names (e.g., *verzuiling* in the Netherlands, *Konkordanz* in Switzerland, *Proporz* in Austria). He replaced these labels with the new concept of "consociationalism" and defined it in terms of common power-sharing arrangements (Lijphart 1990; see also Lijphart 1968, 1969). These shared elements constitute the positive pole of consociationalism. The positive pole also serves to specify a concept's geographic boundaries and avoid what Giovanni Sartori (1970) called "conceptual stretching." Lijphart's subsequent efforts to extend consociationalism to Lebanon, Columbia, and India raised the suspicion that he was stretching his concept too far, ending up comparing apples and oranges (Andeweg 2000).

Identifying the Negative Pole. A concept gains in analytical clarity if it becomes clear what it is not. Lumping together all the dissimilarities that differentiate a phenomenon from others serves to identify the negative pole of a concept. Such a pole clarifies the meaning of the original concept because it elucidates the outer boundaries of the semantic field *within* which that concept operates (Goertz 2012, 27–59). This negative pole is the language equivalent of an antonym that highlights dissimilarities. Lijphart (2012), for example, managed in time to clarify his consociational concept – which emphasizes power sharing, mutual vetoes, and other consensus-enhancing political practices – by defining it in contradistinction to majoritarianism, which lacks these features. Democratic elections are commonly defined in terms of shared features such as holding incumbents accountable or aggregating voter preferences. These core functions become clearer when they are contrasted with earlier, pre-democratic, so-called silent elections that served to affirm social hierarchies (Caramani 2003; Morgan 1988) or with communist, non-democratic elections that functioned to mobilize citizens around the state's ideology (Linz 1978). This grounding of concepts and the specification of their two poles constitute the initial steps in constructing concepts. These initial conceptualization steps freeze history and geography and thus leave unanswered the question about the concepts' validity. Conceptualization therefore involves additional steps designed to evaluate the soundness of those concepts.

Assessing Reliability. Concepts are frequently used to translate categorical textual evidence into continuous quantitative data. This translation typically requires coding historical texts and assigning ordinal scores. To ensure reliability, multiple coders follow a specific protocol, designed to test the clarity of coding criteria and how closely the codes are linked to specific dates.

Identifying Content Validity. Concepts often have multiple attributes, and turning them into measurements involves using multiple indicators. The composite nature of such concepts carries the risk that different indicators capture the same empirical characteristic, and thus count it more than once. Some indicators of democracy, for example, include a general measure related to the openness of elections and to freedom of association. Since freedom of association makes elections automatically competitive, competitiveness indicators and freedom of association indicators measure the same attribute. The resulting *redundancy problem* produces measurement errors, because the overlapping indicators distort the overall value of a variable. Concepts can also include non-essential attributes that muddle their analytical sharpness by conflating features that should belong in separate concepts (Munck and Verkuilen 2002, 13–14). This *conflation problem* often results from a desire to have comprehensive measures that provide a single metric for evaluating often complex and heterogeneous phenomena (e.g., university ranking) (Gladwell 2011). It compromises the content validity of a concept because it lumps together attributes that, albeit co-occurring sometimes, really are so different that they should be ascribed to different concepts. This contributes to concept stretching – the operation of adding attributes to concepts so as to expand their capacity to travel to more cases, while at the same time compromising their analytical precision (Sartori 1970, 1033–6). Including economic rights in a definition of democracy is understandable, since some countries indeed consider these rights to be democratic. But this inclusion conflates two qualitatively different attributes, which make it difficult to analyze, at a later stage, the economic effects of democracy, given that its conceptualization already includes an economic factor. Eventful analysis helps us identify these problems of redundancy and conflation (Munck and Verkuilen 2002, 13–14).

Assessing Temporal Validity. Eventful analysis pays close attention to historical continuities and discontinuities and is very attuned to how *unchanged* a phenomenon remains over time (Schaffer 2015, 67–72). It plays a significant role in identifying the historical boundary conditions of concepts and serves as a "useful reminder that problem of concept stretching arises not only from movement across cases, but also changes over time within cases" (Collier and Mahon 1993, 845). The degree to which a concept is historically bounded, inappropriately stretched, or in need of updating depends on the rate of historical change itself. The Dow Jones almost continuously changes the companies it tracks, to capture both structural changes in the economy and the organizational changes of corporations. The GDP updates its index every twenty years or so, to capture slower moving structural changes in the economy (Coyle 2015; Karabell 2014). GDP has been criticized for reflecting an outdated productivist understanding of economics that ignores more contemporary concerns about human fulfillment and ecological sustainability.

Assessing Operationalism. The need to measure and the availability of an ever-increasing number of data sets often lead to what Becker (1998, 109–13) called "operationalism." He uses this term to describe situations where scholars avail themselves of quantitative indicators without having first engaged in a proper conceptualization, thus violating Sartori's (1970, 1038) principle that "concept formation stands prior to quantification" (see also Swedberg 2018). US News and World Report Best Colleges Ranking, for example, compiles all sorts of admissions metrics (GPA, SAT scores, acceptance rates, retention rates), human resource data (percentage of faculty members with a doctorate, class sizes), and development data (size of endowment, annual giving) to rank colleges, without telling the reader what core attributes it used to identify educational excellence (Gladwell 2011). The company measures without proper prior conceptualization. This makes it difficult to figure out how the number of faculty members with a doctoral degree or the size of the endowment improve the educational outcomes of first-generation college graduates (Gladwell 2011). Eventful analysis serves as a corrective to this kind of operationalism: it provides enough contextual details and historical scale for us to figure out what those indicators do or do not measure. A closer qualitative analysis of those US News and World Report indicators makes it clear that they capture the wealth and reputation of those institutions more than anything related to their capacity of increase students' mastery of new skills and information (Gladwell 2011).

Let me pivot again to the PR literature to illustrate how eventful analysis assists in the formation of concepts.

5.4 Application of Conceptualization

The idea of a "left threat" – a threat emanating from the political left – is the principal concept in the eponymous theory about the origins of PR. Neither Rokkan nor Boix engaged in any systematic conceptualization, but they defined this idea according to two readily available measures: the electoral strength of socialist parties; and the party fragmentation index (Boix only). This rudimentary conceptualization subsequently become the subject of various reconceptualizations that involved grounding, identifying positive and negative poles, and assessing temporal validity and operationalism.

Grounding. Rokkan and Boix loosely grounded their concept in late nineteenth-century demands for a widening of the franchise and in the electoral rise of socialist parties, both of which threatened Conservative and Liberal incumbents. Subsequent scholars grounded the concept in a more eventful context, which situates the left's electoral threat in the broader and longer-standing conflict between the established liberal order – emphasizing free, global markets, private property, constitutional and anti-majoritarian checks and balances, and a limited but not necessarily fully democratic government – and the newly emerging working class, which wanted to limit markets and private property, modify unequal market outcomes, remove checks and balances, and expand democracy to accomplish these goals. In this larger conflict between liberal constitutionalism and majoritarian democracy, PR became one of the political instruments that Liberals and Conservatives used to contain the left threat (Ahmed 2013; Barzachka 2014; Pilon 2013). Placing the left threat in this broader context helps with the next three steps of conceptualization.

Strengthening the Positive Pole. This grounding helps identify two non-electoral attributes that the original conceptualization overlooked. Incumbent Liberals and Conservatives used a wide range of strategies to contain the left before settling on PR. Those strategies included outright repression, imposing restrictions on the labor union's organization, limiting the franchise, plural votes, malapportionment, gerrymandering, and various forms of electoral malfeasance. These pre-PR containment strategies had an important radicalizing effect on the left and thus, ironically, enhanced its threat. Furthermore, Socialists did not pose just an electoral threat but also a larger, ideological one. Some Socialist parties were far more radical in their economic and political demands than others. This led Amel Ahmed (2013) to incorporate ideological threats in her definition of the left threat.

Strengthening the Negative Pole. The grounding points to elements that did not threaten incumbents and thus indicate a negative pole. Ahmed points to the emergence of Lib–Lab coalitions, in which Socialists and non-Socialists formed electoral alliances. Or she discusses various labor incorporation strategies that involved labor unions in the economic decision-making process, or the adoption of early social policies or tariffs that protected workers from the vagaries of markets (Ahmet 2013, 13–63). Such incorporation strategies were the opposite of repression strategies or partisan institutional engineering, and thus point to attributes that define the negative pole of the left threat, making it easier to identify what it is not.

Assessing Reliability. The codings of the left threat thesis raise a few reliability issues, because the original left threat was linked to official election returns. Those returns are widely taken to be reliable, and the unavailability of the original ballots makes assessing their reliability anyway impossible. Ahmed (2013) uses a careful study by Gary Marks (2009) to add ideological radicalism as an extra indicator to her version of the left threat. Thomas Cusack, Torben Iversen, and David Soskice developed a brand-new indicator of labor market coordination that involved a protracted back-and-forth over its reliability (Cusack, Iversen, and Soskice 2007; Web Appendix 2010; Kreuzer 2010; 2022).

Assessing Temporal Validity. The conflict between existing liberal constitutional and newly emerging democratic orders was reasonably stable before 1914 but changed dramatically through the effects of World War I, particularly after the Russian Revolution. Any conceptualization of the left threat ought to pay heed to these dramatic changes. The left threat increased with the demonstration of the potential success of an extra-institutional revolutionary strategy, with the split of the left into Socialist and Communist parties, with the active support that Communist parties received from the Soviet Union, and with the greater propensity of workers to protest in the streets and strike to advance their demands. The original conceptualization of the left threat needs either to incorporate these new elements or to be more transparent about its temporal boundness (Alesina and Glaeser 2004; Barzachka 2014).

The combined effects of eventful analysis on describing phenomena properly make it a crucial first step toward identifying broad patterns of historical change, as well as toward developing the concepts we need if we wish to compare such patterns across larger sets of cases. The next chapter, on longue durée analysis, discusses how time series data expand the temporal range and geographic reach of the initial patterns of historical change identified through eventful analysis. After that, the chapter on macro-causal analysis discusses how to generate the theories that explain those patterns.

Exercises

5.1. The goal of eventful analysis is historical description, which offers a journalistic description of events and starts differentiating historical continuities from historical discontinuities. Eventful analysis is particularly important when we try to make sense of tumultuous, crisis-like moments in history such as the one we currently are living. So take the political crisis around the populist outburst led by Trump, Brexit, the Covid-19 pandemic, Putin's invasion of the Ukraine, or whatever happens to be the latest crisis at the time of reading this book. You probably read enough newspapers or listen to enough podcasts to conduct an eventful analysis without having to head for the archives.

Try to answer the following questions, which are typically asked in eventful analysis. 1. Are we dealing with highly contingent one-time events, or with culminations of long-term trends? 2. What has been unprecedented in the last four years? How likely is it that these unprecedented new elements will endure throughout the next decade? In what ways will the Trump presidency/Brexit/Covid/Ukraine's invasion have lasting consequences? Or are those events just the latest iteration of long series of populist outburst in US history, British nationalism, pandemic history, or military history? Will Covid-19 transform our future economy qualitatively – how and where we work, global supply chains, expectations about government interventions, concerns shifting from efficiency to equity – and, if so, how? 3. Come up with a periodization scheme for the rise of right-wing populism in the United States. If Trump is the final period, what would be the preceding ones? (Or do the same for the crisis of your choice.) 4. What new research questions must be investigated? What older research question could be abandoned?

5.2. Convert Earl Cook's monochronic periodization scheme into a multi-chronic intercurrence pattern. How could the different periods bleed into one another? Use Thelen's intercurrence typology to refine Cook's analysis by making it more eventful – by turning it from one single typology into multiple concurrent processes.

5.3. Let's apply eventful analysis to E. H. Carr's car accident story. Proceed in the following steps.

Part I: Fact Finding and Chronicling. How have car accidents changed since 1939? Ignore for now that the original accident occurred in Lerwick, Scotland and assume that accidents could have occurred in any location. Try to answer the following questions:

Antecedents	Then (1939)	Now	If there were changes, how did they alter the probability of road fatalities?
Who drives?			
What motivates driving?			
How far do we drive?			
How have cars changed?			
How has road design changed?			
How has drinking changed?			
How have traffic regulations changed?			
How have pedestrians changed? Distance walked? Where they walk? Addictions?			
How have responses to accidents changed?			
How has the treatment of traffic victims changed?			
Add further categories if necessary.			

Part II: Concatenation and Periodizing. Can you translate these changes into historical patterns? This would require linking those changes to specific dates, and then coming up with a periodization scheme (e.g., 1940–60, no safety inspections or car safety features; 1970–2020, car inspections, seat belts, airbags; 2021–present, self-driving cars). Propose a periodization for the other categories of change. How closely do these periodizations match that of car technology? Do you detect any intercurrences?

Part III: Conceptualization. The historical description alerted you to all sorts of new factors affecting traffic fatalities. Let us assume that you currently measure traffic fatalities as deaths by car per 100,000 population. How would you want to update or refine this measure, to capture some of the insights gained from historical description? For example, how would you modify the measure after finding out that people drive longer distances, or that urban transportation shifted from cars to bicycles? Or if new research showed that more and more people commit suicide by jumping in front of cars?

6 Longue Durée Analysis
Looking for Serial Patterns

History begins when men begin to think of the passage of time in terms not of natural processes – the cycle of the seasons, the human life-span – but of a series of specific events in which men are consciously involved and which they can consciously influence.

(E. H. Carr 1961, 157)

Time series analysis is the form of quantitative analysis most complementary to historical analysis.

(Janoski and Isaac 1994, 44)

Starting in the 1930s, the French Annales historians led by Marc Bloch, Lucien Febvre, and Ferdinand Braudel tried to shift their discipline's traditional focus from noisy, non-repetitive events such as those alluded to by Carr to quieter and recurrent structural factors, thereby drawing attention to what they called *la longue durée*, the long time span; and the label stuck. They sought to build a bridge between event-filled political history and the rather repetitive natural history studied by evolutionary biologists, geologists, and environmental scientists. To Braudel, who was one of the Annales School's most influential members, this turn to longue durée history was more than just a theoretical pivot. He boldly declared:

> An incredible number of dice, always rolling, dominate and determine each individual existence: Uncertainty then, in the realm of individual [eventful] history; but in that of collective history ... simplicity and consistency [prevails]. History is indeed a "poor little conjectural science" when it selects individuals as its objects ... but much more rational in its procedures and results when it examines groups and repetitions.

> (Braudel, as quoted in Moretti 2005, 4)

Braudel's epistemological ambition of upgrading history from a "poor little conjectural science" to something more systematic required slowing down and ultimately freezing history by shifting historical inquiry to the domain of natural history. He contended that its repetitions were more fundamental than the events that disrupted them and thus should become the primary focus of historical analysis. A bold vision, indeed, carried on through comparative historical analysis (CHA) in economic history, demography, cliometrics, evolutionary psychology, and economic institutionalism (Conrad 2017; Henrich 2020; North 1977). Longue durée history's focus on repetitions and serial events allows it to describe and redescribe historical change in manner that is distinct from that of eventful analysis. There are three major aspects of this difference.

First, longue durée history conceptualizes historical change differently from eventful analysis. It defines it as the fluid unfolding of trends that are readily visualized, rather than the choppy alternation of continuities and discontinuities that produce lumpy periodizations. Second, it describes historical change using theory-laden, thin, and hence measurable variables rather than complex events to be explored. Finally, it shifts the explanatory focus from specific events as the central engine of historical change to quieter, eventless, hidden mechanisms such markets, human cognition, or biology, which are all linked to an evolutionary or demographic logic of change.

The first part of this chapter draws on the tools that descriptive statistics and exploratory data analysis use to visualize univariate, bivariate , and multivariate trends. I also follow CHA nomenclature and refer to multivariate trends as developmental typologies. These tools serve to describe undescribed trends, redescribe already described trends, and thereby generate new research questions. Next, the chapter discusses three factors contributing to misdescriptions: improper baselining; miscalibrations of time scales; and mismeasurements. Understanding the sources of misdescriptions is important for evaluating longue durée history's highly abstract and hence thin accounts of historical change and their validity as descriptions of the more complex and disorderly change captured by eventful analysis.

6.1 Univariate Trends: Time Series Analysis

Longue durée analysis uses time series data and line graphs to track long-term univariate patterns. Larry Griffin and Larry Isaac (1992, 167) recognize the historical quality of time series, which they define as "time ordered data about historical events or processes that represents far more than the numbers contained in those markers. ... Such data are thus historical in the most fundamental sense of the terms." Later in this chapter I will show how historical time series indeed are by discussing the elements of historical change that they capture and pointing to the ones they miss. We will get to revisit Sartori's concern about conceptual stretching. A time series is *historical* because dates still matter – they link the measurements to historical contexts – and because measurements remain *inter*dependent – they link the value of an earlier to the value of a later one. But a time series is *less historical* than eventful analysis because it shifts from historical to serial comparisons and from events to be explored to indicators to be visualized. It thus partially freezes history. However, it is this very freezing that permits comparing historical processes across longer time spans, and thereby exploring the rhythms at which they unfold.

Time series analyze historical patterns by trends. Figure 6.1 shows that these trends fill the space between bounded history – which focuses on causal patterns – and noisy, eventful history – which studies (dis)continuities and the directionality of historical change.[1]

Figure 6.1 underscores the precise vocabulary that time series uses in order to differentiate between three types of univariate trends. It uses *random walks* as its baseline. These are the historiographical equivalent of Henry Ford's conception of history as "one damn thing after another." In random walks, observations oscillate randomly enough for the order of data points not to form any distinct upward or downward pattern. It produces a *trendless trend line* in which points that are close together in time are also close in value and thus do not translate into any pattern. As trends become less random and less reversible, they acquire structure and come to reflect three potential trends: seasonal, cyclical, and secular.

Seasonal and cyclical trends are recurrent because they describe patterns that repeat themselves, and thus are reversible. *Seasonal trends* recur at fixed calendrical moments and are linked to the seasons or to religious events. They typically describe cultural, weather, or consumption patterns. *Cyclical trends* are slightly less predictable because they repeat themselves independently of the calendar. Business cycles are the best-known example. Climate change deniers, for example, cynically dismiss the current warming trend by claiming that it merely represents the temporary upward slope of a larger cycle of global warming and cooling. Global warming is, in short, an artifact of the time used to graph it. Seasonal and cyclical trends are intricately linked to cyclical notions of historical time. CHA views them skeptically because they freeze history to the point where it devolves into historical tourism.

---

[1] Before elaborating on those patterns, I should point out that serial patterns at times involve notions of cyclical or eventful history. Recurring, serial trends overlap cyclical history, for example, and developmental typologies patterns overlay the periodization of eventful history. These fluid analytical boundaries underscore a tension in longue durée analysis. On the one hand, it tries to reduce the past to natural history and thereby make it sufficiently eventless to be analyzed with the tools of natural science. On the other hand, it tries to embed natural history sufficiently in societal processes to make it relevant to the more eventful human history. We therefore must remain alert to what longue durée analysis can and cannot deliver and recognize when, in the hands of its most orthodox advocates, it ceases to contribute to CHA and wanders off into historical tourism (March and Olsen 1984; Sewell 1996).

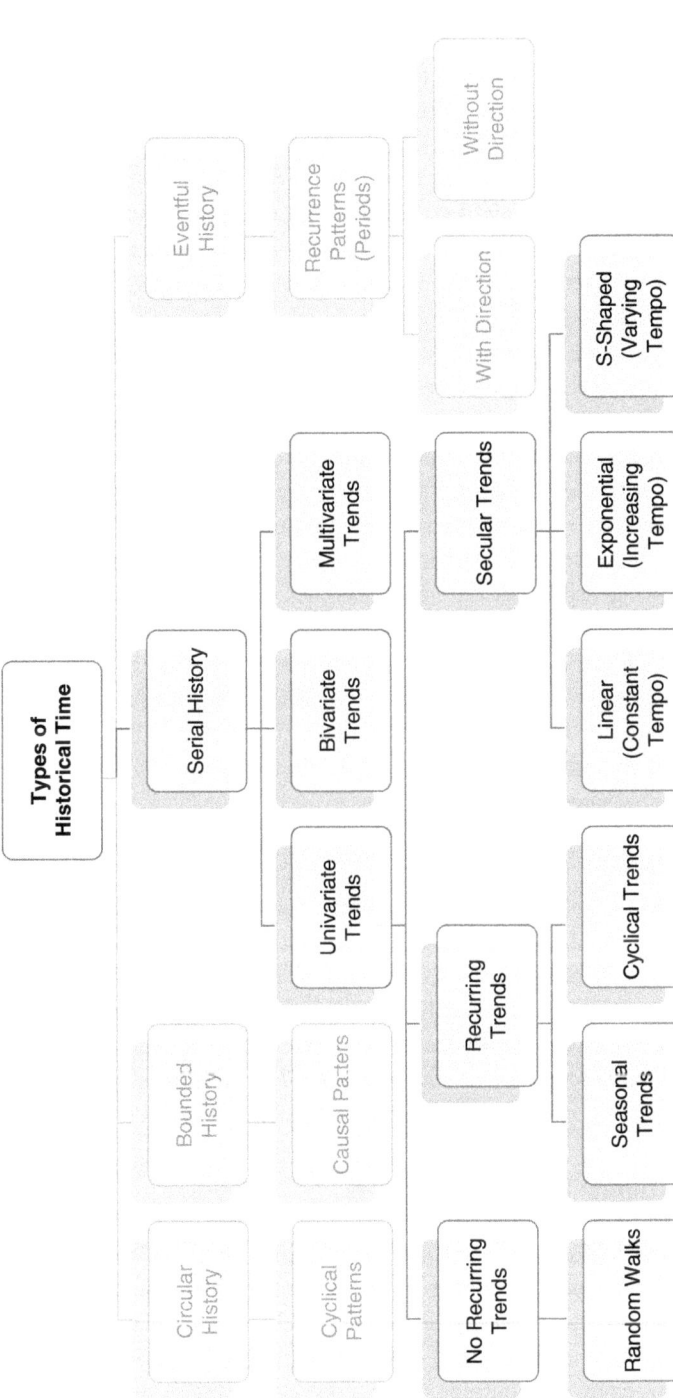

Figure 6.1 Longue durée, trend-based patterns

Here the patterns that CHA explores are organized on the basis of corresponding notions of historical time. Longue durée analysis uses serial history to explore univariate, bivariate, and multivariate patterns. Multivariate patterns are also referred to as developmental typologies. These three serial patterns freeze history less than circular and bounded history but are more frozen than eventful history. The boundaries between these notions of history are porous, as some of the serial patterns overlap with the patterns explored by other notions of historical time.

Finally, *secular trends* capture cumulative and hence qualitative patterns of change. Such patterns are less reversible and thus involve a thicker version of serial history than cyclical patterns do. Gross domestic product (GDP) times series, for example, show a long-term secular trend in the growth of overall economic output in industrialized countries. This output corresponds to qualitative transitions from an agricultural economy to an industrial, service, and eventually knowledge economy. The trend lines do not identify those specific qualitative transition points, which require eventful analysis to determine when exactly changes in degree produce a change in kind. Such qualitative changes can be highlighted in line graphs by adding specific events (historical discontinuities), which elucidate the changes in question in the slope of the line, or broader periods (historical continuities) such as presidential terms, recessions, or wars. William Playfair once again pioneered such contextualized line graphs. In Figure 6.2, in order to contextualize England's growing national debt from 1688 to 1800, he adds the reigns of English monarchs and the wars they fought. This presentation underscores the fact that the wars contributed more significantly to the growing debt than the individual monarchs' profligacy during peacetime. Such contextualized line graphs have two benefits. First, they assist readers in interpreting their meaning by demonstrating how faster-moving eventful history is linked to the fluctuations of the slower-moving serial history. Second, data sets are not infallible, hence the ability to match trendlines with events increases one's confidence in the trend, while the failure to do so can point to potential measurement errors.

The line graphs are also useful for differentiating variations in the tempo of secular trends. Few secular trends progress in a strictly linear fashion, like England's public debt during the eighteenth century. Some start slowly and then unfold more quickly, and thus accelerate. If this acceleration slows down at a later point in time, the secular change becomes S-shaped (slow start and finish, with a fast middle). S-shaped trends are frequently associated with tipping point phenomena. Secular trends can experience serious setbacks, known as "structural breaks." These breaks often point to qualitative changes captured by periodizations.

6.2 Bivariate Trends: Serial Scatterplots

Univariate trends unfold concurrently with other trends and raise the possibility of exploring the covariation between them. Scatterplots visualize these bivariate relations, but they typically freeze time and space to focus on the strength of the correlation, regardless of historical or geographic contexts. The principal takeaway from a scatterplot is the slope of the regression line. It

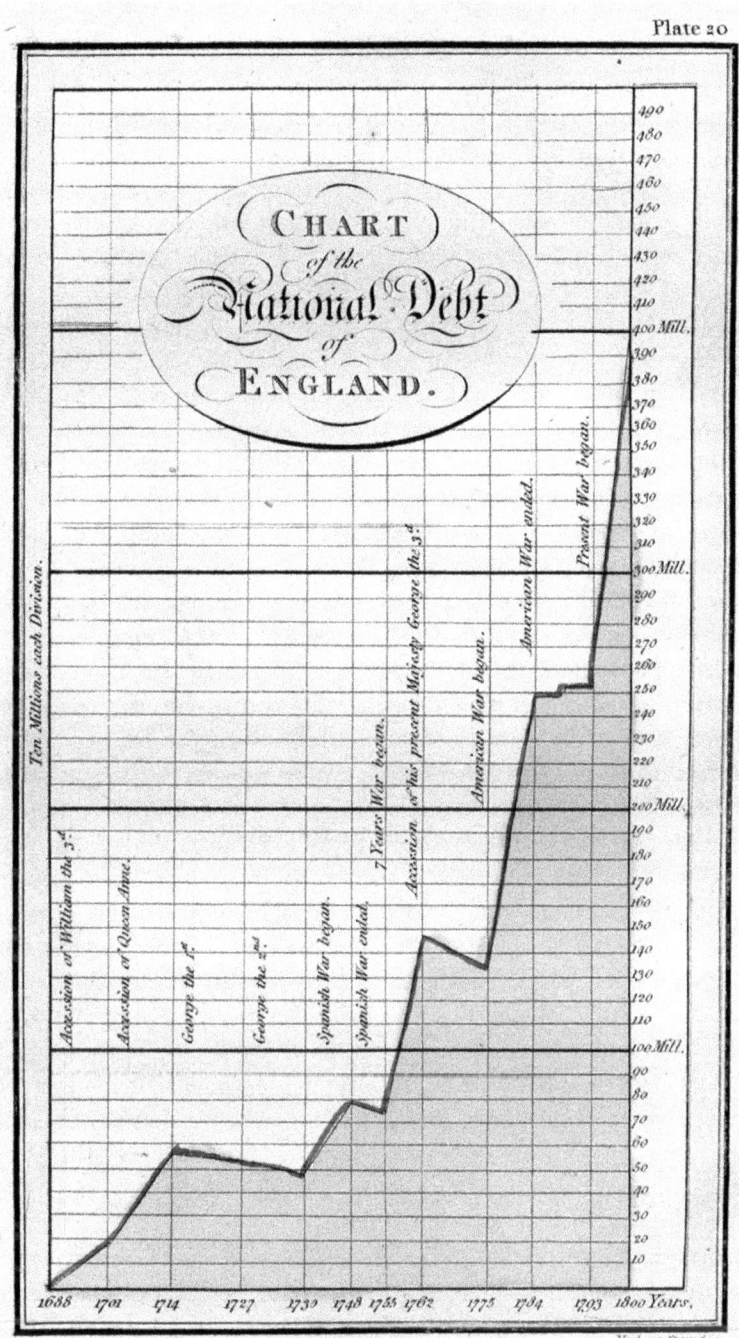

Figure 6.2 A contextualized line graph
William Playfair's contextualized line graph helps readers better understand England's national debt by adding vertical labels that indicate the reigns of kings and the wars that contributed to its growth.

summarizes the aggregate effect across all the cases and thus serves as a benchmark for evaluating how much individual cases deviate from this overall effect. Scatterplots help us place individual cases in the context of a larger population, but they pay little attention to changes across time and to geographic variations in this population.

Serial scatterplots, also referred to as connected scatterplots, reinsert a time and space dimension and visualize historical and geographic trends within a given sample. Hans Rosling, a Swedish public health professor, popularized serial scatterplots with the help of his Gapminder software, Gapminder Trendalyzer. Gapminder is the statistical equivalent of a time-lapse camera, as it stitches together scatterplots at different points in time. It contains a time slider, which allows moving scatterplots forward or backward in time to create stunning bivariate serial patterns. Serial scatterplots thus explore the interplay of two trends in the same visualization. Gapminder also unfreezes geography by color-coding data points, according to geographic origins. This makes it possible to compare bivariate trends across spatial units of analysis.

In a 2013 TED (technology, entertainment, design) talk that made him famous, Rosling focuses on the correlation between income and life expectancy to illustrate how growing prosperity over the last two centuries improved the human condition. Figure 6.3 shows snapshots from six different points in time; the years are shown in the background. The overarching trends reveal how, in 1800, differences in income between Eurasian countries and other regions of the world did not translate into any significant differences in life expectancy. This gradually began to change from 1850 to 1950, when Eurasian countries experienced a gradual increase in life expectancy while other regions did not. Over the next seventy years, this disparity declined – so much so that in 2018 life expectancies varied far less than one would have expected on the basis of continued income differences. Gapminder permits refining this very large pattern by tracking individual countries, or even variations within countries. It thus demonstrates an ability to explore patterns by unfreezing history and geography. It is important to underscore the exploratory function of serial scatterplots of this kind. Rosling does not link his analysis to a well-specified theory that would permit any causal inferences. Instead, his analysis is descriptive and points to patterns that raise interesting questions.

Scholars continue to publish on paper, an analog medium whose static and monochromatic limitations prevent harnessing the potential of software like Gapminder. Since it will not be possible to add a time slider to a printed page, the next best thing is to create panels of different moments in history that convey, in a choppier manner, bivariate serial patterns.

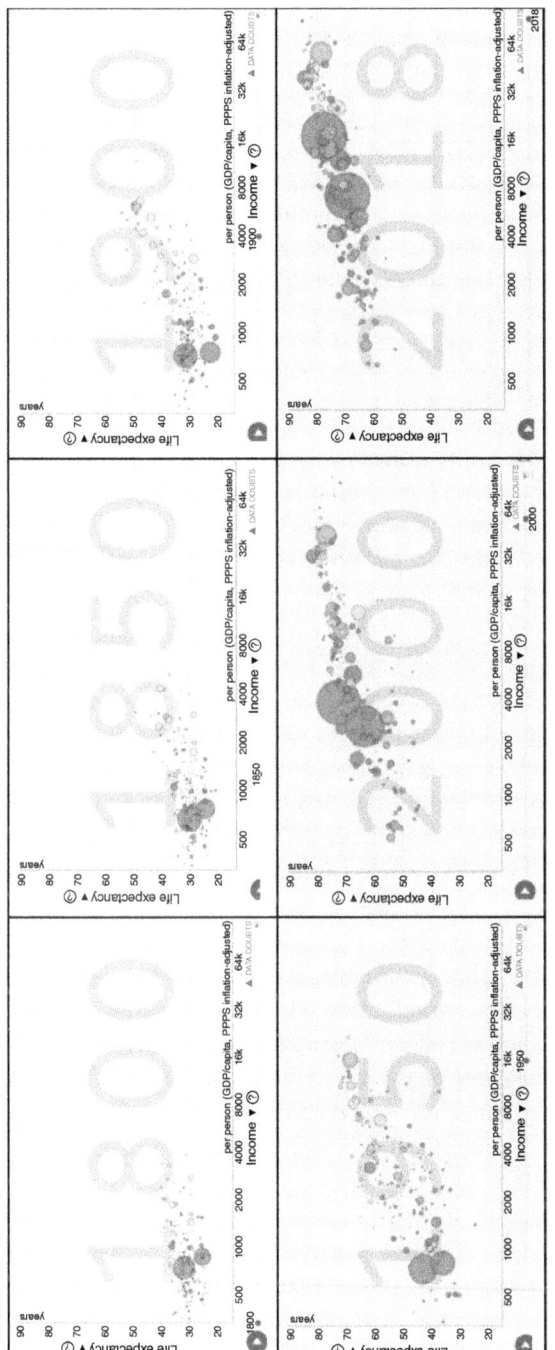

Figure 6.3 Serial scatterplot

This graph shows how growth in national income improved life expectancy between 1800 and 2020 in fifty-year intervals. The six panels track China, Argentina, Japan, the United States, and the United Kingdom. The opaque bubbles in the background track the rests of the world. The diameter of the bubbles indicates population size. The Gapminder software used to generate these graphs allows visualizing annual changes in these scatterplots. It also uses colors to differentiate regions in the world.

6.3 Multivariate Trends: Developmental Typology

Stein Rokkan (1968b), one of the CHA grandees, introduced the term "developmental typology" to describe his effort to retrace the pattern of European countries' transitioning from feudal institutions to modern mass democracy. Developmental typologies can be viewed either as an extension of bivariate to multivariate trends or as a repurposing of regular typologies by substituting cross-sectional with longitudinal or serial classifications (Gerring 2012a, 726). Developmental typologies track long-term, multiple, and complex trends that are so interrelated that they become difficult to visualize. They make categorical historical differentiations that resemble periodizations quite closely. However, developmental typologies differ from periodizations in four ways.

First, developmental typologies pay more attention to continuities than to discontinuities. They reflect the primary interest of longue durée analysis in slowly moving, and thus in rather continuous serial patterns. They do not capture the noisier and faster-moving events that mark the transition from one continuity to the next. The party literature, for example, employs a developmental typology to differentiate various phases in the organizational transformation of parties. Notable parties were anchored in the networks of socially prominent notables; socialist mass mobilization had mass-based membership and formalized internal decision-making structures; catch-all parties substituted membership with loose alliances with interest groups and telegenic party leaders; and, finally, cartel parties became increasingly reliant on public funding to support themselves and block new entrants (Katz and Mair 1995). This developmental typology foregrounds the organizational continuities of parties and their temporal order, but pays little attention to the transition from one phase to the next. It thus freezes history, attempting to paint with a broader brush than eventful analysis.

Second, developmental typologies freeze geography and have a more explicit cross-sectional focus than periodization. The periods of American history, for instance the antebellum era or the Gilded Age, do not travel easily to other parts of the world. Developmental typologies break the past into more formalized stages, which are presumed to occur across a larger set of countries and thus are more readily comparable. The stages are the equivalent of a type in regular typology; they differ only by marking qualitative differences over time rather than across geography. Third, the stages in developmental typology are only loosely linked to dates. The five stages of party development can occur at different historical dates, in a way that a historical period cannot replicate. Catch-all parties, for example, developed far earlier in the United States than in Europe, and mass mobilization parties endured much longer in some European countries than in others. By contrast, the interwar period is always strictly delimited by the years 1918 and 1939. However, developmental typologies remain bounded by broad historical background conditions. Notable parties were the product of late nineteenth-century mass democracies and thus are very unlikely to be observed in the late twentieth century.

Fourth, developmental typologies typically imply a stronger historical directionality than periodizations. The idea of stages is linked to the idea that discontinuities – the source of change – are cumulative over time and thus move history along a particular path. And, as all discontinuities have the same transformative effect, their contingencies and particularities require less attention. Ascribing to history a broader arc always carries the risk of teleology or functionalism because it marginalizes the role of human agency and the impact of historical contingencies. To avoid historical tourism, it becomes important to demonstrate the plausibility of such arcs. Broadly speaking, the longer the arc, the higher the threshold for demonstrating its plausibility. For example, stipulating a smaller, more medium-term arc linking industrialization to greater economic outputs or democratization is less problematic than linking nineteenth-century voting patterns to the aftereffects of the Black Death in the fourteenth century (Gingerich and Vogler 2021). Scholars have used different graphs to visualize developmental typologies. Their selection depends on how many dimensions the typology includes and what data are available. I adduce here three brief examples to illustrate these visualization possibilities.

Tables are a widely employed tool when it comes to visualizing developmental typologies. Referring to tables as visualizations might be a stretch, because they are a crude tool for summarizing complex information. Peter Mair and Richard Katz (1995) extrapolated from the party literature the aforementioned developmental typology (see Table 6.1). They tracked the organizational transformation of parties on the basis of a set of categories listed in the left column: time range, type of membership, linkage between civil society and the state, and resources. Each of the four stages is defined by qualitative changes in those categories.

The columns correspond to the time ranges during which parties shared certain organizational characteristics. Notice that the four stages overlap to indicate that different countries passed through these stages at different historical dates while still being subject to broader historical boundary conditions. For example, catch-all politics emerged in the United States in the 1950s, a good twenty year earlier than in Europe, and cartel parties started earlier in Europe and their arrival was still awaited in the United States.

Tables are helpful for tracking complex, multidimensional developmental typologies; but they do not offer much in terms of actual visualizations. Such visualizations require reducing the number of dimensions that can be tracked over time with serial bar graphs.

Table 6.1 Party developmental typology

Characteristics	Notable Party	Mass Party	Catch-All Party	Cartel Party
Time range	Nineteenth century	The 1880s to the 1960s	1945 to the present	1970 to the present
Type of membership	Small and elitist	Mass-based, organizationally tightly integrated	Small, reliant on consultants and interest groups	Small, reliant on consultants and interest groups
Linkage between state and civil society.	Minimal linkage, limited to elite-based networks	Party belongs to civil society and links to stage	Party is broker between civil society groups and state	Party becomes part of state
Principal source for mobilization	Personal contacts	Membership fees and volunteering	Diverse sources, especially interest groups and media	State subventions

This table identifies the four stages in the organizational transformation of parties from the nineteenth century to the present. It uses three characteristics to create a typology and links each type with a distinct time period, to produce four stages in an overall trajectory. (Adapted from Katz and Mair 1995, 18.)

Serial Bar Graphs. Longue durée analysis is always on the lookout for continuous measures that track cumulative changes over extended time periods. It uses GDP, urbanization, literacy rates, battle deaths, energy consumption, and other measures as proxies for tracking various aspects of economic, political, or human development (Morris 2013). As the next section shows, line graphs are the typical tool for visualizing continuous measures of this sort. Some scholars also use serial bar graphs to translate continuous time series trends into developmental typologies. Earl Cook (1971) uses a serial stacked bar graph to demonstrate how changes in the mode of energy production mark distinct qualitative breaks in the overall growth of energy consumption and distinct stages of economic development. Cook manages to refine the line graph that illustrates the dramatic increase of daily per capita energy consumption over the past 1 million years (solid line) by breaking this long period into six distinct stages and by complementing the division with stacked bar graphs. He labels the six periods of economic development, anachronistically by today's standards, "primitive" (East Africa ca. 1,000,000 years ago), "hunting" (Europe ca. 100,000 years ago), "primitive agricultural" (the Fertile Crescent ca. 5,000 BC), "advanced agricultural" (Northern Europe ca. AD 1400), "industrial "(England ca. 1875), and "technological man" (United States in the 1970s). The time scale of Figure 6.4 is miscalibrated, as it gives the last half-century period the same amount of space as the 1,000,000-year first stage, even though the latter is one hundred times longer. These periods

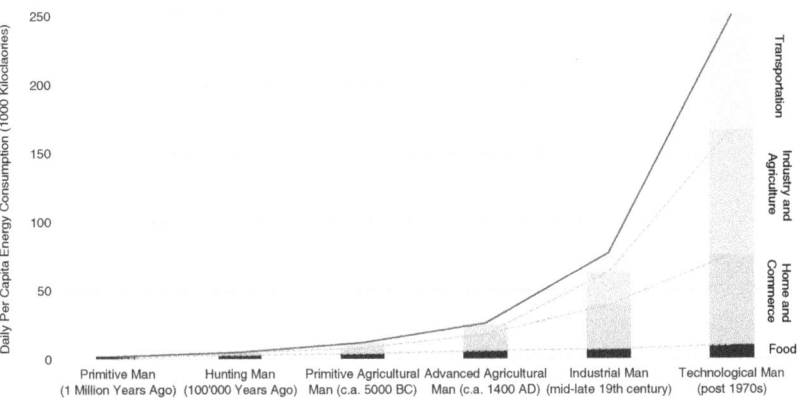

Figure 6.4 Serial bar graph
In order to show a secular increase in per capita energy consumption, Cook breaks the line graph into six distinct stages of economic development. He grounds this periodization in the changing mixture of energy consumptions, as well as in the expanding locus of economic activity to which the latter allude. (Adapted from Cook 1971, 136)

also mark broad time ranges that leave open the specific dates during which individual cases reached this developmental level. The stacked bar graph links the periods to distinct modes of energy production, as well as to four categories that loosely specify the expanding geographic locus of economic activities: food, home or commerce, industry and agriculture, transportation. Cook's serial bar graph could easily be adapted to show how secular increases in GDP are linked to structural changes in the economy; this could be done by using a bar graph to show the changing importance that the agriculture, manufacturing, service, and knowledge sectors played in generating overall wealth.

Jennifer Dixon developed a slightly different serial stacked bar graph, which is particularly ingenious in that it visualizes ideational changes that are difficult to track over time. In her book *Dark Pasts* she follows how official narratives of the Turkish and Japanese governments acknowledged respectively the Armenian genocide and the Nanjing massacre and expressed contrition for them. She develops a carefully crafted scale, which ranges from denying or not speaking about these atrocities to acknowledging them in various forms, which in turn range from admitting responsibility to commemoration. The full ordinal scale is shown in Figure 6.5. Dixon then uses bar graphs to indicate through which of nine stages of contrition a country advanced. Countries in Dixon's graph, unlike in Cox's, can occupy several stages simultaneously, which makes her developmental typology more continuous. Turkey, for example, engaged in denials and mythmaking from

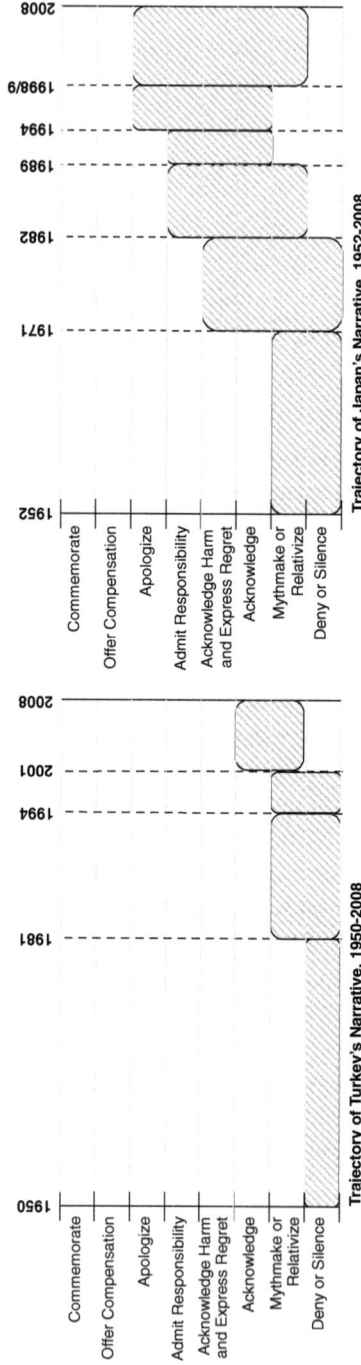

Figure 6.5 Serial bar graph

The vertical axis differentiates eight different levels of contrition in countries' official narratives about past atrocities. The graph plots the levels against the horizontal timeline, thus visualizing the relative stages of contrition that countries reach at specific historical points. It also visualizes the tempo and the reversals of this contrition process. (Dixon 2018, 40, 103. Reprinted with permission)

1981 to 1994, but denials stopped after the acknowledgment of the Armenian genocide in 2001. Dixon's stacked bar graphs thus track more gradual changes than Cox's graph. What makes her visualization so effective is the timeline that allows comparing Turkey and Japan's official narratives. The graph also permits some physical time differentiations. It shows that the denial of atrocities lasted far longer in Turkey than in Japan, and contrition also proceeded at very slow pace. And it even captures a small reversal in Japan between 1998 and 2008.

6.4 Redescribing Misdescribed Trends

Trends are constructed and, as such, are no different from periods built by events. Their very construction makes them prone to misdescribing social processes – a tendency that results from construction errors. Longue durée analysis pays attention to three potential misdescriptions: improper baselining, unfreezing time scales, and mismeasurements.

6.4.1 Baselining: Are Trends Fractal?

Baselining is important because the length of the time scale that a data set covers determines the trend that will be discovered. The most common misdescription results from extrapolating trends from a short time scale and assuming that those trends repeat themselves at a longer time scale (Taleb 2007, 186–7). Short-term trends cannot serve as baselines for long-term ones because trends are not fractal. The mathematician Benoit Mandelbrot introduced the concept of fractals to draw attention to the fact that certain geometric forms reproduce themselves across different scales, large and small. He pointed out, for example, that the individual florets in a head of broccoli have the same shape as the entire head. Gaddis extends Mandelbrot's fractal concept from geometry to history to underscore the non-fractal nature of historical patterns. He contends that short-term temporal patterns do not necessarily repeat themselves at longer time scales, and thus lack "self-similarity across scale" and require baselining (Mandelbrot 2002, 82). Longue durée analysis addresses this baseline problem through *temporal broadening*, that is, by shifting the baseline for interpreting a trend from a data set on a short time scale to one on a longer time scale. (I borrow the term "termporal broadening" from Singh Grewal 2014, 630–3).

Longue durée analysis is full of examples where scholars challenge the validity of existing descriptions by elongating the baseline. Let me offer three examples. (1) Reinhard and Rogoff's (2011) work (discussed earlier) challenges the claim that each new financial crisis is different. The two authors extended their data back to the twelfth century. This temporal broadening revealed the cyclical nature of financial crises and pointed to a misdescription in the existing literature. (2) Piketty challenges Kutznets' secular downward inequality trend by contending that it becomes cyclical if observed over a longer time scale. Kutznets linked this secular downward trend to the fact that industrialization would make economic development more equitable and would provide more well-paying jobs. Piketty (2017, 16–18) extends the original time series, which was benchmarked against the 1913–48 period, by taking it to the present; thus he broadens it by seventy years. He shows that Kutznets' downward trend continued until the late 1980s, at which point inequality increased again, reaching by 2000 the same levels it had during the interwar period (Piketty 2017, 31). He thus redescribes Kutznets' optimistic downward trend and turns it into a worrisome cyclical one. (3) Finally, environmental sciences talk about a *shifting baseline syndrome* in order to explain why we misdescribe the rate at which we lose biodiversity. The initial availability of only short-term data allows the public to benchmark its expectations against recent history. Thus the public uses as benchmark a period with an already significantly depleted biodiversity, which suggests a modest and linear decline. Shifting the benchmark further back, to a time of richer biodiversity, transforms a linear downward trend like this one into a rapidly accelerating decline (Soga and Gaston 2018, 223–4).

6.4.2 Unfreezing Time Scale

What a trendline describes is always a function of the calibration of the time scale against which the trendline is plotted. A timeline graphed on a centennial scale will look much less complex on a decennial scale. The longer the time units, the larger the part of history that becomes frozen and the more likely it is that the trends will be linear and thus will overlook fluctuations that could point to relevant subtrends. In consequence, longue durée analysis unfreezes time scales to assess whether shorter-term fluctuations deviate sufficiently from longer-term trends to warrant separate attention.

We already discussed in Chapter 2 Gordon's critique of the linear, neoclassical accounts of economic change on account of its functionalism. He shows that the century-long time scale used in conventional accounts contributes to a linear trend that overlooks important variations that emerge when we use shorter time intervals. The United States' economic growth over the nineteenth and twentieth centuries, for example, was much slower before and after the period 1920–1970. These varying tempi "represent a rebellion against models of 'steady economic growth' that have dominated economic thinking about the growth process since the 1950s" (Gordon 2017, ix). Gordon uses annualized growth rates, output per hour, and hours per person to unfreeze the existing time scales. He describes America's economic development by dividing it into three periods: 1870–1920, 1920–1970, and 1970 to the present. The period 1870–1920 was marked by major technological breakthroughs such as electricity, railroads, or public sanitations, which all increased economic growth. But their most dramatic effects were time-lagged; they did not come to full fruition until 1920, and they lasted until 1970. Finally, also the post-1970 period witnessed major technological breakthroughs – in telecommunications and computing – that produced economic growth. However, this growth was not nearly as deep: it only touched entertainment and communications but left many other domains unaffected. Gordon uses his periodization to explain the different rates of economic growth (Gordon 2017, 9–12).

6.4.3 Mismeasurements

Measures to describe trends vary in their capacity to capture the historical complexities, undergirding those trends. Longue durée historians evaluate this capacity by assessing historical boundary conditions and by proposing to use stock instead of flow indicators whenever possible.

Historical Boundary Conditions. The chapter on eventful analysis discussed how concepts are historically grounded and thus have attributes that are historically bounded. Indicators such as age and risk misdescribe phenomena if they are not updated. Zachary Karabell (2014, 7) points out that "[i]ndicators have a history – a reason that they were invented in the first place" and that "history reveals their strengths and limitations." Their aging is a by-product of the historical changes they measure. Indicators measuring social media consumption or stock market activities must be updated quickly to capture rapid technological or corporate change. By contrast, changes from agricultural to manufacturing services and to the knowledge economy were slow and required intermittent updating of the GDP indicator (Karabell 2014, 155, 168). Indicators measuring natural phenomena such as temperature or weight do not have to be updated because they do not measure human events but recurrent natural phenomena. Or at least so they did before global warming began blurring the boundary between human and natural history. Finally, indicators that measure coin tosses are even more context-independent, as the probability of a head or tail toss has remained the same since antiquity.

In other instances, updating one's indicators is subject to intensive debates. Psychometrists and developmental psychologists, for example, discuss whether human intelligence is unchanging and merely fluctuates within a given range reflecting differences in age and demographic factors, or whether it changes qualitatively over time as nutrition and education improve, thus producing a secular increase in IQ or what has come to be known as the Flynn effect. This led to debates on whether to update IQ measures so as to capture such qualitative changes in human cognition, or to keep using the existing measures so as to preserve the intertemporal comparability of the measurement (Flynn 2009; Gladwell 2007). Sociologists face a similar challenge in measuring the size of the middle class, a task complicated by the changing cultural definition of this concept. David Singh Grewal (2014, 649) asks: "Would you rather be a 'middle class' consumer in 1960, with a reasonable hope of owning your home, or a middle-class consumer today, living in a rented flat with a personal computer and internet access?" There are no easy solutions to how to address the temporal validity of time series measures. So, it is best to recall that longue durée historians' fondness for natural history is intended to "make history less ideographic discipline by having as its object that which repeats itself" (Krzysztof Pomian, as quoted in Moretti 2005, 2). This freezing of history limits what times series can describe with validity, and thus requires a constant dialogue with eventful history in order to assess this validity and fill the gaps of what cannot be validly described. Historical thinking is the best remedy against conceptual stretching.

Updating the indicators is a difficult undertaking and takes two forms: recalibration or renorming. GDP or Dow Jones are recalibrated by adding or removing attributes or companies to capture qualitative changes in the economy. Recalibrations have an additive quality and thus are more readily capable of tracking qualitative changes over time. Recalibrating GDP is technically challenging because the existing data must be recoded to make the indicator backward compatible (Karabell 2014, 215). By contrast, indicators like IQ are renormed. Test takers in the fiftieth percentile, those exactly at the median, get a score of 100. But, as the test takers' cognitive ability improved over time, the IQ test was renormed on three occasions since the 1940s. This made it difficult to compare test scores across time, because somebody with an IQ of 100 in 1940 would have a score of 70 by today's benchmark, and thus would be technically considered mentally retarded (Gladwell 2007, 5). So ultimately only indicators that are recalibrated are useful for tracking historical changes.

Give Preference to Stock over Flow Indicators. Time series analysis uses flow and stock indicators without fully reflecting on the difference between them. The distinction is used in the finance literature and has important implications for their capacity to capture the transformations that define historical change (see Table 6.2).[2] Economic indicators like the NASDAQ, the Dow Jones, or

---

[2] I was unable to find works that elaborate more fully on the difference between stock and flow indicators and identify criteria specific to each type. Some authors refer to them as level and change variables (Janoski and Isaac 1994, 34). This might explain why there is disagreement over whether certain indicators measure flows or stocks. Principally, the stock and flow analogies serve to show us that indicators vary in their ranges; but they are not always clear as to which attributes make an indicator measure stocks as opposed to flows. The general tendency seems to

Table 6.2 Stock versus flow indicators

	Attributes			
Indicators	Units of Analysis	Time Scale	Range	Trend Variability
Stock	Additive, connected process	Long-term	Expands with time, no upper bounds	Sticky and asymmetrical. Slow, incremental upward trends. Occasional, rapid drops.
Flow	Sequence of unconnected snapshots	Short-term	Fixed across time, but variable across indicators	Fluid and symmetrical. Quick and frequent alternation between up- and downward trends.

The finance literature distinguishes between stock and flow indicators that differ in their unit of analysis, time scale, range, and trend variability.

GDP capture attributes that can be "stockpiled" over time. The stockpiling is an additive, slow, and incremental process with no upper limits. Corporate stocks represent the cumulative worth of a company's prior production or services. They typically rise more slowly than they drop. They also do not have an upper ceiling, as their range expands over time. This lack of an upper bound and their sticky, upward movement – marked by occasional dramatic reversals – makes them well suited to capturing secular trends.

By contrast, inflation or unemployment are flow indicators because they capture fluctuating flows of temporary rate changes between two discreet points in time. They consequently track changes over shorter time spans and describe rates of change among snapshots rather than across long-term additive processes. A time series of such snapshots captures short-term fluctuations in that flow. The snapshots are much more likely to describe seasonal or cyclical changes than secular trends. They have the same ontological properties as coin tosses, whose frequencies are utterly context-independent and do not require paying attention to history.

link stock indicators to variables with a wider range. GDP, for example, has a wider range than inflation and thus is generally viewed as a stock indicator, while inflation is considered a flow indicator. But inflation can gyrate upwards during periods of hyper-inflation and thus dramatically expand its range as well. Such an expansion is nevertheless different from that of GPD in three respects. GDP expansion is incremental rather than rapid; it is linked to changes in self-sustaining capacities rather than to a disequilibrium; and the widening of the scale is the norm rather than an aberration. In short, the stock analogy is linked to longer-term continuities that, while reversible, are associated with what we commonly think of as historical changes. It would be more plausible to draw inferences about structural economic changes (e.g., agricultural to industrial to service economy) from changes in GDP than from inflation. In this sense, GDP is more of a stock indicator that can capture historical changes.

6.5 Application of the Tools

The literature on the origins of proportional representation (PR) is firmly rooted in eventful and macro-causal analysis. It views institutional choices as singular moments of high politics in which actors' short-term strategic choices matter far more than slow-moving long-term processes. Institutional choices are too complex to be readily measured and tracked with time series data. The literature therefore does not contain a direct illustration of longue durée analysis. Let me nevertheless use two tools of longue durée analysis – temporal broadening and developmental typologies – to describe longue durée-style contributions made by the existing, more eventful accounts.

The PR literature treats the adoption of electoral systems as singular events and rarely extends the time frame beyond a few near-miss events that precede them. It overlooks that the first adoptions of PR were preceded and followed by other electoral reforms. Those reforms provide an opportunity for temporal broadening, because together they create a long durée perspective on electoral system change. The trend that results from connecting these reforms makes clear that later reforms involved institutional innovations that addressed flaws or anachronisms in previously existing institutions. In this context it is useful to think of electoral institutions by analogy with technology, because they are subject to innovations that are driven in part by shortcomings in existing institutions or by the discovery of new alternatives. This temporal broadening tracks the long-term pattens of these institutions by following the qualitatively changes in the choice sets available to actors. It shows that these changes were accompanied by normative arguments used to defend the various electoral systems under consideration. It ultimately presents a multivariate trend, too complex to visualize other than by explicating a four-stage developmental typology: electoral systems used to divine God's will, election by lot to maximize office rotation, majoritarian systems that emphasize geographic representation, and finally a proportional system that facilitates the descriptive representation of social groups.

When Thomas Hare first proposed the PR system in 1859, it was neither the first nor the last new voting technology to be introduced. Josep Colomer's history of electoral system choice makes it possible to place this invention in a broader historical context. His perspective makes it clear that elections predate modern democracies by a long margin, since they served to appoint kings and popes. During all that time, the criteria for electoral decision changed from unanimity to lottery, to majority, and finally to proportionality. In the eleventh century the Catholic Church adopted the principle that "he who governs should be elected by all," only to face the risk that the formation of factions could lead to schisms. It viewed elections as a mechanism for divining God's will that required the losing, minority candidate to endorse the majority candidate and thereby to secure this winner's election by unanimity (Hare 2004, 16–17). Medieval local democracies and Italian city states elected their representatives by drawing lots, because this method maximized rotation in office and dispersed the knowledge of how to govern. The difficulties of reaching unanimity and the inability of lotteries to vet the actual governing competence of the elected led to their gradual replacement by absolute majorities, then by relative majorities (e.g., pluralities). And, from the late nineteenth century onward, plurality systems and majoritarian systems were increasingly displaced by systems of proportional representation: the idea was to translate votes into seats more fairly and to represent social groups more effectively (J. Colomer 2004; J. M. Colomer 1998; Morgan 1988). This elementary developmental typology broadens the existing short-term accounts temporally and points to two new research questions.

First, the pattern highlights the role of uncertainty. The very idea that electoral systems have a history of their own, marked by major structural breaks, underscores that some choice sets included a brand-new, first-time electoral system. This confronts actors with more uncertainty than choice sets that contain established and hence well-known systems. For example, the choice of an electoral system between the 1880s and the 1920s involved far more uncertainty than the choices available to postcommunist democracies. The former played out between old and new voting technologies, while the latter were choices between century-old voting systems. Second, actors' willingness to invent a brand-new system rather than to alternate between already existing ones should draw attention to the shortcomings of a status quo system that motivated experimenting with a new electoral system. The established non-PR systems produced disproportional outcomes because of gerrymandering, malapportionment, and, in the case of the blocked vote system, supermajoritarian features that awarded multiple seats to parties on the basis of winning a simple plurality of the votes (Emmenegger and Walter 2019). So the unequal translation of votes into seats was the result not just of the disproportionality inherent in the "winner take all" formula but also of other features of the electoral system that were open to naked partisan political engineering. The invention of PR and its subsequent widespread adoption appear to be partially linked to the previous system of partisan, engineered disproportionality. This is a point that existing theories do not consider.

Exercises

6.1. Use William Playfair's diagram *Universal Commercial History* (Figure 2.1) to identify the various trends summarized in Figure 6.1. 1.

What is the most common trend if you look at countries individually: secular, cyclical, or seasonal? 2. How would you characterize the meta-trend across twenty-one countries? In other words, how does the trend change if you assess individual country trends collectively? 3. Playfair offers the following periodization scheme: 1550 BC to AD 300, 300 to 1100, 1100 to 1650, and 1650 to 1805. How would you characterize the trends in each of these periods? Particularly, what sets the trend in the later period apart from the earlier ones? Conjecture about how historical changes might be linked to these patterns.

6.2. Both Earl Cook and Jennifer Dixon use serial bar graphs, even though Cook tracks a technological, physical phenomenon (energy consumption) while Dixon tackles a cultural phenomenon (state narratives). They consequently raise questions about the ability of such graphs to track historical, qualitatively changing phenomena with ontological qualities that are very different from ahistorical, stationary phenomena. They invite reflection on the context independence and hence temporal validity of their graphs. To better understand Dixon's graph, read her brief explanation (Dixon 2018, 15–19). Try to reflect on those differences by engaging the following questions:

Assume that you have time series that record the frequencies of head–tale coin tosses for the same fifty-year period as in Dixon's serial bar graph. How would those two time series differ in their ontological characteristics? Why would one be a flow indicator and the other a stock indicator? Now contrast the ontological properties of contrition with those of energy consumption. How are they different? How are they similar? How feasible would it be to extend Dixon's contrition scale back by a century? Would this pose challenges? If so, what would they reveal about the historical quality of her indicator? Why does Cook have little difficulty in extending his energy scale to a 2 million-year period? In what ways is Cook's indicator more context-independent than Dixon's? Why are differences in kinds of energy assumption (e.g., food, home, commerce) more easily translated into differences of degree (Cook's trend-line) than differences in kind of contrition are translated into differences in degrees of contrition? In what ways are both these indicators (Cook's and Dixon's) stock indicators – that is, additive, growing over time, and with no potential upper bounds? In what ways are they less so? And in what ways would coin tosses be even more context-independent?

6.3. Read Malcolm Gladwell's (2007) excellent article on the Flynn Effect, which foregrounds the role that history plays in psychology – a discipline that eschews historical thinking, not unlike economics. The Flynn

Effect – the propensity of IQ scores to show a secular increase over time – generated debate between psychometrists, whom Gladwell labels IQ fundamentalists, since they view human intelligence as unchanging (it fluctuates only across demographic groups or across individual life stages). Developmental psychologists like Flynn see it as varying cross-sectionally but also as changing qualitatively over time. You can think of them as cognitive historians, playing a role comparable to that of economic historians in neoclassical economics. Engage with the following prompts:

What factors does Gladwell point out in order to demonstrate the historical nature of human intelligence? How do these factors differ from the elements emphasized by psychometrists? What other factors can you think could explain secular increases in IQ? What would make them historical? What elements of time do psychometrists and developmental psychologists employ? How does Flynn's critique of the psychometrists' treatment of IQ involve a critique of conceptual stretching?

How do the psychometrists treat IQ as a flow indicator and developmental psychologists as a stock indicator? What assumptions of cognitive capacity would be linked to treating IQ as a stock indicator? What assumptions would be associated with IQ's being a flow indicator? What would be the parallels between IQ and GDP as two stock indicators? How did psychologists explain variations in IQ before the discovery of the Flynn effect? In what ways were those explanatory factors context-independent, and thus ahistorical?

How does the baselining or renorming of IQ tests affect their validity, particularly the intertemporal comparability of scores? How does the renorming of IQ scores differ from the recalibration of GDP – that is, from adding property rights to measure new economic outputs? Why are recalibrated intertemporal GDP measures more readily comparable than renormed IQ scores? What does this tell us about the historical qualities of the attributes used to measure IQ and GDP?

In his rebuttal of Murray in the Forum sponsored by the Manhattan Institute, Flynn disaggregates the IQ of whites and African Americans. How does this disaggregation add a temporal element to his analysis? What patterns does this temporal treatment add to Flynn's analysis? And how do such patterns help him undermine Murray's static and aggregate qualities?

7 Macro-Causal Analysis
Physical Time and the Temporal Construction of Theories

> If you torture data long enough, Nature will confess.
>
> (Ronald Coase quoted in Leamer 1983, 37)

Chapter 2 linked macro-causal analysis to bounded history – a notion of history far more frozen than those informing longue durée and eventful analysis – and thus raised an important question. What kind of historical thinking is possible in such a static and unchanging past? What patterns are there to be explored when macro-causal analysis all but eliminates historical change? The answer is simple: macro-causal analysis explores complex, non-linear causal patterns linked to physical time. Consequently it is uninterested in patterns of historical change that eventful and longue durée analysis study. It investigates how tempo, duration, timing, and sequencing structure the order and rhythms in which causal factors unfold. Paul Pierson illustrates the connection between physical time and non-linear causal effects with a suggestive gastronomic analogy. He invites his readers to compare a meal prepared in the avant-garde social science café – whose chef champions parsimonious cooking that disregards the seasonality of ingredients (i.e. timing), the sequence in which they are added, and the duration of cooking them – with a dinner cooked in the less cutting-edge CHA café, which follows time-honored recipes and that does not mind the complexity that physical time adds to the cooking process (Pierson 2004, 4). At the culinary level, the implications of these two cuisines "taste" for themselves. At a methodological level they are more difficult to understand because they are entangled with different notions of causality. The social science café operates under the standard linear notion of causality – also referred to as potential outcome, average treatment effect, or Granger causation – which freezes physical time and thus backgrounds its confounding effects (Goldthorpe 2001). The CHA café, for its part, employs a non-linear, rather historical notion of causality (Ermakoff 2019), which is the object of this chapter.

Macro-causal analysis' embrace of non-linear, historical causation harks back to CHA's nineteenth-century founders and their ambition to develop theories as bold as the pattern they described. Incidentally, this kind of theorizing pre-dates the advent of statistical analysis and its linear conceptualization of causality by half a century – and I will elaborate on the significance of this historical pecularity in the Conclusion. This attention to causal complexity is linked to concerns about p-hacking, specification searching, data mining, or, as Ronald Coase put it entertainingly, torturing the data with the latest and most inquisitorial causal inference strategy. Among these efforts, *causal process tracing* has shown a predilection for adopting historical causation in order to capture the causal effects of physical time and generate hypotheses that are testworthy enough to produce results *and* answers (Beach and Pedersen 2013; Bennett 2014; George and Bennett 2004; P. Hall 2008; Fairfield and Charman 2019).

The chapter starts by discussing the temporal construction of theories. It elaborates on how freezing physical time produces causally linear explanations and demonstrates how unfreezing it makes it possible to generate more complex non-linear explanations that employ historical notions of causality. At the next stage, understanding this temporal construction of theories helps identify the two strategies that macro-causal analysis employs in foregrounding the causal effects of physical time: elongating the causal chains; and elongating the outcomes. These two strategies permit capturing what Pierson calls slow-moving causal processes and outcomes by redescribing existing linear processes, by identifying the confounding effects of physical time, and ultimately by updating the underlining theories. It is this exploratory, theory-developing, and abductive quality that is the hallmark of macro-causal analysis (Abbott 2004; Rueschemeyer 2009; Swedberg 2014; Yom 2015). The chapter concludes with an illustration from the proportional representation (PR) literature. Its overall goal is to make the abduction process more transparent, to present theorizing as an *actual* causal identification strategy, and to ensure that theorizing generates testworthy empirical hypotheses.

7.1 Causal Linearity and the Freezing of Physical Time

Macro-causal analysis extends to causality the exploratory logic of eventful analysis and serial analysis applied to identify patterns of change. Where eventful and serial history unfreeze bounded and cyclical history, macro-causal analysis unfreezes physical time, which allows it to explore temporally complex non-linear causal patterns. As it unfreezes physical time, macro-causal analysis foregrounds tempo, duration, timing, and sequencing and explores their confounding non-linear causal effects. More specifically, macro-causal analysis relaxes four key assumptions of linear causality – simultaneity, addition, immediacy, and symmetry – and in the process shifts to a non-linear, historical notion of causality, which pays heed to physical time (Ermakoff 2019; Goldthorpe 2001). Let me expand on these four elements of linear causality, to demonstrate how they differ from non-linear, historical causality and how the freezing of physical time constructs these two different notions of causality.

Simultaneity stipulates that all causal factors occur simultaneously enough for it to be safe to ignore the order in which they unfold. This idea is linked to the conditional independence assumption, which freezes history, and to its claim that observations are independent of one another, which makes it possible to ignore when and in what order they occurred. Macro-causal analysis relaxes the simultaneity assumption and views causal factors as embedded in a causal process. The temporal location of the factors in this longer process – the when – becomes causally relevant and requires attention to two elements of non-simultaneity: timing and sequencing. The non-simultaneity captured by timing is *early or late*, while that captured by sequencing is *before or after*.

Addition. The additive nature of causal effects is a corollary of the simultaneity assumption because, if the order of causal effects does not matter, then it becomes possible to assess their overall effect simply by adding them together. By contrast, macro-causal analysis stipulates that causal factors can also interact with the factors that precede them and with the factors that follow them; the joint result is a drawn-out generative process that produces an outcome. This generative process is non-linear or incremental: it generates either tipping points or path dependencies. Tipping points are non-linear because initially the causal effects accumulate without producing an outcome, unless or until they reach a threshold necessary to trigger the outcome. Path dependencies involve causal effects that are small at the beginning and that accumulate over time through increasing return mechanisms. The causal effects of tipping points and path dependencies are linked to physical time in that they require attention to tempo and to the duration of causal effects (Abbott 1988; P. Hall 2003, 382–3; Jervis 1998, 39–68; Pierson 2003, 181–2).

Immediacy stipulates that causal effects occur *immediately*, that is, in close temporal proximity to the cause itself. Macro-causal analysis pays attention to non-immediate effects. Effect can be non-immediate because they emerge only over time, and thus are lagged; or because they materialize only partially, by producing near misses; or because they do not endure and produce reversals. Again, these non-immediate effects require attention to the tempo and duration of causal effects (Abbott 1988; P. Hall 2003, 382–3; Jervis 1998, 39–68; Lieberson 1985, 63–82; March and Olsen 1984).

Symmetry stipulates that a change in the value of the independent variable produces a change of equal magnitude in the dependent variable, regardless of whether the value increases or decreases. Lieberson famously pointed out that this symmetry assumption frequently does not hold, because causes also have one-time and historically contextualized effects, which are irreversible and survive even after the cause disappears – thus becoming asymmetrical. He writes that asymmetric causes will "generate changes that virtually guarantee that the earlier conditions will never again be duplicated. . . . Change in the

Y variable will create new changes in other X variables that do not change back in the same way" (Lieberson 1985, 82). This asymmetry is simply a by-product of eventful history. Eventful history, it may be recalled, focuses on qualitative and hence irreversible transformations, which all but eliminate symmetrical causation. Symmetrical causation is possible only in cyclical history, where the past repeats itself and changes therefore become reversible and potentially symmetrical. This kind of causation is not *motionless*, since it involves *changes as fluctuations*. But such variations are different from *changes as transformations* insofar as variations are *processless*: they involve snapshots whose causal effects are independent of one another, and thus they make it possible for us to ignore *when* they happened in relation to one another. It is this interdependence and the resulting interactions across time that define the process and is subject to the dynamics of physical time (Abbott 1988).

The connection between physical time and linear causality is admittedly abstract and raises questions about the practical strategies that macro-causal analysis offers for analyzing the non-linear effects of physical time.

7.2 Unfreezing Physical Time and the Temporal Structure of Theories

Paul Pierson provides very useful advice for exploring the causal effects of physical time. He suggests that we stop treating theories as temporally unstructured amalgams of atomistic snapshots and start conceptualizing them instead as processes or causal chains. He develops this idea most fully in a stimulating study titled "Big, Slow-Moving and Invisible: Macrosocial Processes in the Study of Comparative Politics" (Pierson 2003). There he treats theories not just in terms of their substantive claims – the types of empirical predictions they make – but in terms of their temporal structures. He makes clear that theories are constructed not only through an abductive dialogue with new inductive insights but also through latent conversation with physical time and its potential causal effects.

Pierson summarizes this interplay between the temporal construction of theories and the resulting nature of causality with the help of an ingenious and easy to understand time matrix (Table 7.1), which differentiates theories according to the time scales they ascribe to causal factors and outcomes. This matrix permits classifying theories into four temporal structures.[1]

---

[1] Pierson's time matrix closely resembles the causal 2 × 2 contingency tables that cognitive psychologists use to illustrate cognitive biases and identify causal fallacies. The causal contingency tables try to counter the humans' propensity to favor causal symmetry and thus to jump

Table 7.1 Pierson's time matrix

		Short	Long
		Time Horizon of Outcome	
Time Horizon of	**Short**	I. Tornado	II. Meteorite/Dinosaur Extinction
Cause	**Long**	III. Earthquake	IV. Global Warming

This table unfreezes theories and categorizes them according to four temporal structures. The categories are defined by the time horizon of the outcome to be explained and the antecedent causes that do the explaining.
Source: Pierson 2003, 179.

Pierson illustrates the logic of his time matrix through four examples. Tornadoes are created by very short-term meteorological configurations and cause physical damage for an equally brief time. Meteorites – which hit the Earth 65 million years ago – had a truly brief time horizon, but their effect, which was to trigger a climate change that led to the extinction of dinosaurs, unfolded through a very lengthy process. Earthquakes have short but devastating effects and their cause relates to slow-moving long-term geological processes. Finally, climate change involves the slow-moving, cumulative effects of decades of carbon emission that is gradually transforming atmospheric temperatures and weather patterns (Pierson 2003, 179–81).

Pierson contends that most of the contemporary actor-centered and linear theories fall in cell I of the table and that their short–short explanations overlook the more complex, non-linear effects of physical time that are observable in the other three cells. He therefore suggests that exploring physical time requires us to shift our attention particularly to cells II and III. Cell II permits elongating the causal chain by relaxing the assumptions of simultaneity and additive causation and to conceptualize causation as a non-linear, generative process. Cell III permits elongating outcomes and thereby paying attention to lagged effects, near misses, reversals, and asymmetric effects. Pierson's time matrix is thus an enormously useful starting point for exploring the non-linear effects of physical time, on which the next two sections elaborate more fully. For now, let me first refine the time matrix further.

---

from correlations – which are symmetrical – to causation. This cognitive bias leads to faulty causal inferences, because causation is inferred without first checking for false negatives (causes are absent even though the effects are present) and false positives (causes are present but not the effects) (see Cummins 2012, 115–37; Gilovich 1993, 13–30; Silver 2012, 47–69). Pierson's table applies the same logic to the potential role of those temporal assumptions in biasing causal inferences.

The attentive reader may have realized that all four illustrations in Table 7.1 contain examples from natural history and the disciplines studying it – meteorology, geology, paleontology, and environmental science. All these disciplines pay close attention to physical time and its non-linear effects. Let me turn to the social science equivalents. The Annales historians' famous distinction between environmental, structural, and eventful factors can be crafted onto the time matrix and thereby make it more specific. Social science does not have a periodic table into which different theoretical claims can be firmly placed, but these broad categories provide useful theoretical frames or heuristics that are readily adaptable to different literatures (Braudel 1980; see also Barry 1988; Little 1991; Parsons 2007; Rueschemeyer 2009; Elster 2015). And these frames are helpful also for elongating causal chains and outcomes.

Environmental factors are very long, as they go back far in history, are semi-durable, and change at the glacial pace of natural or serial history. They define explanations over a very long term in which human action is constrained by strictly material, environmental, cognitive, or genetic factors. These factors change at a glacial pace and decelerate history so much that it freezes and literally repeats itself. Geology or biology obviously do not stand still by the standards of geologists or evolutionary biologists – but they do when bench-marked against the history of our everyday lives. These environmental factors have such a wide horizon that they become part of natural history, in which human agency is largely irrelevant (Bjornerud 2018). Some historians refer to natural history as prehistory, so as to differentiate it from the more human-centered history they analyze. They consider "prehistorical" everything that stretches back in time to the point where no written records are available. They deem such records necessary to writing human history, which they differen-tiate from natural histories, "written" as they are with the help of geological or biological records (Gosden 2018). Environmental factors include aspects of geography as well as of biology.

Structural factors are socioeconomic or institutional structures that are rather "long" and sticky enough to endure; they change only episodically and thus have a constant but historically bounded effect. They encompass medium-term explanations of human actions that are frequently (though not always) constrained by either institutions or social structures. Institutions include organizations (corporations, parties, civil society groups), formal pol-itical bodies (rule of law, constitutions, bureaucracies), coercive bodies (the military, the police), and economic bodies (property rights, markets, the WHO, the IMF). Social structures include collective identities (nationalism, race, religion), resources (financial, cultural, social capital), and demographics (age, gender, ethnicity). This typology does not place material constraints under structure, as some do, but puts them instead in the environmental

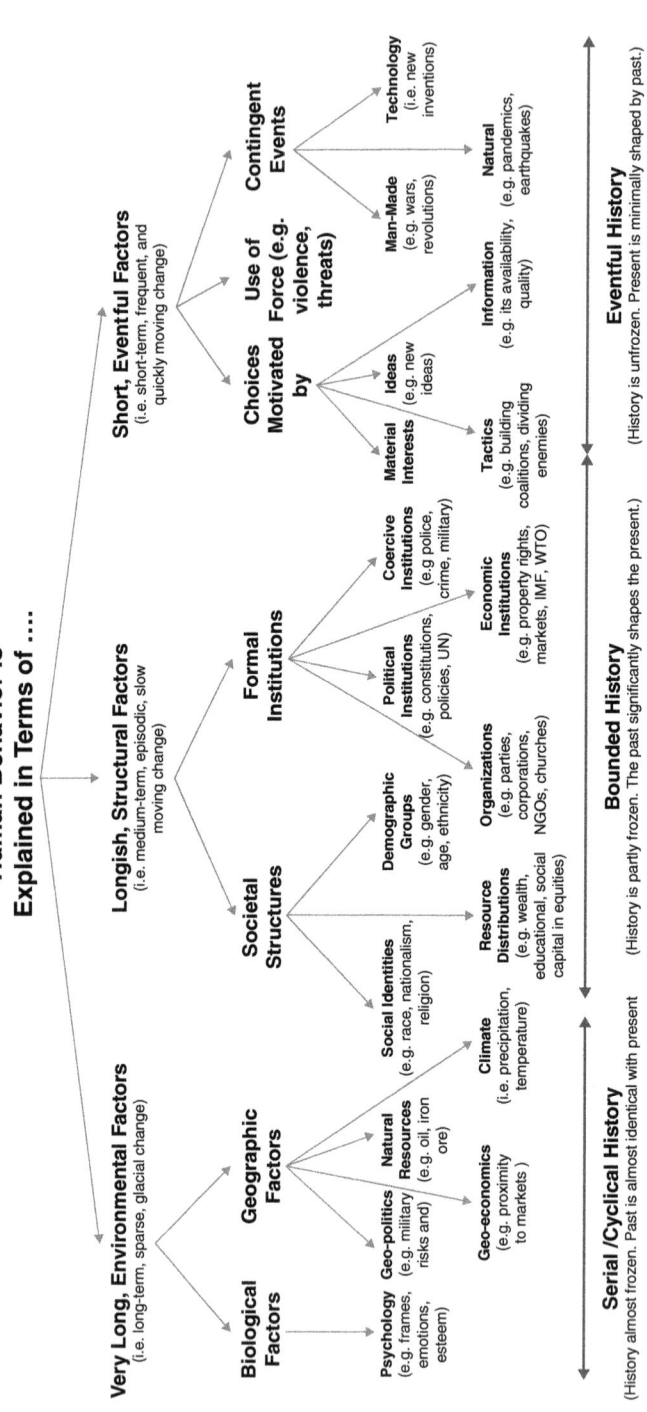

Figure 7.1 Theory map

Theories are typically presented as coagulated history, in other words as being without history or temporal structure. This figure maps theories on the basis of their latent historical time assumptions, grouping them into three categories: theories that focus on very long environmental factors and subscribe to serial or cyclical history; theories that focus on rather long structural factors and employ bounded history; and theories that focus on short, contingent, eventful factors and rely on eventful history.

category (Parsons 2007, 49–65). Institutions and social structures are themselves the result of earlier human choices that reproduce themselves and become durable constraints on subsequent human choices. While they are durable, they are not permanent; they can always change and make room for discontinuities that will give rise to a new set of structures. Their human origins mean that they are always subject to change, which ultimately constitutes their historical nature and distinguishes them from environmental factors.

Eventful factors are contingent and hence change frequently and quickly and follow the rhythms of eventful history. They characterize contexts in which human actions are explained by contingent events, by a range of motivational factors, or by brute coercion. The brief time window during which contingent factors of this sort are relevant implies that human actions are unaffected by more distal, and hence more structural or environmental factors. Actors therefore have a high degree of decision-making autonomy. Motivational theories differ in their assumptions about how much actors optimize their material or their ideational interests, or about how much these are shaped by more complicated cognitive frames.

Taken together, Pierson's time matrix and the theory map provide the key tools that macro-causal analysis employs to explore non-linear causal patterns. These two strategies correspond to using cells II and III in Pierson's time matrix and in his discussion of slow-moving causal processes and outcomes.

7.3 Elongating Causal Chains: Looking for the Causal Effects of Physical Time

Many classics of macro-causal analysis use history to elongate the causal chain of existing explanations and to uncover overlooked causal factors. They keep outcomes frozen – limiting analysis to static of cross-sectional variations – but unfreeze physical time in order to explore lengthier, non-linear causal processes. This unfreezing involves moving the starting date of causal factors back into the past and thereby shifting the theoretical focus from eventful to structural or environmental factors. Daniel Ziblatt, for example, points out that "greater physical distance can expose patterns that were once invisible . . . In analogous fashion *temporal* distance – moving out from single events and placing them within a longer time frame – can also expose previously undetectable social patterns. . . . [It also] can identify and elaborate new explanations for those patterns" (Ziblatt 2017, 3). By elongating causal chains, macro-causal analysis draws attention to the confounding effects of physical time.

The elements of physical time – tempo, duration, timing sequencing, and stages – are of theoretical interest because their temporal attributes have non-linear causal effects. But these causal effects become visible only if we pay closer attention to the temporal order of causal factors and the process through which they unfold. The journalist Malcolm Gladwell developed a knack for identifying non-linear social explanations. His first bestseller, *The Tipping Point* (2006), explains how small, slow-moving changes, after being inconsequential for a long time, produce a large and fast change once they reach a threshold. And oftentimes a small number of individuals have a disproportionate effect in producing big changes. Arguably Gladwell's *Outliers: The Story of Success* (2008) is his most impressive book because it demonstrates how elements of physical time explain the outsized financial success of business leaders. To draw attention to physical time, he elongates the causal chain of the existing short–short explanation – the so-called talent myth explanation, as championed by business titans themselves – which attributes outsized economic success to hard work, risk-taking intelligence, or whatever personal attributes make somebody an entrepreneurial overachiever.

Gladwell does not dismiss the relevance of personal attributes but simply explores what we could discover if we elongated the causal chain from the proximate, short, contingent, talent-related factors to more distal, structural ones. His first discovery is duration: he points to the so-called 10,000-hour rule, the time one is required to practice an activity if one is to become a potential outlier. Those 10,000 hours, in turn, are the result of socioeconomic opportunities that afford individuals the resources necessary to invest the time to practice. However, 10,000 hours plus talent still fall short of explaining outliers, because they overlook their sequencing with technological breakthroughs. The invention of computers or railroads created entirely new industrial sectors that opened once-in-a-lifetime entrepreneurial opportunities. So, individuals born shortly before such technological breakthroughs could amass far more wealth than those born later, because they did not face established companies that created entry barriers (Gladwell 2008, 34–68). Ultimately, the causal effects of the 10,000 hours of practice and technological breakthrough are non-simultaneous and non-additive, since they are detected only by paying attention to the temporal order in which they unfold.

In another chapter, Gladwell uses timing to explain success among hockey players. Seventy percent of all National Hockey League players were born in the first half of the year. This clustering is linked to Canada's January 1 eligibility cut-off, which gives athletes born earlier in the year a small but significant physical advantage that makes it more likely that they end up in the travel team, thus getting more ice time and better coaching. This small initial difference, inadvertently caused by timing, accumulates over the years, giving early-born athletes a significant advantage in the long run (17–34). This non-linear path-dependent outcome, in which a small, seemingly inconsequential event like the birth date produces a significant long-term effect, becomes observable only if causal processes are tracked over a long period. Overall, Gladwell's simple elongation of the causal chain produces a far more complex explanation, one where causal factors are not just additive but embedded in a more complex causal process. Paying attention to such processes makes it easier to detect the confounding effects of physical time and to use them to update existing linear short–short explanations, such as the talent myth.

7.4 Elongating Outcomes: Looking for Lagged, Asymmetrical and Near-Miss Causal Effects

Macro-causal analysis elongates outcomes less frequently than causal chains do, because its use of bounded history privileges explaining cross-sectional, and hence short outcomes. It consequently treats outcomes as singular, static, and historically frozen snapshots that vary cross-sectionally along fixed and readily observable dimensions. Moore's three paths to political modernity exemplify this static notion of outcomes, which encompasses only contextual varieties. However, causal effects very often have a mind of their own and do not reveal themselves with the immediacy, transparency, symmetry, and permanence that linear theories ascribe to them. Elongating the outcomes draws attention to more complex causal effects by unfreezing the snapshots stipulated by theories. It seeks to foreground three causal effects that are frequently overlooked: lagged, asymmetric, and near-miss causal effects.

Lagged Causal Effects. Some outcomes, just like some causal factors, involve slow-moving processes where the effects of antecedent causes become apparent incrementally, or with a time lag (Pierson 2003, 181–9). Such effects are non-linear because they do not manifest themselves immediately and thus require elongating outcomes to become observable. Time lags typically point to complex causal processes. Steven Levitt and Stephen Dubner (2005), for example, attribute the rapid decline in US crime rates during the 1990s to the 1973 *Roe v. Wade* Supreme Court decision that legalized abortion. They explain this twenty-year time lag with a demographic argument. They point out that the legalization of abortion led to the termination of unwanted pregnancies, which reduced the number of children born into broken families.

Such children had a higher probability of becoming criminals because they lacked proper parenting and socioeconomic opportunities (Levitt and Dubner 2005, 115–46). Time lags are common in social policies, where the expenditure effects of some policies are visible only after a considerable period. Contributory pensions, for example, can be quickly introduced, but their financial implications become fully apparent only after a fifty-year period, when all contributors will have retired (Jacobs 2008; Pierson 2003, 191).

Asymmetric Causal Effects. Causal effects oftentimes are asymmetrical because they persist even after the cause disappears, or at least its direct effects. Structural factors typically have asymmetric causal effects. They often are themselves the result of contingent, eventful factors and endure after their disappearance. Conversely, causal effects are occasionally reversed, and those reversals are not easily explained because the very factors that produced them have long since disappeared and thus should have caused the reversal at a much earlier stage. For example, the democratic backsliding in various postcommunist democracies was caused by factors very different from the ones that produced those democracies in the first place. The origins and persistence of a phenomenon are subject to different causal processes, thus making causality asymmetrical. Macro-causal analysis pays close attention to this asymmetrical causality. Chapter 9 elaborates on so-called historical explanations that pay attention to asymmetrical causation. The key point for now is that the analysis of such historical explanations requires elongating the outcomes so that we observe more systematically the long-term interactions between causes and effects and assess the symmetry between them.

Near-Miss Causal Effects. Such effects constitute a theoretically important but conceptually somewhat muddled category for exploring slower-moving, drawn-out outcomes. Near misses share an affinity with counterfactual explanations that leverage potential outcomes in order to assess the robustness of causal inferences (Edward Kiser and Levi 1996). They can be thought of as observable rather than strictly hypothetical potential outcomes. The conceptual confusion comes from the fact that there are four different near misses: near-miss events, near-miss cases, negative cases, and counterfactual cases (see Table 7.2). Each of these near misses relies on a distinct type of comparison and makes a distinct contribution to theorizing.

Political defeats constitute actual *near-miss events* that provide observable outcomes. Such outcomes tend to be ignored because, unlike political victories, they seem less directly relevant to understanding historical change. But this neglect of political defeats overlooks the fact that they frequently are part of the prehistory of subsequent political victories and, as such, provide important

Table 7.2 Near-miss typology

	Near-Miss Events	Near-Miss Cases	Negative Cases	Counterfactual Cases
How it specifies units of analysis	Negative outcome is an observable event. Events are interdependent, with earlier ones shaping subsequent ones	Negative outcome is observable, but events treated as independent and uniform cases providing within case variations	Negative outcome is not observed but likely given partial presence of theorized causal factors	Negative outcome is not observable and highly unlikely
Role of dates	Matter	Don't matter	Don't matter	Don't matter
Type of comparison	Historical	Quasi-cross sectional	Cross-sectional	Counterfactual, imaginary
Methodological contribution	Helps observe generative processes, reading history forward	Increases variation on dependent variable, reduces selection bias, Identify omitted variables	Increases variation on dependent variable, reduces selection bias, identifies omitted variables	Limited to theorizing heuristic
Examples	Russia 1905–7 interacting with Russia 1917	Russia 1905–7 in Skocpol	Germany and Japan in Skocpol	What if Hitler had not been elected in 1933?

Near misses are typically treated as a single type of outcome, when in fact they involve four types that vary in their use of dates, comparisons, and methodological objectives.

inductive clues for better explaining actual outcomes. Near-miss events could be, for example, a bill that never made it out of committee, a bill tabled but then withdrawn, a bill defeated in the legislature, or a bill signed into law but defeated in the courts, say, by a presidential veto, by a referendum, or by some international agency. They unfreeze history and encourage reading it forward in a less deterministic manner and gaining better insights into generative processes (Møller 2021). The degrees of failure, for example, offer insights into the power dynamics of actors who push for or react against proposed changes. As the trying history of US healthcare reforms shows, defeats are rarely final, and thus set the stage for the next events. Near-miss events invariably interact with subsequent events by reshaping actors' preferences, and this leads to the re-evaluation of strategies, the reshuffling of coalitions, or the elucidation of new options. Jeffrey Tulis and Nicole Mellow studied four major defeats in US political history. They show, for example, how Barry

Goldwater's crushing 1964 defeat contributed to Ronald Reagan's victory sixteen years later. They point out how his critique of New Deal liberalism and his emphasis on states' rights, free markets, and strong defense, albeit electorally costly in the short run, proved to provide the ideational glue that united conservative activists outside the existing Republican infrastructure. This new electoral coalition gradually displaced many incumbent Republicans and helped elect Ronald Reagan in 1980 (Tulis and Mellow 2018, 102–31).

The other three types of near misses differ largely by shifting from eventful to bounded history, ignoring dates, and employing cross-sectional comparisons. *Near-miss cases* dehistoricize near-miss events by stripping them of dates and converting them from events into cases, thus treating them as being historically independent of each other. Near-miss cases are methodologically interesting because they increase the number of observations within a single case by treating earlier outcomes within a case as the equivalent of other cross-sectional outcomes. In *State and Social Revolutions*, Skocpol uses the Russian revolution of 1905 as a near-miss case on the grounds that it did not amount to a full-fledged social revolution. She employs this as a shadow case, to both increase the number of observations by leveraging variation within Russia and to counter charges that she based her selection on a dependent variable (Skocpol 1979). Had she been interested in how the 1905 revolution interacted with the 1917 Revolution, she would have had to unfreeze history and treated it as a near-miss event.

Near-miss cases have an empirically more anemic cousin: *negative cases*. This type starts to assume a counterfactual quality. Jim Mahoney and Gary Goertz (2004) define negative cases as involving an observable near miss, but that near miss is an artifact of the theoretical possibility or probability of its occurrence. A negative case is assumed to have a probability of occurring (hence its being a near miss) as a result of the partial presence of the theorized causal factors that explain the outcomes in the positive cases. It thus differs from a near-miss case by being counterfactual – it did not occur – but it is empirically possible by virtue of having some theorized factors present. Skocpol, for example, uses Germany and Japan as negative cases. These countries did not experience failed social revolutions (i.e. an actual, empirical near miss) but had some of the factors present that produced social revolutions in France, China, and Russia. They were near misses in the sense that revolutions were theoretically possible, even though none was observable – as in the case of Russia's first revolution in 1905 (Mahoney and Goertz 2004). Negative cases reduce selection bias and permit observing omitted variables. Finally, *counterfactual cases*, at least in their purest, most parlor-like fashion, imagine alternative historical paths of events that could have happened even though the possibility was very slim. Examples includes musings of what would have happened if Hitler invaded England successfully or defeated Stalin (Ferguson 2000; for a more nuanced treatment, see Tetlock 1999).

The PR literature provides a long series of illustrations of how exploring causal patterns helped its theoretical development.

7.5 An Illustration of Exploring Causal Patterns

The PR literature elongated causal chains and outcomes to update the original left threat thesis. This thesis makes conventional linear causal arguments where the effects of the franchise explanation, the left's electoral strength, and the right's fragmentation all occur almost simultaneously, produce additive causal effects, is in close temporal proximity to the PR adoption, and symmetrically explain its reversal and endurance.

Table 7.3 elongates the causal chain with data gathered by Bartolini. It uses a ten-year threshold (column 6) to differentiate between short–short and long–short explanations. It shows that the short–short assumption, which states that

Table 7.3 Elongating the causal chain of PR adoption

	(1) Socialist Party Founding	(2) Year of Manhood Suffrage	(3) Year of Universal Suffrage	(4) Year of PR Adoption	(5) Years between (1) and (2)	(6) Years between (2) and (4)
Germany	1863–75	1871	1918	1919	+4	+47
Denmark	1871–8	1848	1918	1919	+23	+61
Belgium	1864–85	1893	1949	1899	−8	+6
Austria	1874–89	1907	1919	1918	−18	+11
Switzerland	1880–8	1848	1971	1918	+39	+61
Norway	1885–7	1900	1912–15	1920	−13	+20
Sweden	1889	1911	1921	1911	−22	0
Italy	1880–92	1913	1945	1919	−21	+6
Netherlands	1881–94	1918	1922	1918	−24	0
Finland	1893–9	1907	1907	1907	−8	0
France	1880–905	1848	1945	1920	+57	+72
UK	1900–4	1918	1918	n/a	−12/−16	n/a
Ireland	1912–22	1918	1918–22	1922	−4.5	0

Source: Bartolini 2000, 215; information about PR from various other sources.

Table 7.4 Timing of electoral reforms

Pre-1914	1918–1920	Post-1920
Some Swiss Cantons (1890s)	Switzerland (**1919**)	France* (~~1928~~)
Switzerland (1900, 1910)	France (**1919**)	Ireland (1922)
France* (1880s*, 1910, 1918)	Norway (**1919**)	Greece (1926,~~1928~~,1932,~~1933~~)
Belgium (1889, 1899, **1899**)	Denmark (**1918**)	Iceland (1923**, **1959**)
Sweden (1891, 1902, 1903,	Austria (**1919**)	
1906, **1907**)	Italy (**1919**)	
Finland (**1907**)	Luxembourg (**1919**)	
Norway (1911)	Netherlands (**1919**)	
Denmark (1915**)	Iceland (1916*)	
Iceland (1874*, 1908*)		

* Majoritarian list systems. ** mixed system. 1889: Near miss where PR bill is either rejected or not voted on. ~~1928~~: Reversal. **1899**: PR Adopted.

Sources: Ahmed 2013, 139–60; Barzachka 2014; Cox, Fiva, and Smith 2019; Elklit 1992; Hardarson 2002; Lutz 2000; Mavrogordatos 1982, 25–40, Appendix I; Verney 1957.

PR was adopted only shortly after the franchise was expanded, holds exactly for seven out of the fourteen cases: Belgium, Sweden, Italy, Netherlands, Finland, Ireland, and Norway. The longer time lag for the other seven cases mattered because it gave incumbents more information about the changing electoral fortunes of the left and more time to strategize how best to contain it. Furthermore, in four of the seven cases – namely Denmark, France, Germany, Switzerland – the franchise predated the formation of the left. This sequence had a moderating effect on the left, insofar as its members did not have to fight for democracy and economic reforms at the same time. The ability to contest elections also provided Socialists with an alternative to strikes, protest, and revolutionary threats as a way of advancing their agenda (Lipset 1983; Marks, Mbaye, and Kim 2009).

Linear short–short explanations typically treat outcomes as singular snapshots with no prehistory or posthistory. Table 7.4 elongates those outcomes by paying attention to following questions.

- Were there any prior near-miss electoral reforms? If so, did those reforms focus on introducing a full PR system, a hybrid system, or a different, non-PR system?
- Were those efforts successful, and how many of them were there?
- Once PR was introduced, were there reversal efforts and, if so, were they successful?

Table 7.4 powerfully underscores just how much more varied the outcomes were than the existing theories stipulate. It identifies only two reversals (France and Greece), and thus emphasized the overall durability of PR adoptions in other countries. Only six countries (Finland, Ireland, Austria, Italy, Luxemburg, Netherlands) had no near misses before the adoption of PR; and all six were at the end of major political crises such as the fight for independence in Ireland and Finland or the end of World War I. The other countries had complex prehistories that included near misses or other electoral reforms.

Leaving aside the noise near misses add to the analysis, they are theoretically relevant in two ways. First, the cases without near misses suggest that major political conflicts can significantly accelerate the adoption process. Second, near misses are helpful for better understanding the generative process leading up to the PR adoption, as Chapter 6 pointed out.

Exercises

7.1. Exercise 2.3 used Gladwell's chapter on honor killings to explore different notions of historical time. Let us now explore the explanatory factors Gladwell uses in his analysis. Carefully dissect his argument and sort the various explanatory factors according to the typology offered by the theory map (Figure 7.1). Does he propose factors not covered by the map? Can you think of explanatory factors that might be relevant but that Gladwell overlooks? In what theoretical categories would they fall? (See Gladwell 2008, 161–76.)

7.2. Macro-causal analysis leverages the existing stock of theories as well as our knowledge of cases and events, in order to update existing theories. The following stylized example advances several theories that explain Trump's 2016 victory. Use these theories (feel free to add details) as well as your own background knowledge (which would be the equivalent of a case study). Or adapt the example to a comparable case in another country. Read the following theories before using them for theorizing:

Theory 1 (politics): Trump defeated Hillary Clinton because of her unpopularity, his effective communication (use of Twitter, trolling, ability to garner media attention) and Russia's misinformation campaign. *Theory 2 (inequality)*: Growing inequality in the United States since the 1970s contributed to the takeover of the Republican party by wealthy plutocrats. Those plutocrats managed to enforce orthodox neoliberal economic policies (e.g., low taxes, free trade, anti-union policies, deregulation) while making appeals related to cultural issues (e.g., guns, abortion, gay marriage). The plutocrats' stranglehold of the Republican party and enforcement of neoliberal orthodoxies led to disenchantment with party leaders among voters. Trumps broke with those orthodoxies, at least during the election campaign, which allowed him to take over the party and to sideline the older leadership. *Theory 3 (Trade)*: China's admission to the World Trade Organization in 2001 dramatically accelerated the decline of manufacturing jobs in the Midwest and alienated key working-class constituencies from both the Republican and the Democratic Party, making them available to populists like Trump or Bernie Sanders. Trump ultimately proved successful in mobilizing such voters in electorally key swing states. *Theory 4 (Race)*: Structural racism in the United States is going back to slavery, which created a de facto caste system. This historical legacy generates status anxiety and antidemocratic backlash every time African Americans mobilize for greater political inclusion or demand more social justice. The socioeconomic advances of African Americans since the civil rights reforms in the 1960s and the sharp increase in Asian and Latino/a immigrant groups generated increasing status anxiety among white, male, rural, and evangelical voters, whom Republicans managed to exploit ever since Nixon's adoption of the southern strategy in the 1970s.

Use these theories to engage in the following four topics. First, in which of the four boxes of Pierson's time matrix (Table 7.1) would you place those theories? Second, what mix of theoretical factors did they use? Identify the theoretical elements using the theory map (Figure 7.1). What elements on the theory map seem relevant but are not covered by the existing theories? Third, employ the different theories to elongate causal chains and outcomes that macro-causal analysis uses to update theories. Work through the following scenario. How would the politics theory (1) complement the inequality (2) and the race (4) theories? How would the inequality theory (2) complement the politics (1) and the trade (3) theories? How would the trade theory (3) complement the inequality (2) and the politics (1) theories? Fourth, how does elongating causal chains require paying greater attention to the temporal order of causal factors? In what ways are causal effects less likely to be additive, simultaneous, immediate, and symmetrical?

7.3. The political scientist Daniel Ziblatt (2009) and the historian Margaret L. Anderson (1993) both explore the role that electoral fraud played in imperial Germany, but they employ very different kinds of historical thinking. They consequently illustrate how macro-causal analysis, with its largely frozen historical thinking, employs Anderson's unfrozen historical thinking for updating theory. Ziblatt offers the more straightforward argument, where electoral fraud provides evidence that the incumbents used their economic power to undermine democratization. By contrast, Anderson interprets electoral fraud as demonstrating a shift in Germany, between the 1860s and the 1870s, from a deferential to a more oppositional, and hence more democratic political culture. Across the two works, fraud is used as an indicator of both democratic deficit and democratic growth. Despite this difference, the two arguments overlap in complex ways. Macro-causal analysis typically uses the more nuanced analysis of historians like Anderson to update existing theories. This abduction process is slow; it requires close reading and ontological triage. The following prompts serve to guide you through this abduction process.

How does Ziblatt read history backwards while Anderson reads it forward? (See the index for finding the passages that discuss reading history forward and backward.) And how do these readings of history shape the respective research questions? How does Ziblatt employ bounded history and Anderson eventful history? Parenthetically, how mindful is Ziblatt of the boundary conditions of his analysis? Is he offering a German-specific explanation, or is he contributing to a broader, transhistorical literature on democratization? Anderson employs a largely eventful analysis, but how attentive is she to chronology? In what ways does she freeze historical time herself?

How does Ziblatt's the second section (14–18) pay more attention to the temporal order of causal factors than the first part (5–11), thus unfreezing physical time? How does the second section elongate the causal chain? How does it update the original theory tested in the first section? What explanatory elements discussed in the theory map (Figure 7.1) does the case study add? How well does the second section address the two empirical anomalies mentioned on page 12 – that is, the increase of fraud over time and the null effect of 1903 secret ballot?

How does Anderson's even more eventful history help identify causal factors that Ziblatt overlooks? Where do their explanations overlap? Which factors that contribute to electoral fraud does Anderson mention while Ziblatt overlooks them? In what ways do those confounding factors differ from the ones Ziblatt mentions on p. 12 when he explains the longitudinal variation in electoral fraud? How readily could Ziblatt incorporate those confounding factors in his explanation? What do Anderson's various political cartoons add to strengthen her analysis of Germany's changing electoral culture? What insights do they contribute that Ziblatt's analysis misses?

Part III

What about Causality?

So far, our discussion focused on the exploratory contributions of comparative historical analysis (CHA): describing patterns of change, refining research questions, and unpacking non-linear causal effects. I also claimed that such an exploration is necessary for translating results into answers. Description and explanation, exploration and testing are intimately connected and complement each other. The enormous importance that CHA assigns to exploration raises the question of what CHA has to say about confirmation, causality, or testing. How do CHA's contributions to causal inference differ from those variance-based techniques that emphasize the testing of a hypothesis, or from interpretivist approaches that champion thick, ethnographic description?

The concluding section addresses these questions and consequently returns to the more familiar methodological subject matter of causal inference. Chapter 8 assists with this transition by placing CHA's exploratory contributions in a larger methodological context, which highlights its connection with the confirmatory testing stage. The chapter reintroduces an older conception of methodology as *research cycles*. This conception, which emphasizes the close dialogue between exploration and explanation, between description and causal inference, is broader than the contemporary notion of methodology as *research design*, with its narrower focus on causal inference. Next, the chapter expands on the ontological map introduced in Chapter 1. It uses this map to place in a broader methodological context CHA's two principal causal inference strategies – historical explanation and process tracing – by showing how they differ from other methodologies in terms of freezing history and geography. This map becomes the point of reference for aligning the ontological assumptions of different research designs with the ontological characteristics of the question being answers. It guides what I called "ontological triage" in Chapter 1.

Chapter 9 discusses *historical explanations* that are linked to eventful and longue durée analysis and that explain historical change through time. These explanations draw on tools developed by Austrian economists, historical sociologists, and comparative historians and in the literature on path dependency. Historical explanations address the complexity of analyzing change by breaking it down into a two-step process. They employ one set of tools to explain the generative processes or the event chain that produces discontinuities. And, in a separate step, they focus on increasing returns that explain the reproduction mechanisms perpetuating continuities. They make explaining change manageable by analyzing the moments of discontinuity and the periods of continuity *separately*. Chapter 10 focuses on *causal process tracing*, which is widely used in macro-causal analysis to develop and test historically situated theories. Those theories pay close attention to elements of physical time and explicate long and complex causal pathways that can explain variations in cross-sectional outcomes. Causal process tracing draws on tools that have long been used informally in CHA and have more recently been formalized under the label of "process tracing." Historical explanations and process tracing do not exhaust the types of causal arguments used in CHA, but they are the most established ones and consequently will be the focus of Chapters 9 and 10.

8 Situating Comparative Historical Analysis
Heterodox Yet Still Systematic

> Social reality wants rigor and imagination.
>
> (Abbott 2004, 4)

After seven chapters devoted to exploration and description, the three concluding ones return to the standard methodological concern of making valid causal inferences – of linking small, concrete pieces of evidence or data to broader causal claims in a manner that is transparent and replicable enough to inspire confidence. Before elaborating on historical explanations and causal process tracing as comparative historical analysis' (CHA) two main strategies for causal inference, this chapter first situates CHA in a broader methodological context. This is designed to make the transition from exploration to explanation easier and to underscore once more CHA's complementarity with other methodologies. The heterodox label is frequently used to characterize CHA's position and to differentiate CHA from other methodologies. The everyday use of the label "heterodox" implies a degree of non-conformism strong enough for its bearer to deviate from orthodox default norms, but not so strong enough for the bearer to risk being excommunicated as a heretic. The term thus has a certain liminal quality and leaves open whether it is meant as a compliment or in disparagement. The present chapter defines it with greater precision by linking it to CHA's conceptualization of methodology as a series of research cycles and to its embrace of methodological bricolage, which is necessary to align methods with questions.

First, CHA welcomes an understanding of methodology as multistage and iterative *research cycles*. It is less enthusiastic about the recent push to employ multimethod research designs that view methods as offering alternative ways to test hypotheses, and thereby as still competing among themselves (Ahmed and Sil 2012). Instead, it sees different methods as contributing to distinct stages in a *single* research process – stages that complement one another. Furthermore, CHA sees this research process as being iterative and in close dialogue with earlier research. At the risk of stretching the term a bit, the idea of research cycles underscores CHA's view of research itself as having a historical dimension that needs to be factored into evaluating causal inferences.

Second, CHA sacrifices a formalized testing protocol in favor of a more complex methodological bricolage that pragmatically selects the methods that are most appropriate for a particular question. What this methodological bricolage lacks in formal testing techniques, it makes up by subjecting causal inferences to a broader set of validity checks than does variance-based analysis (VBA). Most importantly, it places ontological transparency, together with transparent testing and data collection, at the center of causal inference. Methodological bricolage exhorts scholars to understand *what* theoretical propositions are being tested, not just *how* they are tested; it insists on evaluating causal inferences against prior results and not just against context-independent statistical significance tests; and, most importantly, it uses historical thinking to pay close attention to the confounding effects of history, geography, and physical time.

Together, the idea of the research cycle and methodological bricolage should make it easier to understand how CHA blurs the boundary between exploration and testing, and thus becomes more heterodox than the methods that uphold this boundary.

8.1 Research Cycles

Various scholars have expanded on Skocpol and Somers' original idea of linking the exploratory and confirmatory research stages by introducing the idea of research cycles (Skocpol and Somers 1980, 197). Andrew Abbott (2015) talks about methods of discovery, Sean Yom (2004) about inductive iteration, Richard Swedberg (2014) about abduction, and Evan Lieberman (2016) about the role that research cycle assume in biomedical research. These scholars resist sorting research tools (e.g., description, conceptualization, measurement, testing) by different, competing methodological schools, but instead view them as contributing to distinct and complementary stages of a singular research process. They all take seriously two key precepts: testing without exploration is just as pointless as exploration without testing; and the interplay between exploration and testing makes research itself a historical process in which new results must be evaluated against older ones.

The idea of a research cycle elaborates on those two precepts by linking them to three characteristics.

First, each individual research cycle involves the six stages shown in Figure 8.1. It begins with an exploratory stage that relies on historical thinking to increase the understanding of understudied or misstudied phenomena, to describe and redescribe patterns, to formulate new research questions, to elucidate concepts, to disentangle test anomalies, and to pay close attention to non-linear causal processes. Downplaying the importance of this exploratory stage is, as Skocpol points out, "a conceit of a very dull, overdeveloped

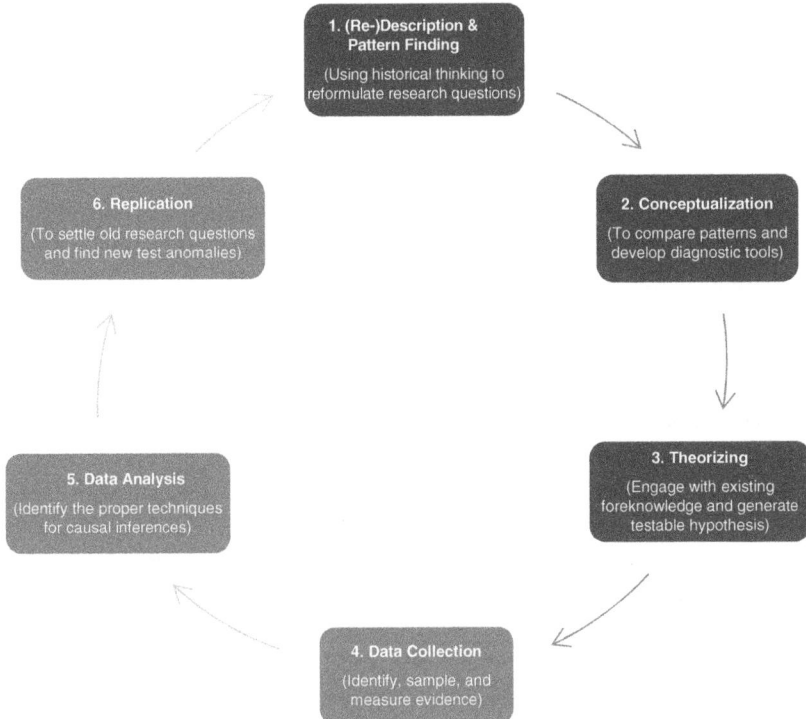

Figure 8.1 Research cycles
CHA is reluctant to arrange research tools by competing methodological schools and prefers instead to view them as contributing to six stages of a research cycle. Light grey cells correspond to the exploratory stage, dark grey cells to the confirmatory stage. The research cycles repeat themselves, and this requires scholars to evaluate new findings by considering earlier ones.

field, one that is confident that it already has all the questions. . . . It is hopeless to approach things this way in the social sciences because our questions and angles of vision change with changes in our society's normative concerns. It is important to test theories rigorously, but the sense of discovery is equally important. And in human terms, the sense of discovery is *more* important, otherwise we get bored with our work" (interview in Munck and Snyder 2008, 678–9). CHA does not limit itself to exploration but uses historical explanations and process tracing also in order to explain. Historical explanations and process tracing follow an abductive logic that pays equal attention to the empirical implications of theories and to the theoretical implications of new inductive insights. Finally, the unidirectional arrows in Figure 8.1 represent a highly idealized sequence of the six research steps, one that overlooks their often non-sequential interplay. Ultimately, Figure 8.1 underscores that research generates genuine answers only to the extent that the exploratory stage produces new research questions, valid concepts, and testworthy hypotheses and that those answers become compelling only to the extent that they are supported by test results.

Second, the idea of research cycles represents a broader and, in many respects, older understanding of methodology. This conception differs from the contemporary one, which concentrates on the technical, more confirmatory elements of methodology that are subsumed under the label "research design." This broadening recognizes that focusing too exclusively on causal inference techniques diverts attention from the research tasks required to identify interesting macro-historical questions (Skocpol and Schickler 2019). Lieberman offers a particularly telling illustration from biomedical research. He points out that randomized controlled trials make up only a part of biomedical research and that this research is in close dialogue with other, lower-tech and more exploratory forms of research. Epidemiology, for example, plays a vital role in accurately describing a new illness, identifying its symptoms, and developing diagnostic tests before other strands of biomedical research develop and test cures (Ankeny 2010; Lieberman 2016). It thus assumes many of the same functions that CHA's historical thinking plays in social science research: investigating, exploring, identifying patterns, developing concepts, and conjecturing about possible explanations.

Third, the iterative nature of research cycles makes research itself historical, whereby new findings must be evaluated against prior research. Lieberman sees research cycles as a corrective against the "go big or go home" research strategy that is increasingly common in social sciences. Scholars are expected to hit a home run with each article by exploring new research questions, explaining them with a novel theory, testing them with fresh data, and providing definitive test results (Lieberman 2016, 1085) – a proposition that is as daunting as it is unrealistic. The individual scholar becomes the research cycle itself rather than contributing a small piece to it. Lieberman thus underscores that research is a process, which – as historians of science point out – has its own history: as one cycle ends, another begins, and together they advance knowledge. What distinguishes individual cycles is defined, just as with periodizations, by clear changes in research patterns. A new phenomenon, for example the collapse of communism, global warming, or the Covid-19 pandemic, starts brand-new research cycles; this is because a new phenomenon is, of course, a previously unstudied phenomenon. Or an already well studied phenomenon might be re-studied by having a new theory or method imported into it from another discipline. Discontinuities in research cycles mark qualitative breaks in the larger knowledge production process to which the genealogy of the PR literature in Chapter 6 alluded. Parenthetically, I should point out that CHA's engagement with the existing foreknowledge manifests itself in emphasis on a close, careful, and empathetic reading designed to find new theoretical connections. It is also evident in the fondness for lengthy footnotes (Grafton 1999; Lustick 1996; Trachtenberg 2015), in the efforts to develop new footnoting technologies, (Moravcsik 2010), and in the willingness to perish a little professionally rather than publish too much or too early.

8.2 Methodological Bricolage: Aligning Methods with Questions

CHA's mantra – the imperative to put questions before methods – requires aligning the strategies for causal inference with research questions rather than following a single, all-purpose testing protocol. This alignment requires skillful bricoleurs/bricoleuses to solve the ontological triage dilemma of how much to freeze history and geography to render social reality methodologically tractable without making it so static and uniform that important confounders get overlooked. Or, to put it differently, methodological bricolage grapples with the question of how much methodological orthodoxy scholars are willing to give up to foreground history and geography, and how many historical and geographic particularities they are willing to background to give up heterodoxy.

Few mastered this methodological bricolage more nimbly than Skocpol, who repeatedly aligned her methods with her questions. In *State and Social Revolutions* she employs macro-causal analysis and an early form of process tracing to explain cross-sectional variations in social revolutions. In *Protecting Mothers and Soldiers* she switched to eventful analysis and historical explanations to retrace the origins of the first social programs in the United States. In *Diminished Democracy* she employs longue durée analysis to retrace the changing trends in American associational life during the past two centuries and, again, uses historical explanations. In each of these works, Skocpol figured out what ontological qualities defined the questions she was exploring and then, in true bricoleuse fashion, purpose-built the methodological tools appropriate for answering the question. Such bricolage requires both ontological literacy and transparency to effectively communicate to readers which research strategy is most appropriate to a given research question.

Figure 8.2 provides guidance for bricoleurs/euses in this alignment process. It refines the ontological map introduced in Chapter 1. It places on the horizontal x-axis the four notions of history or historical time discussed in Chapter 2. The vertical y-axis plots methodologies according to how much

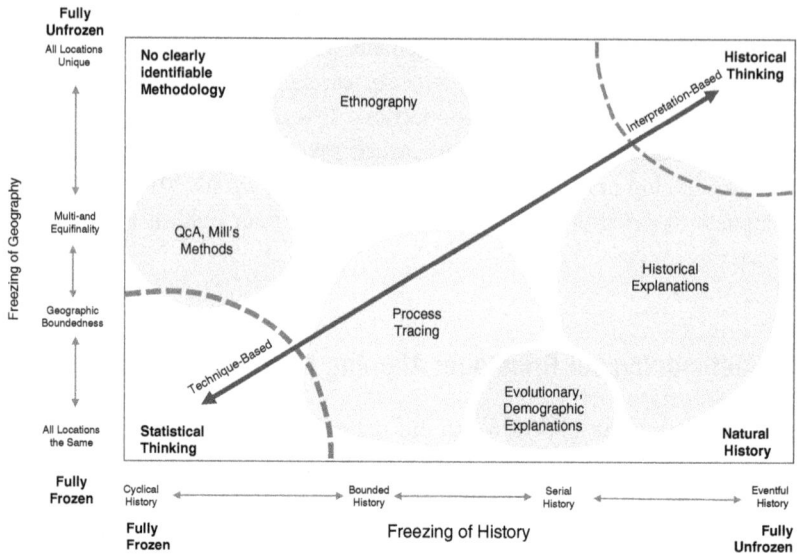

Figure 8.2 Ontological map

Different methods are mapped on the basis of their ontological assumptions. The horizontal axis differentiates between methods according to the degree to which they freeze history; the vertical axis, according to the degree to which they freeze geography. CHA's two principal causal inference strategies – historical explanations and process tracing – are thus situated in a broader context. The map includes evolutionary and demographic explanations as a third, less well-established inference strategy. It also offers guidance into selecting the causal inference strategies whose ontological assumptions are the ones most appropriate for the ontological characteristics of the question under investigation.

they freeze geography. It treats geography in an ordinal manner and differentiates between three notions of geography: physical, bounded, and cultural. *Physical geography* is the geography specified by unit homogeneity: a world so uniform that spatial particularities no longer exist, and thus can be ignored. Geology does not make any allowance for varieties of geography but instead focuses on variations of uniform elements across space. *Bounded geography* makes some allowances for broad, but not universal, geographic patterns. In the social sciences, it features in discussions of geographic boundary conditions invoked to qualify the external validity of test results. Or it is used in qualitative comparative analysis (QCA), in the discussion of equifinality and multifinality. QCA admits that geographic particularities make it possible for the same outcome in two different set of cases to be explained by different causal factors, which renders those outcomes equifinal. Or it points to instances in which the same causal factors might be present across cases but produce different outcomes; this kind of occurrence renders them multifinal. Equifinality and multifinality thus make allowances for a world that is more heterogenous than the one permitted by unit homogeneity, but not so heterogeneous as to make it impossible for us to look for geographically bounded generalizations. Finally, cultural geography is the counterpart to eventful history. It unfreezes geography to such a degree that the world becomes exceptionalist. Each unit of analysis is sui generis, and its study has to be thickly textured to capture local meanings. It becomes difficult to generalize, and attention therefore shifts to thick, experience-near description, which tries to convey the meaning of a context related to people.

Figure 8.2 maps different methods on the basis of their ontological assumptions. The horizontal axis differentiates methods according to the degree to which they freeze history, and the vertical axis according to the degree to which they freeze geography. The figure situates in a broader context CHA's two principal strategies for causal inference: historical explanation and process tracing. It also includes evolutionary and demographic explanations as a third, less well-established inference strategy. The map provides guidance for selecting the causal inference strategies whose ontological assumptions are most appropriate for the ontological characteristics of the question investigated.

Three of the four corners correspond to three well-established modes of analysis: regular historical (top right), variance-based (bottom left), and natural history analysis (bottom right). CHA covers a broader intellectual terrain than VBA, natural history, and regular history and this terrain is not circumscribed by any ontological boundary. CHA does not define itself in narrow ontological terms; it pivots instead between the three ontological corners defined by statistical, regular historical, and natural historical thinking. This pivoting requires the aforementioned bricolage skills and allows CHA to align methods with questions. For this alignment process, CHA draws on process tracing linked to bounded history and macro-causal analysis, historical explanations connected to eventful history and analysis, and evolutionary or demographic explanations associated with serial history and longue durée analysis. The next two chapters will expand on historical explanations and process tracing. I will not cover evolutionary or demographic explanations that play a role in institutional economics, evolutionary psychology, and persistence arguments. These explanations have received too little attention in CHA for me to report anything useful in this connection. They are frequently dismissed for being functionalist, too (Beck and Witt 2019).

The remaining fourth corner (top left) is a bit more ambiguous and also does not have a border. Ethnography certainly rests on thick, geographic-culture assumptions, but mostly employs bounded notions of history; thus it is shifted slightly to the right of that corner. To find an example that fully freezes history but unfreezes geography, I had to go outside the social sciences. Biology has a subfield called "biogeography," which explores how specific geographic conditions explain variations in particular species. It freezes history because any pattern it finds repeats itself if benchmarked against human history. Biogeographers report that islands have a most powerful geographic impact, to the point where two closely related species live on one island on treetops and on others on the ground. Since biogeography focuses on physical rather than cultural aspects of geography, the geographic particularities will not be as great as when we are dealing with the cultural particularities that ethnographers study. Put differently, there are more dialects spoken in a given geographic unit than mutations in bird species.[1]

The graph provides three insights for aligning methods with questions. First, it underscores a trade-off between the technical complexity of causal inference procedures and the robustness of their ontological assumptions. VBA trades off high-tech causal inference techniques against reductivist ontological assumptions. These assumptions are fragile because they background history and geography, and thus produce numerous confounding effects. Historical analysis, in turn, trades off low-tech, narrative-based explanations against more complex and robust ontological assumptions, where dates and zip codes matter. For the other methodologies, the trade-off is not as stark. Qualitative comparative analysis (QCA) is still high-tech, even though it makes more allowances for geographic particularities. Ethnography is low-tech too, even though it recognizes the historical boundedness of its narratives. CHA minimizes this trade-off more than any other methodology, by employing historical explanations and process tracing as two distinct strategies.

Second, the arrow going from the lower left to the upper right corners marks the shift from the ontologically least complex, most frozen terrain – which permits using formalized, technique-based causal inference strategies to explain clock-like phenomena – to the ontologically most complex and liquid terrain – which requires judgement-based, interpretivist strategies to analyze cloud-like phenomena. CHA combines technique and judgement-based strategies that fill the unoccupied, liminal space between the other types of analysis. Historical explanations concentrate on explaining discontinuities and continuities. They assume events to be interdependent, and this interdependence produces either generative processes that explain discontinuities or

---

[1] I would like to thank Dennis Wykoff for sharing this example.

increasing return mechanisms that reproduce the status quo and account for persistence. Historical explanations differ from conventional historical narratives by assuming that these generative and increasing return processes can be compared and repeat themselves across some cases – but certainly not all. As for causal process tracing, it looks primarily at interdependencies related to timing and sequencing that are less directly historical. It limits its historical attention to emphasizing the historical boundedness of findings. However, it is more comparative as it tests hypotheses across a larger number of cases. I include QCA as another ecumenical, heterodox research design that is occasionally linked to CHA (see Mahoney 2004). It emphasizes the pecularities of geographic units of analysis that can produce equifinal or multifinal outcomes. But, given its inability to address elements of time, its relevance to CHA is limited. Overall, then, historical explanations and process tracing clearly are the most ecumenical and heterodox, which makes them CHA's causal inference strategies of choice.

After this bird's eye perspective, let me return to the more technical aspects of historical explanations and process tracing that are directly relevant to the research process.

Exercises

8.1. The ontological map serves to place different research designs in the larger methodological landscape. Place the following examples: coin tosses, psychometric treatment of IQ, developmental psychology treatment of IQ, social psychological treatment of IQ (the Cole experiment referenced in Gladwell), Dixon's analysis of the degree of contrition of state narratives, the middle class, and GDP on the ontological map (see Figure 8.2; use the index to locate the discussion of these examples in the text). Where would you place conventional cancer treatment vis-à-vis the newly evolving, more targeted treatments discussed in Mukherjee's (2016) article? How has the ontological status of cancer changed? Did geneticists come to realize that cancers are historical and change with time? Or did they recognize that they differ "geographically" (i.e. cross-sectionally) across demographic groups?

Place the following subdisciplines on the updated ontological map (Figure 8.2). Economics: neoclassical economics, economic history, economic institutionalism (i.e. Douglas North). Medicine: etiology epidemiology, medical randomized control trials. Can you identify similar subdisciplines within your own field, or even literature? What are they and where would you place those literatures onto the ontological map? What role do the more historical subdisciplines play in relation to the more ahistorical ones? Is this balance appropriate, given the ontological characteristics of the phenomena being studied?

8.2. Read Evan Lieberman's (1980, 196–7) treatment of the research cycle and discuss how it differs from related notions of research originally proposed by Skocpol and Somers. They understood research cycles, just like chapter 8 does, as involving the complex interplay between the different strands of CHA during a singular cycle, as well as an even more complex interplay across multiple cycles. Does Lieberman offer a more linear, almost teleological sequence, which starts with qualitative exploratory approaches and culminates in randomized controlled trials? Or does he conceive of the different stages of research cycles as offering complementary causal inference strategies rather than distinct exploratory and confirmatory research tasks? How clearly does he delineate one research cycle from another?

8.3. In his thought-provoking *Methods of Discovery*, Andrew Abbott stresses the importance of exploration and imagination in social inquiry and discusses their complex interplay with explanation (Abbott 2004, 1–40). How does his understanding of this interplay differ from the one laid out in Evan Lieberman's discussion of research cycles? Abbott does not embrace the idea of research cycles; but in what ways could his account be reconceptualized as forming a research cycle? How do his three research programs overlap (29), and differ from, the contributions that the three strands of CHA make to social inquiry? In what ways can he be said to advocate methodological bricolage?

9 Historical Explanations
Making Sense of Continuities and Discontinuities

> History does not crawl, it jumps.
>
> (Taleb 2007, 8)

It is easier to analyze static objects than objects in motion, which explains the appeal of freezing history and physical time. Historical explanations unfreeze history and physical time just enough to capture change and non-linear processes but not so much as to impede broader generalizations. The term "historical explanation" is itself is closely related to other, less widely used labels such as punctuated equilibrium (Krasner 1984), critical juncture (Collier-Berins and Collier 1991), and etiological (Sewell 1996, 273), ecological (Gaddis 2002), path-dependent (Aminzade 1992), or genetic (Rustow 1970) explanations. Historical explanations rest on the assumption that history sometimes crawls and other times it jumps. Explaining historical change therefore requires separate approaches for analyzing these two types of change: one identifies the generative process that produces discontinuities, the other focuses on the reproduction mechanisms that explain continuities.

These separate approaches mirror the efforts of eventful analysis to make unfrozen history analytically manageable by assigning events to periods of continuity and periods of discontinuity and thereby distinguishing analytically between static and changing time intervals. They also reflect the efforts of macro-causal analysis to elongate causal chains and outcomes and to employ historical notions of causality that capture the causal effects of physical time.

Parenthetically, I should point out that evolutionary explanations play a role in longue durée analysis by explaining slower-moving long-term trends. Institutional economics, for example, employs such explanations in tracing the evolution of private property, of parliaments, and of other institutions that gave rise to capitalism. Unfortunately, comparative historical analysis (CHA) has paid insufficient attention to such evolutionary explanations. Many scholars dismiss them on account of their alleged functionalism, while others try to ground them in the literature on complex adaptive systems (Gaddis 2002; Jervis 1998). These efforts, interesting as they are, are insufficiently understood and remain too preliminary to provide tangible research advice.

This chapter discusses historical explanations in four steps. First, it identifies three key elements that give them coherence. Second, it elaborates the causal mechanisms by which historical explanations account for discontinuities. Third, it demonstrates how historical explanations adapt path-dependent arguments to account for continuities. Fourth, it illustrates historical explanations with examples from the PR literature.

9.1 Core Elements of Historical Explanations

Just as eventful analysis is the most interpretive CHA strand, so historical explanations constitute the most heterodox causal inference strategy, far less formalized than process tracing or variance-based analysis (VBA). Three elements define this field: historical causation, the simplification of historical change, and making events the central unit of analysis.

Historical Causality. The chapter on macro-causal analysis already introduced historical, non-linear causation as an alternative to the ahistorical, linear notions of causality that are also known as "potential outcomes" or "average treatment effects." Historical causation unfreezes four elements of linear causality, namely simultaneity, addition, immediacy, and symmetry, in order to explain historical transformation more clearly. Parenthetically, I should point out that linear causality tacitly acknowledges historical causation when the problem of collinearity is at stake. In statistics, collinearity refers to the confounding effects that result when causal factors are insufficiently independent of one another to meet the four conditions of linearity. It is an artifact of frozen physical time that backgrounds particularly timing and sequencing, which make causal factors interdependent. Thus collinearity is another way of acknowledging history; and, just like an exogeneous shock, it is presented as something problematic that requires fixing rather than as something essential that should be embraced.

Historical causation parses causality into *generative mechanisms* or originating causes, which explain discontinuity, and *increasing return mechanisms* or sustaining causes, which explaining the durability of the legacy effect. It is fundamentally processual because it requires close attention to temporally interacting causal chains, to the causal process that they produce, and to the non-linear causal effects of physical time. Thus the terminology of originating and sustaining causes or generative and increasing return mechanisms can be a bit misleading, as it suggests a more mechanistic, atomistic, and static notion of causality. But these entities are temporal in that they play close attention to physical time. It is to this temporal quality that the qualification "historical" in "historical explanations" alludes – a connotation that admittedly blurs my distinction between historical and physical time. But this semantic ambiguity seems worth accepting, given that "historical explanation" is an already well-established term.

Simplifying Historical Change. Historical explanations face the challenge that change itself is a moving target that needs to be frozen and simplified before it can be explained. They consequently construct a history that is orderly enough to align with theories that stipulate more general causal mechanisms. Historical explanations borrow from eventful analysis and, to a lesser extent, from longue durée analysis the idea that change becomes more orderly and analytically more tractable when we break it into periods. The periods, in turn, are divided into intervals of continuity, when history crawls, and intervals of discontinuity, when history jumps. With this simplified pattern of change in place, historical explanations offer different theories for explaining continuities and discontinuities. They point to so-called genetic or originating causes, which explain the generative process that brings about discontinuity, and increasing return mechanisms or sustaining causes, which explain the reproduction mechanisms that produce continuities (Cowan and Rizzo 1996, 285; Mahoney 2000, 512). This analytical separation between explaining discontinuities and explaining continuities has a distinguished lineage. It first surfaced in the late nineteenth-century *Methodenstreit* (methodological dispute) over idiographic versus nomothetic explanations, then became central to Austrian economists' efforts to explain economic change (Boettke, Coyne, and Leeson 2013; Cowan and Rizzo 1996; Palagashvili, Piano, and Skarbek 2017), and more recently has been at the center of path-dependent arguments (Mahoney 2000; Pierson 2000a).

But historical explanations have important limitations. They offer little guidance for analyzing the more complex intercurrences between multiple and concurrently unfolding processes that are also part of eventful analysis. Historical explanations also provide few insights into how to explain slowly unfolding trends, which longue durée analysis tries to account for using evolutionary or demographic explanations. Parenthetically, I should point out that demographic arguments constitute a subcategory of historical explanations that focus more narrowly on population-centered change. They account for demographic changes in terms of the intercurrence of three processes, each one closely related to a distinct notion of history. *Life cycle effects* are recurring, biology-related changes across different life stages or major life events (e.g., gaining weight with age as a result of lower metabolism). *Generational effects* are historically bounded effects shared by a particular age cohort (e.g., declining religiousness among younger cohorts). Finally, *period effects* are related to contingent large-scale historical events that have an impact across all generations and life cycles (e.g., increased fear of terrorist attacks after 9/11). These three kinds of effects are closely linked to cyclical, bounded, and eventful history; they also combine natural history where dates do not matter (life cycles) with regular history where dates do matter (generational and period effects). Demographic explanations are well suited to analyzing social or group changes, but are less relevant to actorless, institutional, or economic changes. In such changes, the past casts a longer shadow because history has long-term legacy effects that are not fully captured by the short-term generational and period effects. Nevertheless, demographic explanations are well established and are relevant to CHA (Duffy 2021, 1–15; Stinchcombe 1968, 60–79). But, since CHA has not explored their relevance, I will not elaborate any further on demographic explanations.

Centrality of Events. Historical explanations make events their key unit of analysis and employ analytical narratives in accounting for the continuities or discontinuities that a series of these events produce. They recognize that historical causation severely restricts the usefulness of variables and the ability to test hypotheses formally; it requires instead focusing on events and theoretically structured narratives. Bill Sewell (1996, 262) writes that "most happenings reproduce social and cultural structures without significant changes. Events maybe be defined as that relatively rare subclass of happenings that significantly transform structures." And Ivan Ermakoff (2019, 591–2) points out that focusing on events draws our attention to "generative and reproduction processes" that ultimately help us "address the question of 'why?' through the question of 'how?' It tackles this question by specifying a set of mechanisms, defined as 'specific causal patterns that explain individual action in a wide range of settings.' And it explores the empirical relevance of these mechanisms in light of primary historical evidence." The challenge is therefore to identify the event-centric generative processes, find possible mechanisms, and construct causal narratives that explain discontinuities and continuities (Capoccia and Ziblatt 2010; Edgar Kiser and Hechter 1991, 939).

With the broad contours sketched, let me turn to the practical steps of explaining discontinuities and continuities.

9.2 Explaining Discontinuity: Spotting Generative Processes

Explaining discontinuities is difficult because it involves qualitative changes and generative processes; and these do not comfortably align with theories and methodologies that assume a static (and hence devoid of change), snapshot-like, and ultimately linear world in which physical time remains frozen. Explaining discontinuities also requires a narrative mode while at the same time avoiding what Sewell (2009, 11) called "narrative overconfidence," which substitutes "a welter of narrative details" for conceptual clarity and theoretically grounded causal statements. CHA debates on the proper admixture of narration and analytical explicitness (Bates et al. 1998;

Bryant 1994; Elster 2000; Goldthorpe 1994; Hart 1994; Mann 1994) amount to four practical recommendations:

1. Identify discontinuities.
2. Explicate generative processes.
3. Beware of historical tourism.
4. Use the annotations for transparent inquiry (ATI).

Identifying Discontinuities. Change is ongoing and too fluid to be readily explained. It therefore must be made tractable by identifying events that together mark broader moments of rupture. As the chapter on eventful analysis showed, such discontinuities are not historically given but are constructed by scholars as they lump non-recurring and recurring events together, in broader chronological containers, namely periods (de Carvalho, Leira, and Hobson 2011). Explaining discontinuities starts with the identification of the liminal in-between moment when an earlier period of continuity ends and a subsequent one begins. Differentiating such discontinuities is crucial: this helps us recognize what Ermakoff (2019, 583–4) calls "phenomenal patterns," which provide clues for the underlying generative processes. Those patterns indicate to us whether the generative process involves a single chain of events leading up to a rupture-like discontinuity or multiple concurrent and interacting processes – that is, intercurrences.

CHA draws on eventful and longue durée analysis to look for empirical clues of discontinuities, and on macro-causal analysis for theoretical leads. Eventful and longue durée analysis look for historical and serial patterns that provide clues for rupture-like discontinuities. The efforts of eventful analysis to periodize lead to the discovery of crises, critical junctures, or reversals and thereby point to discontinuities. Historical institutionalists caution against relying too much on well-known historical switching points such as wars, economic crises, or regime changes and overlooking more complex intercurrence patterns, in which the discontinuities of multiple, concurrent, and multi-chronic processes interact (see Bernhard 2015; Capoccia and Ziblatt 2010, 941). Longue durée analysis locates structural breaks – sudden and significant changes in the slope of trendlines – that point to discontinuities. Eventful and longue durée analysis therefore play a central role in identifying patterns of continuity and discontinuity. However, given that such patterns are not just the result of inductive historical thinking and pattern identification, CHA also looks for theoretical clues suggested by macro-causal analysis.

Various CHA scholars suggest looking to micro-foundations – identifying actors and their available choice sets, or what I called in Chapter 7 eventful factors – to locate historical discontinuities (Capoccia and Ziblatt 2010, 935; Ermakoff 2015, 2019; Mahoney 2000, 515; Capoccia and Kelemen 2007).

For Ira Katznelson, human agency clarifies to what extent discontinuities result from contingent factors, human choices, or slower-moving structural and environmental factors. He points out that discontinuities are "unusual moments when the space for human agency opens wide" and agency "can come to possess an unusual capacity to determine outcomes. Of course, even at such times, the conditions under which preferences and agency operate are not simply of their own making. Events at such moments, the actual existence of competing possibilities, 'the universe of possible discourse,' occupies a more constrained space than the full universe of hypothetical options" (Katznelson 2003, 282). In a similar vein, Mark Blythe (2006, 495) points out that rational choice is well suited because it "assumes a world to be far more stable (and hence predictable) than it actually is. Specifically, it assumes that agents in the social world face tractable and normal probability distributions, that they face a world of risk, when in fact they face a world of uncertainty." He suggests that we think of discontinuities in broader probabilistic terms, as shifts from actors who operate in a world of risk (e.g., continuity) to actors who operate in a world where they face uncertainty (e.g., discontinuity). But how are we to identify this "universe of hypothetical options" or "periods of uncertainty?" CHA recommends elongating the causal chains and paying close attention to the near misses discussed in Chapter 7. Such an elongation in effect explores the prehistory of a discontinuity to describe what choice sets were available to actors and how structural changes widened the set for some actors while narrowing it for others. A significant change in the actors' choice sets, then, is tantamount to a widening of the "space of human agency," as Katznelson's calls it, and to a "period of uncertainty" in Blythe's language.

Explicating Generative Processes. Generative processes – also referred to as reactive sequences or originating causes – are an element of historical, non-linear causality (which was discussed in Chapter 7). They involve "chains of temporally order[ed] and causally connected events. ... each event in the sequence is both a reaction to antecedent events and cause of subsequent events" (Mahoney 2000, 526). Explicating such generative processes is closely related to the narratives that historians offer. The different labels signal CHA's effort to make these narratives more analytical by bringing them in closer dialogue with theories and by not overburdening them with too many historical minutiae. The chapter on macro-casual analysis already introduces the key tools for explicating generative processes: elongating causal chains by paying attention to events, and elongating outcomes by paying attention to near-miss events and reversals.

Events come with dates that are necessary for retracing the interactions between earlier and later events, and consequently for explicating the process that generates the discontinuity (Ermakoff 2019, 594–5). They are far less theory-laden than variables deduced from pre-existing theories, and thus permit the historical thinking necessary to *generate* inductive insights into explaining the patterns of discontinuity. As Capoccia and Ziblatt (2010, 934) point out, the analysis of events (or "episode analysis") "identifies the key political actors fighting over institutional change, highlights the terms of the debate and the full range of options that they perceived, reconstructs the extent of political and social support behind these options, and analyzes, as much as possible with the eyes of the contemporaries, the political interactions that led to the institutional outcome."

Readers may recall that near-miss events are a subtype of other near-miss outcomes. Near-miss events can be thought of as semi-discontinuities, because they fail to bring about full change but instigate enough change to break the continuity of a status quo. This liminal quality makes them interesting for two reasons. First, they protect against reading history backwards by connecting only to those events that form the causal chain producing a final outcome (Capoccia and Ziblatt 2010, 939; Ermakoff 2019, 594–5; Møller 2021). Near misses could have taken history down a different path. Paying attention to them guards against what Baruch Fischhoff (1982) called "creeping determinism": our propensity to connect only the dots that produced the outcome directly. Second, near-miss events involve defeats that often have causal effects, and thus are necessary for understanding generative processes. Near-miss events are interdependent insofar as an earlier failure shapes the outcome of subsequent events. Understanding for example the generative processes that led to the adoption of Obamacare benefits tremendously from analyzing all the unsuccessful healthcare reforms that preceded it.

Beware of Historical Tourism. CHA does not have a monopoly on historical explanations, and thus faces the challenge of differentiating its own from ahistorical and hence deficient alternatives. The ultimate step of explaining historical discontinuity involves looking for the ahistorical alternatives discussed in Chapter 2. This step does not directly contribute to developing sound historical explanations, but it guards against functionalist and evolutionary arguments that make history tidier and more linear than it actually is.

Using Annotation for Transparent Inquiry (ATI). Explaining historical discontinuities requires lengthy interpretations that run up against journals' strict word limits and, in all honesty, are of little interest all but to the most dogged readers. ATI offers the perfect solution: it has reinvented the old discursive footnotes, where these interpretive elaborations can be offloaded. ATI has been developed by the Institute for Qualitative and Multi-Method Research in conjunction with various foundations (Elman and Kapiszewski 2018). ATI citations can be thought of as the qualitative equivalent of the data appendices in quantitative analysis, since they link specific empirical claims made in articles to original source material, now stored online at the Qualitative Data Repository (QDR), and they elaborate on the judgments that support the inferences drawn from this source material.[1] And, since these footnotes and sources materials live entirely online, they do not count toward word limits.

Overall, these five suggestions for explaining historical discontinuities do not add up to a formalized causal inference strategy; but they are more analytical than the thick descriptive narratives favored by historians, make transparent the various inferential judgments, and thus increase readers' confidence in the conclusions reached.

9.3 Explaining Continuity: Spotting Reproduction Mechanisms

Continuities involve the absence of change, which needs to be explained just as much as change itself. Explanations of change and the notion of historical causality have rightly been criticized for assuming continuity rather than explaining it. The sociologist Arthur Stinchcombe points out that it is "considerably more difficult to explain why many types of organization retain structural peculiarities after their foundation without falling into tautological statements about 'tradition,' 'vested interests,' or 'folkways' not being changeable by formal regulation" (quoted in Pierson 2000b, 76n). And Katznelson (2003, 288) indicates that "moments of origins to transformations of state, economy or society should be joined to assessments of their aftermath and persistent effect. This reproduction of the consequences ... is a subject that clearly would benefit from the specification of how they shape human preferences that in turn ... sustain their outcome."

In recent years, CHA has drawn on the path dependency literature to address this concern. Originating in economics and sociology, this literature avoids the standard black box explanations of continuity that invoke naturalist, actorless analogies such as freezing or crystallization (Thelen 1999, 391). To avoid such empty analogies, the path dependency literature introduces theoretically grounded mechanisms – varyingly labeled "positive feedbacks," "self-reinforcing sequences," or "increasing returns" – in explaining the reproduction of continuities. While these terms are employed interchangeably, I use "increasing returns" because it is the one most widely adopted. Mahoney (2000, 508) defines an increasing return as a sequence that delivers "increasing benefits with its continued adoption, and thus over time, it becomes more and more difficult to transform the pattern or select previously available options,

---

[1] For an early example, see Kreuzer (2019).

even if these alternative options would have been more efficient." Broadly speaking, increasing returns reconceptualize continuity as a process of reproduction and identify a mechanism with causal properties that explain why things recur (and hence do not change). "Increasing returns" is frequently used as a generic umbrella term, which led the path dependency literature to specify five increasing return mechanisms: learning effects, coordination effects, adaptive expectations, socialization, and institutional engineering – all of which reproduce continuity.

- *Learning effects.* Learning is a key element in explaining why one-time originating causes produce irreversible effects and make causality asymmetrical. It involves a change in human consciousness, norms, and the acquisition of skills that endure well beyond the event that triggered the learning. Learning effects thus become locked in and make it less likely for actors to pursue courses of action that require norms or skills different from the ones that they recently acquired. The path dependency literature uses the QWERTY keyboard as its go-to example. Once people started using the standard QWERTY keyboard, the time invested in learning the requisite fingering technique made it less likely that they switch to the subsequently developed and allegedly more efficient Dvorak keyboard (Aminzade 1992, 464; Pierson 2000b, 76).
- *Coordination effects.* The multiplication of small first mover advantages often results from strategic interactions among actors that produce so-called coordination effects. Such interactions involve the strategizing, coalition building, or resource mobilization necessary to defend initial advantages. Russian oligarchs, for example, formed alliances with politicians to lock in the advantages they gained during the privatization process. Or coordination effects involve larger, more impersonal network effects where the benefits of a new institution or technology become conditional on the number of people who use it. Social media platforms gain in value the more people use them, because an increase in usage raises the entry barriers for potential competitors (Pierson 2000b, 76).
- *Adaptive expectations* are a by-product of learning effects. Learning can have coordinating effects for actors who are not immediately or directly involved in acquiring new norms or skills. Once such bystanders see in what direction the winds of change are blowing, they will adapt their expectations and become late adopters. Pierson (2000b, 76) likens adaptive expectations to some band-wagoning process: "if options that fail to win broad acceptance will have drawbacks later on, individuals may feel a need to pick the right horse." Civil rights activists acquired new organizational skills that helped them mobilize new recruits. Their early organizational success made it easier

for them to mobilize new recruits at a later stage because the civil rights movement's growth gave it some protection against the most brutal forms of repression. This organizational success also transformed public opinion about the injustices of the political exclusion of African Americans in the South, and this made the new civil rights legislation irreversible.

- *Socialization* is similar to adaptive expectations; but it is a slow-moving, impersonal, intergenerational demographic process when older generations reproduce their value systems through parenting and on a broader scale. Avidit Acharya, Matthew Blackwell, and Maya Sen (2016) point to the socialization of racial attitudes in the American South to explain their stunning continuity between the end of the Civil War and the present. They argue that the emancipation of black people at the end of the Civil War threatened white plantation owners in the "cotton belt" states, which possessed many slave-owning plantations. The emancipation of former slaves increased labor costs and posed an economic threat for plantation owners. This motivated them to encourage violence against blacks, anti-black sentiment, and the implementation of racial policies. The violence and racist sentiments passed on to generations of whites through schooling, cultural practices, and other socialization mechanisms. This explains the strong partisanship for Republicans, the lower support for affirmative action, and the stronger racial resentments of whites in these states.
- *Institutional engineering* involves changing the rules of the game so as to lock in a group's advantage permanently. It assumes that political change is a highly contested power-based undertaking with winners and losers. Winners will use their legislative majorities or coercive control to hardwire their advantages by changing the institutions (Mahoney 2000, 523). After the end of Reconstruction, southern segregationists undermined the gains of African Americans by restricting their civil and political rights. Augusto Pinochet tried to safeguard military or economic privileges of the Chilean military by protecting them from legislative reforms. He promulgated a new constitution to this effect.

Arguably, the path dependency literature contains more theoretical contributions than empirically applications; it consequently leaves a gap in how to analyze increasing returns. This gap can be filled by paying heed to four analytical steps that make the path dependency analysis empirically more tractable:

1) Specify early mover advantages.
2) Particularize increasing return mechanisms.
3) Look for intercurrences among different mechanisms.
4) Check for reversals.

I illustrate these four steps with the development of Germany's postwar party system. Its stability stands in stark contrast to the instability and polarization of the Weimar party system, and thus raises the question of how the refounding of the party system in 1945 – a moment of critical juncture and discontinuity – set in motion the increasing return mechanisms that contributed to its consolidation by the late 1950s and then reproduced this stability into the 1990s.

First Mover Advantages. Explaining increasing returns requires identifying the small initial advantage that ends up being reproduced. Some scholars refer to it as the first mover advantage in order to highlight that some actors acquire early advantages that are the result of contingent one-time factors that occurred during the pre-continuity period – the so-called critical juncture phase. Explaining such critical junctures is the task of historical explanations, and hence is analytically distinct. However, the analyst should consult those explanations so as to identify the initial small advantages that eventually got reinforced through mechanisms of increasing return. In the German example, this first mover advantage involved the Allies' licensing of new German parties before the first national election in 1949. The ability of licensed parties to operate in the open, recruit candidates, build their logistical infrastructure, and introduce themselves to voters in the initial state elections gave them a first mover advantage over parties that received only partial licenses or whose licenses were delayed altogether (Kreuzer 2009, 677–8).

Particularizing Increasing Return Mechanisms. Neither the party literature nor the historical accounts of the party system in postwar Germany talk directly about learning effects, adaptive expectations, or any of the other increasing return mechanisms. Nor do those mechanisms, primarily developed to explain technological change, fully capture the reproduction of every phenomenon studied. The analyst must therefore particularize the increasing return mechanisms to the context at hand. The broader theoretical literature or the thick descriptive historical accounts provide the necessary translation clues for this operation. In the German case, the link between institutional engineering and the actions of German politicians was easily established. In 1953 the incumbent parties tried to solidify their electoral advantages by requiring that parties meet a national 5 percent electoral threshold, which in prior elections parties had to pass only in one of the counties or estates (*Länder*) (Kreuzer 2009, 685). By contrast, the learning effects were less directly evident. In 1945, it was at first unclear what German politicians could have learned after having experienced seventy-five years of electoral competition, twenty of them under a system of proportional representation (PR). However, historical narratives contained repeated references to early mover parties deliberately recruiting politicians who had electoral experience at the local level or during the prior Weimar period. This pointed to a learning effect. Overall, then, increasing return mechanisms should be thought of as playing more of a heuristic role; they indicate possible empirical implications that have yet to be specified rather than making directly observable empirical predictions.

Look for Intercurrences. Path dependency accounts often are quite macro and attribute continuity to a single mechanism of increasing returns. This was particularly apparent in the earlier socialization example of how slavery in the 1860s accounts for political and racial attitudes in the twenty-first century. Such macro accounts risk being reductionist and deterministic. It is therefore important to look for multiple increasing return mechanisms and be attentive to their intercurrences with one another over time. These interaction effects can be detected only by paying close attention to them through time. In the German example, the institutional engineering and learning effects interacted not just with each other but with two other increasing returns mechanisms. Elite coordination played a key role as early mover parties used their electoral advantage to form electoral alliances with smaller parties, whose seats were threatened by the rise of the electoral threshold in 1945. They then undermined those smaller parties by encouraging their leaders to switch parties and promising them prominent cabinet posts. Non-linear causal processes usually are complex and thus require causally complex, multilayered explanations that pay close attention to the events that move the causal process forward.

Reversals. Continuities vary in their duration, given that not all increasing return mechanisms have the same reproduction or sustaining effects. They will consequently experience reversals, which can be thought of as the analytical counterpoint to the role that near misses play in discontinuities. Looking for reversals is important because they guard against overly deterministic accounts of continuity that devolve into historical tourism. In the German case there were no reversals, as the German party system reproduced itself well into the 1990s. At that point, the end of the Cold War, German reunification and globalization initiated economic and demographic trends that weakened the postwar mechanisms of increasing returns. Given that this case offers no reversal, I turn to another example.

Kurt Weyland's study of the reactionary backlash to the 1848 revolutions illustrates the benefits of paying attention to reversals and checking for the absence of increasing returns. Not all critical junctures produce increasing returns, as the initial loser can also learn and reverse the early mover advantages of the initial winners. The outbreak, in February 1848 in Paris, of the revolution that lead initially to the abdication of Louis Philippe I and establishment of the Second French Republic, triggered a riptide of similar revolutionary uprisings, which reached almost all other European countries by March. This revolutionary wave was surprising, because the political conditions in individual countries varied – and they also differed greatly from the ones that set off the revolution in Paris. This demonstration effect explains how the initial revolutionary outbreak in Paris served as a template for later cases, in which countries started revolutions even when local political conditions would have made such events unlikely (Weyland 2016, 216–18). These revolutions, however, did not produce increasing returns and were reversed as the incumbents managed to overturn many of the constitutional concessions that the revolutionaries had won. The counter-revolutions moved more slowly than the initial revolutions, stretching over a sixteen-month period by comparison with the one month of the initial revolutionary wave. The counter-revolutions were also staggered, which allowed reactionaries to learn from earlier repressions and adapt their strategies to their country's political circumstances (220). The counter-revolutionaries resisted copying the playbook that French reactionaries laid out in 1848 by repressing the short-lived Second Republic (221). Instead they proceeded very incrementally, building coalitions, exploiting splits in their opponents, and learning from what had worked in earlier repressions (222–4). Paying attention to such reversals is interesting because they provide a null finding for the increasing returns and raise the question of what makes discontinuities temporary when increasing returns do not materialize.

Overall, it is important to resist the temptation to use path dependency to lend theoretical credence to vague claims that history matters and that the past shapes the present. It is also important to differentiate path-dependent from so-called persistence arguments, which have gained currency among economists (see Cirone and Pepinsky 2021). Both kinds of argument are interested in how historical events of long ago produce long-term causal effects. They differ, however, in what they explain. Path dependency analyzes continuities, and thus focuses on the lack of historical transformations. Persistence, on the other hand, studies cross-sectional variations by identifying long, complex causal chains that extend over centuries. The labeling is confusing here, because path dependency focuses on the persistence (i.e., continuity) of an empirical outcome, while persistence arguments focus on the persistence of long-ago causal effects to explain distal cross-sectional variations at some future point in time. Persistence arguments thus elongate causal chains to offer more complex explanations; but they have no interest in explaining historical change, and therefore do not qualify as historical explanations, as defined at the outset of this chapter.

9.4 PR Example

Both Nina Barzachka and Amel Ahmed use Belgium as a case study for their historical explanations. They carefully specify the discontinuity, focus on events to elucidate the generative process, and guard against determinism by providing a detailed inventory of near misses. They pay less attention to the durability of PR, and thus provide fewer insights into the reproduction process that might explain its continuity.

Boix stipulates that the adoption of PR constitutes a discontinuity, but he does so without demonstrating historically the rupture that this event is alleged to mark. Ahmed (2013; 2014) fills this gap by exploring the prehistory of Belgium's PR adoption. She goes back to the 1860s to demonstrate the ineffectiveness of the efforts of Belgian Conservatives and Liberals to weaken the left threat by incorporating workers through educational programs, by forming Catholic labor unions, by including workers on liberal electoral lists, or by making half-hearted attempts to expand the male franchise. By the late 1880s, the ineffectiveness of these incorporation strategies lead to a political crisis in which franchise expansion and PR adoption became the only remaining options.

Ahmed's retrospective demonstrates how the ineffectiveness, in the 1880s, of earlier incorporation strategies turned the 1890s into a critical juncture. She highlights the underlying structural shift in political strength from the right to the left, a shift that significantly narrowed the right's choice set to expanding the franchise and experimenting with electoral system reform in order to protect itself against the left's expanding electoral threat (Ahmed 2013, 167–70). This background information elucidates the decreasing returns or viability of antidemocratic strategies that the right used to reproduce the status quo, and the growing pressure to contain the left threat by making actual concessions and drawing on new electoral technologies with a less antidemocratic pedigree, such as PR. It provides the forthcoming analysis with microfoundations, in the sense of demonstrating how the PR adoption marked a liminal moment: it was both the end point of a lengthy historical process and the beginning of a new stage in Belgium's democratization.

Ahmed's and Barzachka's analyses also dig deeper to explicate the generative process that is missing in Boix. They both focus on eleven attempts at electoral reform that lead to the final adoption of PR in December 1899. These events include early PR parliamentary discussion in the 1870s, a PR bill in 1888 that never made it out of committee, and various hybrid proposals defeated after the franchise expansion in 1893. Ahmed and Barzachka do not treat these near-miss events as near misses, to increase the number of their observations, but instead analyze them as interdependent events that provide crucial clues for identifying learning as the key generative mechanism. Ahmed points out that PR and single-member district (SMD) were both equally valid alternatives that Conservatives and Liberals entertained, because the status quo block vote system involved a complicated mixture of SMD and large multimember districts. This learning process involved the following elements. First, Conservatives and Liberals wanted to test the effectiveness of the mandatory and plural voting provisions that they attached to the 1893 franchise expansion. They expected that both these mechanisms would blunt the electoral inroads of the left (Ahmed 2013, 172–3). It was only after they deemed those electoral safeguards to be insufficient that they considered changing the electoral system. Second, Belgium was the first country to adopt PR at the national level and thus had to figure out how this new electoral technology would work. Barzachka points out that Conservatives, whose seat share increased after the franchise expansions, began to experiment with what she aptly called tactical seat losses, that is, with how to maximize the overall seat share of the right without appearing to be so overtly partisan in the institutional engineering as to undermine the threat to the regime that was coming from the left and from public opinion, which demanded genuine democracy. The six failed electoral reform bills between 1893 and December 1899 all served to help Conservatives figure out what the optional seat loss strategy would be (Barzachka 2014, 215–20).

What is the value added of such involved analytical narratives and how do they elucidate the generative process? This question merits consideration, given that the analytical narratives confirm Boix's and Rokkans' more expansive left threat thesis. Understanding the generative processes offers three concrete benefits. First, it increases the internal validity of the left threat thesis and expands its empirical footprint. Second, it shows that the adoption of PR was intertwined with other forms of institutional engineering, which incumbents used to protect themselves against the left. It thus suggests that viewing PR adoption strictly in terms of electoral competition and as a rupture might be inadequate; and it indicates instead a more bounded form of change, in which PR was layered on top of other institutional mechanisms. Third, it draws attention to the problem of masking where different generative processes might produce the same outcome (Beach 2020, 173). The generative process, just like the left threat thesis, stipulates a clear sequence: founding of socialists → growing organizational strength of socialists → franchise expansion → growing electoral strength of left → PR adoption. Ahmed's and Barzachka's case studies confirm this sequence, laid out as it is by the left threat thesis. But their analysis could have identified a different sequence, where the franchise expansion predates the founding of Socialist parties, as it did in many countries; or the franchise expansion and the PR adoption could have occurred at the same point in time.

None of the contributors to the PR literature pays close attention to the surprising continuity of PR systems once they were adopted. Apart from France and Greece, no other first-wave countries changed their electoral systems, which might explain why this topic received little scholarly attention. However, the broader literature provides a few clues for exploring possible increasing returns mechanisms. Several scholars have pointed out that PR systems are more permissive and produce multi-party systems that make it highly unlikely that smaller parties that won seats under a PR system would support its abolition (J. Colomer 2005). PR systems, with their lists and larger electoral districts, nationalize and centralize parties' decision-making structures, giving party leaders more leverage over deputies. Party leaders are thus unlikely to give up this control and revert to a more decentralized first-past-the-post system (Kreuzer 2001, 53–69; Schröder and Manow 2014).

Exercises

Background. Historical explanations and process tracing do not follow a formalized causal inference strategy that scholars identify with readily available terminology. Instead they are embedded in narrative modes of explaining and involve complex bricolage. The goal of the exercises in this and the next chapter is therefore to engage in a sort of methodological anthropology by explicating the elements of historical explanation and process tracing discussed. These chapters follow an apprenticeship model of teaching, in which you learn how to do something by replicating how it has been done it before by somebody else. The rather detailed questions serve to guide in this replication process.

9.1. Demographers employ "demographic" or "generational" explanations. In his opening chapter, Robert Duffy (2021, 1–18) explicates the three mechanisms that such explanations use: life cycle, period, and generational effects. To what sort of notions of history do these three mechanisms correspond? How explicit are they in the type of reproduction they imply? (Duffy only hints at them, so try to describe them more fully.) How do demographic explanations differ from historical explanations? How useful are they in dealing with non-demographic phenomena such as institutional or economic changes? How do they differ from the intercurrence patterns, which were developed to explain mostly institutional changes, as discussed in Chapter 5?

9.2. Gladwell's argument about honor killings draws on the work of four psychologists: Dov Cohen, Joseph Vandello, Sylvia Puente, and Adrian Rantella (1999). Read their original analysis on which Gladwell draws (just focus on pages 57–60). What sort of replication mechanisms does it specify? Do those more explicit mechanisms increase your confidence in Gladwell's analysis? If so, how? Do the mechanisms in Cohen et al. overlap or differ from the reproduction mechanisms discussed in the Chapter 9? How? Gladwell's cultural legacy – what is called persistence arguments – shares some features (but not all) with path-dependent arguments. What are the similarities and differences between these types of arguments? What generates reproduction or increasing returns in Gladwell's and in Cohen et al.'s argument that is different from path-dependent arguments?

9.3. Margaret Anderson provides a thick description of imperial Germany's electioneering practices. How could this richly contextualized narrative be converted into a more mechanistic, CHA-like historical explanation, with more explicit generative mechanisms that changed Germany's political culture? Recall that Anderson describes Germany's political culture in the 1860s and 1870s as fluid and the new franchise as a "leap in the dark." She explores the democratization of this political culture as an unintended consequence of the franchise expansion. It was unintended because the German chancellor, Otto von Bismarck, intended the franchise to allow incumbent Conservatives to translate their existing economic power and cultural deference into political power, and thus to contain the rising political threat posed by Liberals. Extract from her narratives the theor-etically more grounded generative mechanisms that characterize what CHA calls historical explanations. What mechanisms can you extract that are generalizable beyond the German case? How could Dankwart Rustow's (1970) influential article on democratization help you translate Anderson's narrative into generative mechanisms? Does Rustow read history forward, like Anderson, or backward, like Ziblatt (1970)? How helpful are Rustow's stages in extracting generative mechanisms from Anderson's narrative? In what ways do those stages freeze history, and therefore make the analysis more generalizable?

10 Causal Process Tracing
Making Testing Symmetrical

> Those who forget historiography are doomed to republish it.
>
> (Paul Macdonald 2009, 45)

Causal process tracing has established itself as the principal alternative to variance-based causal inference. It goes back to Stephen Van Evera (1997), Alexander George and Andy Bennett (2004), David Collier and Henry Brady (2004), and other scholars who pushed back against the claim that qualitative and quantitative methodologies share a single, experimental-based logic of causal inference (Goldthorpe 1991; King, Keohane, and Verba 1994). Many of these scholars engaged in qualitative, historically informed research themselves, underscoring their affinity with comparative historical analysis (CHA). They tried to escape what Pierson called short–short, explanations, which treat outcomes as single snapshots and assume causal effects to be simultaneous, additive, immediate, symmetrical, or, in short, linear. The more recent Bayesian-inspired version of process tracing explicates more fully the role that CHA assigns to abduction and research cycles to validate causal inferences (Beach and Pedersen 2013; Bennett 2014; Fairfield and Charman 2019; Kreuzer 2016; Zaks 2021).

Process tracing and CHA thus share the belief, brilliantly captured in MacDonald's epigram, that causal inferences must be evaluated not just against a singular, context-independent statistical metric, but against the broader unfolding foreknowledge. More specifically, causal inferences are conditional upon the *pre-testing* articulation of testworthy hypotheses, the construction of strong tests during the *actual testing stage*, and the juxtaposition of new test results, at the *post-testing stage*, against prior ones. All this constitutes a more drawn out, heterodox approach to validating causal inferences than standard variance-based analysis (VBA). The present chapter elaborates on these three stages of process tracing. First, it briefly revisits the discussion in Chapter 7 on macro-causal analysis and on the role that theorizing plays in leveraging new inductive insights, particularly ones related to the non-linear effects of physical time, in order to expand the empirical footprint of theories, make their predictions more diverse, and ultimately generate more testworthy hypotheses. Second, the chapter pivots from a pre-testing focus on generating hypotheses to pairing those hypotheses at the testing stage so as to produce so-called strong tests. Process tracing's emphasis on test construction is part of a larger effort to address p-hacking, specification searching, or other forms of ad hoc hypothesis testing, that is, testing that is weak because it does not systematically engage with rival hypotheses (Bennett and Checkel 2014, 26–9; Zaks 2021, 9–11). Finally, the chapter redirects our attention to the post-testing stage: it discusses how process tracing, particularly in the Bayesian version, brings new test results in dialogue with prior ones, thereby updating our confidence in causal inferences with the help of these new tests. It discusses more fully the link between this updating and CHA's historiographical sensibilities, which stress careful reading, emphasize abduction, and embrace a more iterative understanding of causal inference. In short, process tracing and CHA share the conviction that causal inferences have a history and that leveraging this history is crucial for validating causal inferences. They also share the belief that the robustness of causal inferences is the triple result of the quality of the hypotheses generated *before* the test stage, of how those hypotheses are configured *at* the testing stage, and of how the results hold up *after* testing, when compared to earlier results. To keep the length of this chapter manageable, I forgo the concluding illustration of process tracing with the PR literature. I employ instead the literature on populism, introduced in Chapter 1, and use it as an example throughout the chapter.

10.1 Theorizing: Expanding and Diversifying Theories *before* Testing Them

Theorizing is the last step in the longer pre-testing, exploratory stage of a research cycle that we discussed in earlier chapters. Its central objective is to generate hypotheses that are testworthy in the subsequent, confirmatory stage. Process tracing specifies several benchmarks for evaluating the testworthiness of a hypothesis. It links improving causal inferences to increasing the number *and* diversity of empirical implications that a theory has. Both these attributes enhance causal inferencing because they make a theory more falsifiable, that is, they make it more difficult to confirm. It is important to underscore that process tracing shares this insight with VBA. King, Keohane and Verba (1994, 10), three VBA champions, point out that the goal of testing is to "generate as many observable implications as possible which will allow more tests of the theory, with more data and greater variety of data." Checkel and Bennett (2014, 27) further underscore the importance of data variety. They point out that establishing whether an animal is a duck requires more than just checking its proverbial walk; "also considering how it flies, sounds, and looks" will go into it. Theorizing provides the tools for looking beyond the theory, and looking for additional and more diverse empirical implications to test. It improves causal inferences by recognizing that confidence in test results is a function of not just the amount of supporting evidence found but also how qualitatively different those pieces were (Stinchcombe 1968, 19–20). Process tracing contends that confirming a theory with ten pieces of evidence for ten different and substantially distinct implications generates more confidence in the test results than finding one hundred identical pieces of evidence for a single implication.

There is a second, less often acknowledged way in which expanding the empirical footprint of theories improves causal inferences. As discussed in earlier chapters, the robustness of causal inferences is frequently linked to addressing the confounding effects of physical time as well as other confounders. (Bennett and Checkel 2014, 22–3). VBA addresses such confounders after it generates test results by assessing their external validity. Theorizing attends to those confounders by incorporating them into the theory itself, and thus improving its external validity *prior* to testing. Expanding the empirical footprint of theories invariably reduces confounders, enhances external validity, and increases confidence in test results *in addition to* making the theory more falsifiable. Confidence in causal inferences thus depends not just on the techniques used for testing but also on the prior ability of theorizing to make the theory as falsifiable and realistic as possible. It is this theorizing that ultimately translates results into answers.

Chapter 7 already discussed how elongating causal chains and outcomes serves to generate new inductive insights as well as to address the confounding effects of physical time. Typically, these two strategies involve empirically analyzing actual cases in order to identify new or more diverse empirical implications. Sometimes, however, theorizing expands the empirical footprint of theories simply through a more careful reading of existing theories, and thus it obviates the need for empirical research. Existing theories frequently are more comprehensive than the actual statistical models used to test them; thus they have latent implications that become detectable through careful reading. Furthermore, scholars frequently exaggerate the differences between theories by accentuating the novelty of their own theory and dismissing the implications of competing explanations. They engage in what could be called *theory swapping*. This premature dismissal of competing theories overlooks the fact that the implications of another theory, despite a scholar's contrary claims, can be perfectly compatible with that scholar's own theory. So, before prematurely dismissing theories, it is worth exploring possible synergies among them. But this requires a close and empathetic reading – a practice that is less and less frequently employed (Gaikwad and Herrera forthcoming; Lustick 1996; Trachtenberg 2015).

Generating testworthy hypotheses concludes the pre-testing phase of making causal inferences and sets the stage for pairing them so as to construct the strongest possible tests.

10.2 Test Strength: Validating Causal Inferences *during* Testing

If the testworthiness of a hypothesis improves when that hypothesis is made to include more numerous and more diverse predictions, then the inferential strength of the hypothesis in question is further strengthened by its being pitted against another, equally testworthy hypothesis. Test construction concerns itself with the pairing of hypotheses. Process tracing uses test construction to avoid testing hypotheses that have been paired in an ad hoc manner: it maximizes the inferential leverage of every piece of observed evidence by pairing the hypotheses mindfully. Test construction highlights the simple but powerful insight that evidence does not just confirm and disconfirm a single theory but also has the potential to discriminate *among* rival theories. Test construction leverages this discriminatory capacity of evidence, or what it also is called the probative value of evidence (Beach and Pedersen 2013, 87, 129–30; Bennett and Checkel 2014, 16–18). Peter Hall (2008, 310) remarked that "research in social science is most likely to advance when it focuses on a three-cornered fight among a theory, a rival theory and a set of empirical observations." Process tracing is not alone in recognizing that the inferential leveraging of evidence increases to the extent that ad hoc hypothesis testing is minimized (Freese and Rokeach 1979; Leamer 1983; J. P. Simmons, Nelson, and Simonsohn 2011). Christopher Achen (2002, 423), for example, warned that "theoretical models are too often long lists of independent variables from psychology, sociology, or just causal empiricism tossed helter-skelter into canned linear regression packages."

But process tracing has developed criteria – formulated by two CHA scholars, Steven Van Evera (1997, 30–5) and Arthur Stinchcombe (1968, 15–23) – that help directly with the construction of strong tests. These criteria link the strength of a given test to the degree to which the predictions of each theory in a pair are *unique* rather than overlapping and *specific* rather than generic.

- *Uniqueness.* Unique predictions strengthen the inferential leverage of observed pieces of evidence because such pieces can confirm a theory while simultaneously disconfirming its competitor. Unique tests sort empirical implications into mutually exclusive pieces of *supporting evidence*, predicted by the anchor theory, and *counterevidence*, predicted by the rival theory.[1] Supporting evidence and counterevidence are distinct, and thus have the ability of *both* confirming or disconfirming the theory that hypothesizes them *and* discriminating between the two rival theories. Pieces of evidence that overlap between two theories do not have this discriminating potential because they confirm or reject *both* theories. They consequently do not discriminate between the two theories and fail to advance our understanding to the same degree as a unique piece of evidence would (Beach and Pedersen 2013, 102; Stinchcombe 1968, 20–2).

- *Specificity.* Causal inferences are conditional on the granularity or specificity with which a theory details its implications. Specificity is defined by several attributes. We already discussed how theorizing expands and diversifies the empirical footprint of an explanation. It does so by elongating the causal chain and the outcomes. Some theories also make predictions that are very concrete, experience-near, and mindful of temporal dynamics and boundary conditions, and thus have what Heuer (1999, 45–6) called a high diagnosticity. Other theories are more general, experience-distant, ontologically less differentiated, and thus less specific. Specific theories increase confidence in causal inferences because they reduce measurement errors and make it easier to match empirical observations with theoretical predictions (Kreuzer 2019, 129). Specificity can be thought of as the social science equivalent of the legal distinctions between hearsay and circumstantial, eyewitness, and forensic evidence. Law assigns different weights to these kinds of evidence; some of them are not even admitted into court proceedings. There are no ex-ante specificity criteria, as the specificity will always be relative to the available theoretical choices. But specificity is a function of the unit of analysis chosen (supranational, national, subnational, individual), of temporal proximity (closeness to the event), of temporal granularity (daily, monthly, annually), of chronological proximity (attention to historical context), and of the theory's empirical footprint.[2] Specificity ultimately relates to how much a theory freezes history and geography.

---

[1] Stanley Lieberson (1985, 15–40) was, arguably, the first to show the importance of uniqueness, even though he made it in the context of statistical inferences. He pointed out that statistical control variables needed to be exogenous to provide genuine controls. He argued that control variables control – that is, provide quasi-experimental equivalence of randomization – only if they are genuinely exogenous, in other words unique. Control variables lose this effect insofar as they are causally linked to the test variables, and thus less unique. In this way Lieberson pointed to an issue that recently resurfaced with respect to whether the as-if randomization attributed to natural experiments is indeed random (see Kocher and Monteiro 2016).

[2] Process tracers that follow in a more formal Bayesian logic use certainty of prediction as their second criteria, rather than specificity. The certainty refers to how unequivocal a particular prediction is and hence what the implications are for updating confidence in a theory when predicted evidence is absent (Beach and Pedersen 2013, 100–101; Bennett 2014, 279–80; Evera

Table 10.1 Varieties of test strength

		Uniqueness	
		Low (Implications made by both anchor and alternative theories overlap)	**High** (Implications made just by the test or by the alternative theory do not overlap)
	Low (Implications are distal and general)	**I. Straw in the Wind →** Inferential leverage is *inconsequential.* Evidence supports both tests, and in a circumstantial manner.	**III. Smoking Gun →** Inferential leverage is *strong.* Permits differentiation between theories, but only with circumstantial evidence.
Specificity	**High** (Implications are proximate and granular)	**II. Hoop Test →** Inferential leverage is *suggestive.* Still does not allow discrimination among theories but confirmation is now stronger because the supporting evidence is more specific.	**IV. Doubly Decisive →** Inferential leverage is *decisive.* Allows discrimination among theories with strong evidence.

Process tracing differentiates the inferential leverage in terms of its specificity (i.e., how experience-near, how unfrozen) and its uniqueness (i.e., overlap of empirical implications of anchor and alternative hypotheses). These two attributes of evidence translate into four types of tests that vary in the confidence they generate in test results, "straw in the wind" being lowest and "doubly decisive" being strongest.

These two dimensions of test construction translate into four ideal types of tests (which are shown in Table 10.1) and determine the inferential leverage that individual pieces of evidence will possess. The labels were first coined by Van Evera and have been gaining currency ever since. They articulate a rudimentary, ordinal, and strictly judgment-based system of differentiation between test constructions on the basis of their strength. The strength itself is the sum of the uniqueness and specificity of all the implications of theories.

1997, 31) I prefer following Heuer and more generally historians who emphasize the specificity of evidence as an alternative criterion for assessing causal inferences. It is easier to assess than certainty and more attentive to the temporal qualities involved in doing CHA.

Theories will invariably have overlapping and general implications, and thus the question becomes how unique and how specific the predictions are, on average, across a theory. Parenthetically, I should point out that aggregating the uniqueness of individual implications stipulated by a theory to assess that theory's overall uniqueness creates semantic ambiguities. Uniqueness implies a categorical, either–or distinction and should not be used for continuous, more-or-less distinctions. Given that uniqueness has been used to make continuous distinctions of degree, I will follow this practice and ignore the semantic ambiguities it creates. It is important to underscore that test strength should not be confused with the robustness of the actual test results. The test strength provides an *indirect* benchmark that does not take into account the ultimate test results, which are based on the amount of evidence found. The test strength thus provides a benchmark for the amount of confidence related to an actual test result. It becomes an element in Bayesian analysis for deciding how much we should update our confidence in causal inferences, given the test results available. The ultimate confidence in causal inferences is therefore the combined effect of how much evidence was found and the test strength itself. In other words, a strong test could still produce a null finding if no evidence turns up, but that would be a very authoritative null finding.

I elaborate on these four tests through stylized hypotheses borrowed from Morone's account of the waves of US populism, discussed in Chapter 1, and I pair them with other explanations.

Straw in the wind tests involve two conjectures that make a small number of overlapping predictions. Finding some preliminary circumstantial evidence lends credibility to both and warrants their further analysis. The evidence here is *inconsequential* because it permits no inferences about the validity of one theory over another. Straw in the wind tests could be the equivalent of an initial probe, feasibility study, or stage one trial. Finding supporting evidence keeps multiple theories in contention for further, more rigorous testing. The absence of evidence for a theory, in turn, does not definitively disprove it but casts doubt on the value of its continued testing.

Let me illustrate a straw in the wind test with two stylized hypotheses – the trade thesis and the technology thesis – that are used to explain the rise of contemporary US populism (see Figure 10.1). I assume that these hypotheses and subsequent ones are familiar enough to readers not to require elaborating on them beyond the arrow diagram.

The pairing of these two theses produces a weak straw in the wind test. The test is weak for three reasons. Both theses advance journalist-like conjectures that make a small number of broad, hence non-specific, predictions. These predictions are economic on both sides; thus diversity is reduced. Furthermore, four of those five predictions overlap, which reduces uniqueness.

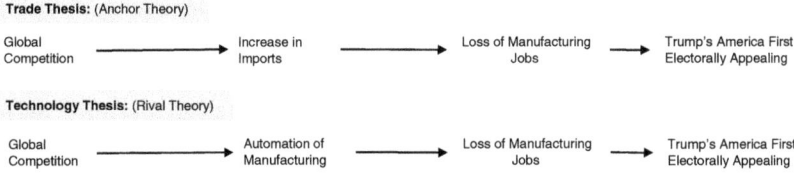

Figure 10.1 Straw in the wind test
This test is weak because it makes only eight general predictions, all of which are economic, and only two are unique.

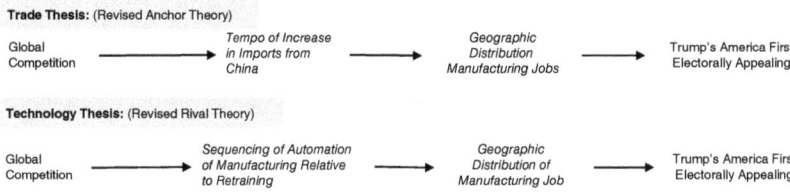

Figure 10.2 Hoop test
This test increases the strength of the straw in the wind test by adding tempo, geography, and sequencing to make the predictions more specific. Updated predictions are shown in italics. The number, diversity, and uniqueness of predictions remain unchanged.

This pairing produces a weak test because not only are both theories easy to confirm but also a part of the evidence will confirm them simultaneously. The inferential leverage of such a test is thus predominantly *inconsequential*.

Hoop tests are about testing a conjecture against a more developed theory, which makes similar predictions but increases their number and diversity, employs more refined measures, pays more attention to elements of physical time, or is more explicit about historical boundary conditions. The evidence found in a hoop test becomes *suggestive* because finding supporting evidence for such a theory increases our confidence somewhat, but the confidence is still limited by our not having tested the anchor theory against a genuine and unique rival theory that makes quite different predictions. Here again, the failure to find evidence weakens a theory but does not eliminate it, given that there is no viable alternative explanation. Hoop tests often involve testing a more developed theory against its predecessor, employing either better data or more refined measurements.

The pairing of the slightly revised trade thesis and technology thesis moderately increases the test's strength by making more specific predictions (see Figure 10.2). Predictions in italics represent updated and more specific predictions. This increases confidence in the results, as more precise measures are used, geographic variations are acknowledged (e.g., the geographic variation of job losses, or in Chinese versus non-Chinese imports), and two elements of physical time are incorporated: tempo (change in the rate of imports) and sequencing (automation versus job retraining). This hoop test therefore increases the test's strength by unfreezing geography and physical time. The number and diversity of predictions remain the same as in the straw in the wind test, and thus the hoop test forgoes two additional opportunities to becoming more specific.

Smoking gun tests involve more "unique" but less specific predictions than hoop tests. The inferential leverage can now be rated as *strong* rather than just suggestive, because evidence can differentiate one theory from another. This head-to-head testing increases confidence in causal inferences more than it increases the specificity of the predictions of two very similar theories; this is because finding or not finding supporting evidence has the dual inferential effect of confirming or disconfirming one theory while discriminating against the other theory. The smoking gun test may at first appear related to the gladiatorial style of hypothesis testing, against which I warned earlier. Such tests are different in that they resist the practice of their gladiatorial counterpart, namely dismissing an *entire* rival theory because there is no evidence for one *single* prediction. A genuinely strong test makes such a dismissal conditional on evaluating *all* the predictions of the rival theory and contrasting them, directly and fairly, with those of the author's theory. In the unlikely scenario of failing to find evidence for both theories, this would suggest having to go back to the drawing board and producing altogether new theories.

The cultural thesis introduced in Figure 10.3 is a loose adaptation of James Morone's (2020) cultural explanation of populism discussed in Chapter 1. The three key cultural factors here are racial prejudice, deeper biological arguments about white superiority that create what Isabel Wilkerson described as a de facto caste system, and immigration. These three factors interact with the post-civil rights political and economic advances of African Americans, a phenomenon that on the one hand accelerated status or racial anxiety in the white population and on the other helped elect Obama. Pairing this new cultural explanation with the updated trade thesis strengthens the testing in three ways. First, it increases the number of predictions from eight in the hoop tests to eleven, thus expanding the empirical footprint of the test. Second, it dramatically enhances the uniqueness of the test by eliminating any overlapping predictions. Third, it makes the predictions more diverse, as it pits a cultural against an economic explanation. The strong inferential

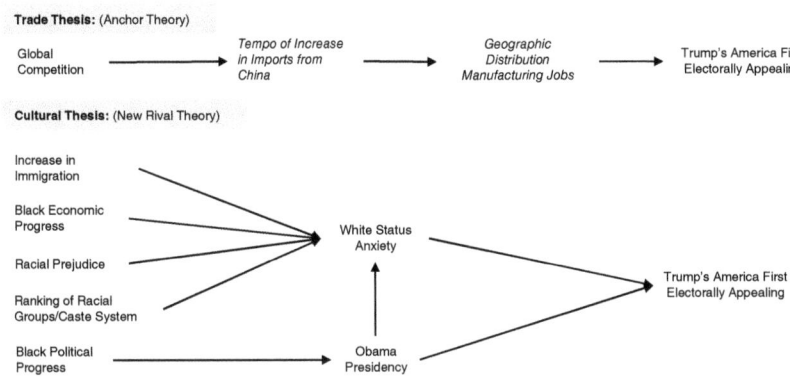

Figure 10.3 Smoking gun test
This test is stronger than the hoop test because it reuses the more specific version of the trade thesis and adds seven new, non-economic predictions that significantly increase its uniqueness. But the new cultural implications remain broad and non-specific.

leverage of the evidence in such a test is held back only by the still broad and non-specific predictions of the cultural theory.

Doubly decisive tests benefit from having both uniqueness and specificity and make the inferential leverage of the evidence *decisive*. They consequently combine the strength of the hoop test with the strength of the smoking gun test. We have so far defined uniqueness as a set of predictions that do not overlap. Another way to think about uniqueness is in terms of control variables that render doubly decisive tests super-decisive. Such controls make in effect the negative counter-prediction that a particular variable will produce a null finding. These counter-predictions become particularly powerful when accompanied by theoretical arguments that the empirical implications of another theory do *not* matter. Identifying control variables can be seen as extending the empirical footprint of a theory by stipulating the absence of pieces of evidence. The inferential leverage of such predictions is particularly strong: more than involving absence of overlap, it provides a theoretically grounded rationale as to why this piece of evidence should not be present.

This doubly decisive test keeps the updated trade thesis and updates the cultural theory by making four of its original predictions more specific (see Figure 10.4). It also elongates its outcomes by considering not just Trump's 2016 presidential victory but also six earlier near misses – unsuccessful populist presidential contenders: Barry Goldwater in 1964, George Wallace in 1968 and 1972, and Pat Buchanan in 1992, 1994, and 2000. All

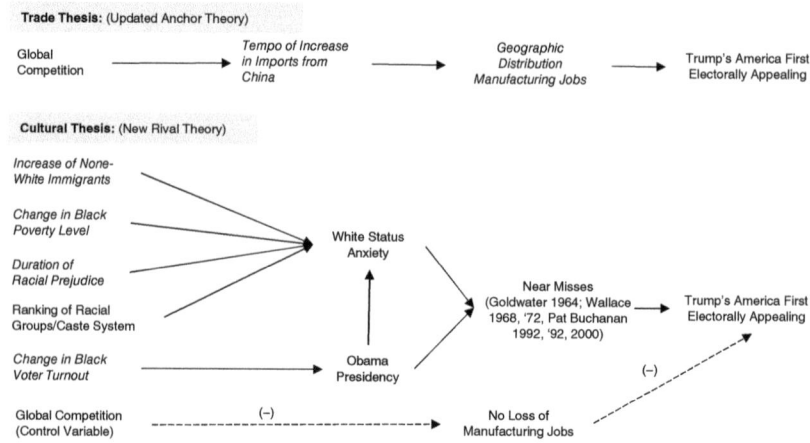

Figure 10.4 Doubly decisive test
This test is very strong because it makes numerous, diverse, specific, and unique predictions. It also elongates the outcome by considering near misses of earlier populist candidacies.

these were failed presidential bids. The cultural theory now resembles more closely Morone's original explanation about the waves of populism in the United States. The cultural thesis further doubles down on its argument by stipulating that global competition played no role in Trump's 2016 victory. It thus challenges the trade thesis not only by making non-economic, cultural predictions, but also by actively claiming that trade was irrelevant. In effect it controls for trade and stipulates a null finding.

These four tests underscore that not all tests are created equal. The process tracing literature is still working out how to translate test strength in some widely accepted robustness metric (Bennett, Charman, and Fairfield 2021; Zaks 2021). And discussions on test strength remain largely confined to methodologists; they have not been widely applied yet to empirical research. (For a rare exception, see Tannenwald 2005.) What, then, is the practical utility of test strength for actual empirical research? Most immediately, it draws attention to the shortcomings of ad hoc testing and offers guidance for constructing tests that leverage the probative value of evidence more effectively. More broadly, the test strength typology clarifies how process tracing mirrors the iterative research logic of CHA, which is reflected in its embrace of abduction and research cycles and informed by a tacit Bayesian or historiographical logic of causal inference. Process tracing follows a similar updating logic, which we already encountered in description. Part II discussed how describing, redescribing, and even undescribing update research questions and concepts. Analogously, process tracing tests, retests (by developing stronger tests), and untests causal propositions (by withholding unconfirmed hypotheses). As the Part III shows, the test strength can be thought of not just as the static typology just presented, but also as a developmental typology that tracks the updating of available foreknowledge.

10.3 Updating: Validating Causal Inferences *after* Testing

Bayesian process tracing makes causal inferences conditional not just on the testworthiness of the hypotheses, the test strength, and the evidence unearthed but also on the validity of test results over time. It recognizes that test results have an inter-temporal – I am almost tempted to say historical – dimension. Or, as Mark Twain would have put it, were he a methodologist, the past rarely replicates, but it updates. The test strength makes this inter-temporal element of causal inferences more transparent and permits tracking such inferences across multiple research cycles. I introduce the *theory ledger* as a new tool for following over time the elements of test strength discussed earlier: frequency (how many), specificity (at what unit of analysis, how experience-near, what granularity of context, how much unfreezing of causal chains and outcomes), and uniqueness (overlap of predictions, number of control variables).[3] These test strength criteria can be thought off as substitutes for the testing criteria that inform VBA: case selection, sample size, randomization, null hypotheses, type of causal identification strategy. Parenthetically, I should point out that this updating process not only imitates a Bayesian logic of causal inference but also informs the rationale of doing historiographies and conducting meta-analysis – two activities also marked by close and empathetic engagement with prior work. Let me illustrate how the theory ledger tracks the updating of causal inferences before reflecting more broadly on its contributions to CHA.

The theory ledger is built on three simple assumptions.

First, it recognizes that a theory is too unwieldy a unit of analysis to track changes in test strength. It therefore unbundles theories into their individual empirical implications and follows these individually, both across time and across other theories. Second, theoretical implications can be classified according to the theoretical frames discussed in Chapter 7 – according to environmental, structural, and eventful factors, as well as according to physical

---

[3] These criteria are not exhaustive. The updating could also include the number of times an empirical implication has been confirmed or what replication strategy has been employed.

time and historical time. These theoretical frames help compare the diversity of empirical implications and foreground their temporal characteristics. Third, the theory ledger reflects a Bayesian process tracing and the CHA historiographical conviction that confidence in causal inferences is ultimately the result of a knowledge production that extends through time and thus requires attention to the history of test results. It therefore lists theories and their implications chronologically, to track how theories update their implications over time. It compares those implications in terms of the test strength criteria discussed earlier, to benchmark the strength of the various tests.

Table 10.2 presents a theory ledger that tracks the updating process of the trade, technology, and cultural thesis used earlier to illustrate the difference between various test strengths. It can be thought of as a more formalized replication of the prior discussion of test strength. Before expanding on how the three hypotheses illustrate the logic of the theory ledger, let me first explain its mechanics.

- *Rows.* The rows provide the timeline for arranging theories and comparing them across time. It in effect converts the test typology, in which each test is independent, into an iterative and cumulative research process that imitates short-term abductive updating and long-term updating across research cycles. The anchor theory typically goes in the first row because it provides the baseline against which subsequent theories are compared. There are no a priori criteria for selecting the anchor theory. It can be the very first theory in a literature, the most prominent one, or the theory most favored by the scholar. The key point is that this theory anchors the author's particular analysis and becomes the benchmark for comparing subsequent theories. I should emphasize that there are no limits to the number of theories to be compared. This is a highly stylized theory ledger, which tracks only three theories and then distributes them into four research cycles that correspond to different test strengths. It thus employs a de facto periodization scheme to track the research history on this topic. The theory ledger could easily forgo such a periodization and track every single contribution to a literature.
- *Columns.* Each column corresponds to an empirical implication contained in a given theory, and thus unbundles the theory in its constituent parts in order to compare them more easily. Individual columns are then bundled into environmental, structural, and eventful theoretical frames outlined in Chapter 7, or according to physical and historical time. The theoretical frame suggested by heading levels is too broad to capture the actual empirical implications. Those implications are added in bold. If one frame contains more than one implication, scholars simply add additional columns. The column categories make it possible to assess the diversity of empirical implications of a theory. They also help identify whether a single frame dominated,

Table 10.2 Theory ledger

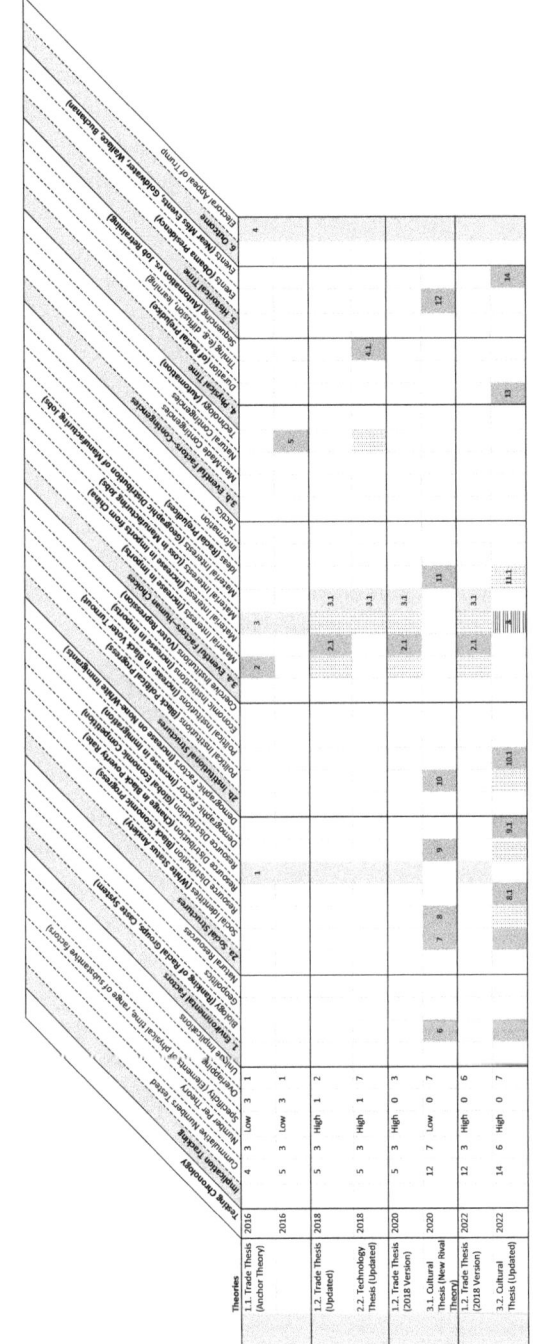

The ledger tracks the theoretical updating over time, here represented by four research cycles. Rows track theories across time and each grayed cell indicates an empirical implication specified at the top of the column. Light grey cells identify overlapping, dark gray cells unique predictions, and cells with horizontal lines control variables. The numbering tracks the increasing number of predictions over time. Numbers with a decimal digit identify more specific updates of earlier implications.

whether there were significant shifts in frames, or whether the frames were layered on top of each other, thus suggesting an abductive updating.

- *Cell shading.* Cells colored in light grey indicate overlapping implications of the two theories being paired. Darker grey cells identify unique predictions. Dotted cells indicate earlier implications that have been replaced by more specific ones. Cells with horizontal lines point to control variables. The strike-through number identifies the earlier prediction, for which a null-finding has been stipulated.
- *Cell numbering.* The number of cells filled by each theory provides a first indication of its empirical footprint. The empirical implications also are numbered across theories; in this way we keep track of their overall number, which the literature has proposed at any given moment in time. The numbering increases each time a theory hypothesizes a new implication. A decimal point indicates updated predictions that become more specific. The first digit identifies the earlier prediction that was updated. Columns with entirely empty cells suggest either an empirically irrelevant causal factor or a latent factor that has not been theorized yet. The theory ledger can serve the counterfactual function of looking for potentially known unknowns, that is, implications as yet untheorized.

With the mechanics now explained, let me apply the theory ledger to the three populism theses to illustrate how it makes more transparent the updating at the center of Bayesian process tracing and the abductive logic of CHA more generally.

In this stylized example, the process tracing began in 2016, after Trump's unexpected presidential victory. It draws on the trade and technology theories used to explain the rise of populism at earlier points in the history and of other democracies. These initial theories had a very small empirical footprint: they made only five predictions, which were not specific, diverse, or unique. This changed by the fourth research cycle, when the literature had grown to fourteen implications that were unique and specific and pitted a cultural against an economic theory. The theory ledger thus simply converts the earlier arrow diagrams into a more formalized framework, making it easier for us to track the updating process.

What, then, are the benefits of devising and populating this theory ledger, which is, after all, a time-consuming undertaking? Moreover, how should scholars think of deploying such a theory ledger, given that this is its first presentation? I have more definitive answers to the first question, about benefits, than for the second question, about how to deploy the ledger. Let me talk about benefits first.

Broadly speaking, the theory ledger underscores that test results are insufficient to generate sound causal inferences, as they also must be converted into answers. And this conversion involves three tacit elements of causal inferences that are frequently overlooked: reading, foregrounding confounders, and a fox-like cognitive mindset. The three elements are so interwoven with the pre-testing, testing and post-testing stages that they are nearly invisible, even though they play a crucial role in making valid causal inferences.

Careful, Analytical Reading. The very costs the theory ledger imposes on scholars is the price paid for the close and careful analytical reading of the various theories. Each theory ledger must be tailored to a specific literature and requires close reflection on what empirical predictions theories make, into what frame they belong, whether the proposed frames are adequate or need to be amended, and how similar, specific, and diverse the predictions are. It forces scholars to apply to theories a set of analytical criteria that those theories do not use themselves. The theory ledger thus requires the sort of translation process that is possible only by carefully interpreting the analytical categories with the particulars of a theory and by bringing them into conversation through attentive reading (Adler and Van Doren 1972, 301–26). Abbott (2004, 18) rightly points out that "reading documents *seems* easy but it *is* difficult." This point applies just as much to reading theories as it does to documents. It compels scholars to be mindful of what they test, and thus increases confidence in causal inferences by assessing the testworthiness of the hypotheses. It also serves as a reminder of how frequently works are cited in support of claims that, on closer inspection, cannot be found in those works.

Foregrounding Confounders. The theory ledger provides a benchmark for identifying overlooked confounders. It requires parsing theories into their environmental, structural, and eventful factors as well as distinguishing between historical and physical time. This differentiation will draw attention to causal factors that a particular theory overlooks and that could bias causal inferences. The ledger – not unlike formal mathematical models – serves the function to impose a degree of analytical or, in this case, ontological rigor. But it has an advantage over mathematical models: it does not require us to freeze geography, history, and physical time to a degree where theorizing becomes empirically so circumscribed that it backgrounds numerous confounders. In so many ways, the theory ledger brings us back where we started as it invites us to make historical thinking more systematic.

Fox-Like Cognitive Mindset. The ability to exercise close analytical reading and to leverage historical thinking in order to evaluate theories from different ontological perspectives adds up to what the psychologist Philip Tetlock (2005), borrowing from Isaiah Berlin, called "a fox-like mindset." Tetlock has spent his career trying first to understand how to measure the quality of predictions and then to identify the factors that explain the variations in their quality. His findings are relevant for process tracing, which also makes predictions and differs only in that it evaluates them with data from the past. Tetlock used the fox analogy to highlight a mode of thinking that shares important elements with process tracing, historical thinking, and CHA more generally. He associates fox-like thinking with a willingness to think inductively (abduction), tolerate complexity (non-linear causality), embrace multidisciplinarity (freezing and unfreezing history and geography), and update (research cycle) (see Silver 2012, 17–45; Tetlock 2005). He links these attributes to the multiple strategies that a fox, living in the wild, employs when evading predators – by comparison with the single one employed by the hedgehog. The theory ledger foregrounds these elements of fox-like thinking that are implicit in process tracing and that play a crucial, albeit tacit, role in improving the quality of causal inferences. It involves a causal identification strategy that does not limit itself to how the data or the cases were selected but incorporates a broader set of equally important factors.

I believe that these benefits are significant enough for us to use the theory ledger to engage more systematically with different theories. The ledger also has the potential to track not just theoretical predictions but also empirical findings. Illustrating this, however, would takes us too far afield.

Exercises

10.1. Process tracing places considerable emphasis on generating tests that are strong because its empirical implications are both specific and unique. So I would like you to generate three tests: each one should pair two hypotheses that vary in strength. Just to underscore, this is largely a make-belief exercise. So do not get too hung up on the particulars of your theories and empirical implications. Be playful and creative.

Proceed along the following steps:

1. Follow the populism example and formulate three theories that explain Mr. Robinson's death in E. H. Carr accident example. Two of the theories should be rather similar and the third should be very different in its substantive claims. Label the theories using catchy titles.

2. Create your own theory ledger on the basis of Figure 10.1. Fill it in and modify it as necessary. Break down each theory into its individual empirical implications. Label each empirical implication and enter it into a cell located in the column closely matching its predictions (e.g., Mr. Jones' speeding might fall under maximizing motivation, the assumption being that he wanted to get home as fast as possible).

3. Construct two tests: the first one should be weak and the second one strong. Identify how the tests differ in the uniqueness and specificity of their implications and how this affects their strength.

4. In which of the four test strength boxes (Table 10.1) would you place them?

10.2. Daniel Gingerich and Jan Vogler's (2021) article on the very, very longue durée origins of German voting behavior offers an interesting counterpoint to the accounts given by Ziblatt and Anderson. Gingerich and Vogler's article is interesting because of its sheer theoretical ambition of linking the Black Death in the fourteenth century with voting outcomes in the 1870s and 1930s. It is part of a genre of so-called persistence arguments. CHA generally views such arguments skeptically, because they tend to be very deterministic and have poorly specified causal mechanisms. But Gingerich and Vogler's argument is particularly explicit about the causal mechanisms, and thereby provides an interesting test case for the validity of persistence arguments. And, if we juxtapose it with Ziblatt's piece, it opens an opportunity to evaluate the testworthiness of their hypotheses and the strength of their tests.

What foreknowledge do Gingerich and Vogler cite that warrants exploring the link between pandemics and voting behavior in section 3 of their paper? How much prior work do they cite that has explored this connection, as opposed to the impact of pandemics on labor markets and institutions? What is the disciplinary background of the works cited in their literature, and how diverse is it? Can you think of literatures and disciplines that have the relevant sort of expertise and were not cited? How many prior research cycles appear to ground their hypotheses? Given the foreknowledge they cite, how would you rate the prior probability that we could have confidence in any subsequent results? How does Ziblatt's literature review differ from that of Gingerich and Vogler? What prior probability would you assign to Ziblatt's default hypothesis? Would you rate it higher or lower? Why?

Now let us turn to the testworthiness of Gingerich and Vogler's various hypotheses. For example, how plausible is it to link the Black Death with voting in the 1870s and 1930s? How effectively do Gingerich and Vogler explain the timing of the Nazis' electoral rise in the 1930s? Gingerich and Vogler identify two reproduction mechanisms, serfdom legacy and participative institutions, to link the labor market effects of the Black Death to subsequent voting outcomes. How plausible are particularly the effects of the participative institutions that emerged between 1300 and 1500 in exerting a causal effect in 1871 and 1932/1933? How does their test of those causal mechanisms differ from Ziblatt's process tracing? How much does their respective empirical analysis of these causal mechanisms increase confidence in their overall test results? How do Gingerich and Vogler address the potentially confounding effects of Germany's territorial reorganization during the Napoleonic Wars, the gradual expansion of Prussia, Germany's unification, and the collapse of imperial Germany after 1918? Conjecture on the role that abduction played in the generation of their hypotheses.

To what extent does Ziblatt's analysis suffer from a potential endogeneity problem, in the sense that landholding inequality is not the uncaused first cause and Ziblatt overlooks the deeper causal origins of the Black Death that Gingerich and Vogler link to landholding inequalities? In what ways does extending the causal chain back to the Black Death improve our confidence in Ziblatt's findings? If you want to explore this problem of infinite regress further, please read the interesting article by Dan Slater and Erica Simmons (2010).

Let us finish up by comparing the test construction. What alternative theory do Gingerich and Vogler present to challenge their persistence theory? How well developed, for example, is the theory of elite reaction, to which they refer on page 8? Are the control variables discussed on page 20 linked to a specific and competing theory, or are they introduced in an ad hoc manner? Do we know enough about alternative explanations to assess the uniqueness and specificity of their empirical implications? How would you contrast Gingerich and Vogler's test construction with that of Ziblatt? How do they differ in terms of strength, and why?

Assign a subjective probability to the confidence you have in their findings on the basis of the test results. By how much does your confidence increase after you have read their 70-page appendix? How extensively does the appendix leverage CHA to turn results into answers? (optional) How much confidence do you place in the theoretical argument? Explain any discrepancy between that confidence and that of the test results. What would be the case for characterizing Gingerich and Vogler's analysis as one that engages in historical tourism? What would be the case against it?

Conclusion
Different Origins and Shared Complementarities

> It would be a mistake to assume that democracy was just invented once
> and for all as, for example the steam engine.... Like fire or painting or
> language, democracy seems to have been invented more than once, and in
> more than one place.
>
> (Dahl 1998, 9)

So here we are, having translated comparative historical analysis' (CHA)
numerous vernaculars into a single grammar of time in order to highlight
how it leverages the methodological riches of history. Where do we go
from here?

Let me look at history one last time and draw the broader implications of
this book.

CHA's distinct origins story, alluded to in the epigraph to this chapter
provides clues for CHA's complementarities with other methodological traditions. Talking about democracy, Robert Dahl (1998, 9) asked whether we
should think about its genesis by analogy with the steam engine, which was
invented once and then copied elsewhere, or by analogy with language, which
was created in different locations independently, and thus in slightly different
ways. CHA fits the origins story of language – hence its many vernaculars –
while other methods follow the steam engine trajectory – having distinct
founders or adhering to a specific notion of causality. The fact that CHA
emerged independently in each discipline helps understand on the one hand
the halting dialogue among its various disciplinary members and on the other
hand its complementarities with other research traditions.

The more fully articulated grammar of time should improve the dialogue
among the variegated CHA vernaculars. It lowers the entry barriers for those
interested in learning CHA by demonstrating that its various charter literatures share a set of practices and a broader conception of social science.
Historical institutionalists, economic historians, American political development scholars, international relation constructivists, historical sociologists,
path dependency scholars, Austrian economists, and anyone else who is
interested in history will more readily recognize their elective affinities and
the opportunities they open for further dialogue. They will appreciate more
fully a common temporal vocabulary, shared exploratory strategies, and a

cogent, albeit broader, conceptualization of social inquiry. The grammar of time should assuage lingering concerns that CHA constitutes an inscrutable craft, learnable only through a long apprenticeship with one of its masters. So much for the book's contributions to CHA.

But what about the skeptics who continue to believe in a narrower, more exclusive steam engine version of social science and whose epistemological aspirations are too ambitious for them to settle for a mere grammar? How to respond to scholars convinced that the arc of social science bends from anachronistic language to modern, mathematically modeled steam engines or, to update the metaphor, to artificial intelligence? The book already hinted at answers to these questions. It did so most directly by refusing to engage the very premise on which they rest – namely that different methods compete for epistemological gold in some unspoken methodological Olympiad. This pernicious premise invariably leads methodological discussions down the same old unproductive rabbit wholes. David Collier, a long-time CHA veteran, together with Henry Brady, David Friedman, Jason Seawright, and, before them, Stanley Lieberson, Theda Skocpol, and Andrew Abbott, have valiantly tried to move past these tired debates by emphasizing the complementarities of different methods (Brady and Collier 2004).

The present book contributes to these efforts by highlighting how historical and physical time – two elements that these earlier scholars overlooked – can improve the dialogue across different methodological traditions. It discusses how the freezing of history backgrounds important confounding factors, just as the freezing of physical time masks the non-linear causal effects of tempo, duration, timing, and sequencing. It repeatedly returns to Christie Aschwande's line: it is easy to get results but difficult to get answers. I found this line so appealing because it eviscerates traditional methodological boundaries and makes it clear that there can be no explanation without description, no testing without exploration. It highlights that the key elements of CHA – historical thinking, abduction, the research cycle – complement rather than compete with the more technical testing strategies of variance-based analysis (VBA). Aschwande's line also recognizes that translating answers – at least tentative ones known as hypotheses – into results is a far better understood process than the inverse – at which CHA excels – of translating results into answers. The book highlights four contributions – historical thinking, ontological transparency, testworthiness of hypotheses, and heterodoxy – that CHA makes in addressing this imbalance and in translating results more effectively into answers.

Historical Thinking. I linked CHA closely to historical thinking – the ability to unfreeze history and geography – and to the opportunities it opens for exploring social reality unconstrained by methodological or theoretical precedents. I pointed out that the key question for different methods is not whether, but when historical thinking takes place in the broader research process. VBA differs from CHA by engaging in historical thinking *after* it has obtained test results. It leverages historical thinking to assess the external validity of results by using history to identify confounders that could in principle bias those results. Natural experiments, regression discontinuity designs, and instrumental variables – the favorite tools of the recent causal inference "revolution" – all leverage historical discontinuities, and hence depend on historical thinking to validate these quasi-experimentations (Kalyvas and Federowycz 2022). This dependence, if adequately acknowledged, amounts to historical thinking being leveraged by its most unlikely champions – economists. Historical thinking is thus inescapable and becomes an element shared across different methods. And CHA's more explicit methodological treatment of historical thinking should facilitate exploring still further the role it plays across methodologies presumed to be ontological strangers.

Ontological Transparency. In acknowledging the inescapability of historical thinking, CHA places ontological transparency at the center of its methodological concerns and recognizes Sartori's (1970, 1033) exhortation to social scientists that they become "conscious thinkers" – being aware of the ontological construction of concepts – and thus avoid "unconscious thinking" – paying no attention to the historical and geographic boundary conditions of a concept – as well as foregoing "over-conscious thinking" – constructing concepts to meet the ontological requirements of a particular method. Ontological transparency contributes to this kind of conscious thinking by highlighting that causal inferences should be subject not just to statistical but also to *ontological robustness checks.* Such checks relate to CHA's insight that freezing historical and physical time is essential to getting results, but unfreezing them is equally essential to verifying whether the results offer answers. Chapter 2 showed that historical thinking is not a single activity but comes in four distinct varieties linked to cyclical, bounded, serial, and eventful history. Each type of historical thinking involves a distinct freezing of history that makes social reality ontologically compatible with the ontological assumptions that a particular method makes. Yet this very freezing also comes with the realization that history must be *unfrozen* if we want to verify the test results. Eventful analysis, as the most unfrozen form of historical time, plays a particularly central role in exploring social reality to identify potential confounders, since it is unconstrained by methodological and theoretical strictures. Freezing and unfreezing history thus constitute a dialectical process designed to first produce results and then translate them into answers. Chapter 7 demonstrated that freezing physical time produces linear causality, which ignores the effects of tempo, duration, timing, and sequencing. Freezing historical time and physical time permits statistical robustness checks, while unfreezing them allows ontological robustness checks. Such checks pay attention to the confounding effects of temporal heterogeneity, just as replications, which extend test results to new cases, consider the confounding effects of geographic heterogeneity. The call for greater ontological transparency is a call to place the confounding effects of historical and physical time at the same level as those of geographic particularities. This slipping in and out of different types of temporal thinking – a key element in abduction – requires ontological transparency to bring readers along when we discuss which notions of historical and physical time are employed and what role they play in validating causal inferences.

It is unclear why ontological transparency and robustness remain in the almost exclusive purview of CHA. The focus on enhancing research transparency has been the proper response to the replication crisis and to placing social science on more solid methodological foundations (Jacobs and Büthe 2021; Lupia and Elman 2014). But those efforts could be further enhanced if they placed on the transparency of ontological choices the same emphasis as they currently place on the transparency of data gathering and data analysis (Kreuzer and Parsons 2021). Choosing the type of history or causality leaves just as many logistical traces as coding or sampling the data, since both involve judgments. So why not talk about ontological judgments with the same frankness as about judgments related to the handling of data? The availability of annotation for transparent inquiry (ATI) makes it possible to document those judgments while still remaining within given word limits.

Testworthiness of Hypothesis. CHA's conceptualization of methodology as research cycles means that it treats its own findings as *epistemological objects in motion*, objects that require a close Bayesian or historiographically inspired dialogue with the existing foreknowledge. CHA is therefore reluctant to treat all hypotheses as being created equal; it pays close attention instead to their testworthiness. It wants to know *what is being tested*, not just how it is being tested. CHA judges testworthiness in two ways. First, it defines itself as problem-driven and treats testworthiness as involving hypotheses that address important substantive issues. Second, its abductive logic – its focus on theorizing and test strength – requires a close dialogue across theories. This dialogue is central to avoiding the ad hoc testing of hypotheses that received little support in prior research and are theoretically poorly grounded, paired against weak alternatives, and untestworthy. CHA's abduction shares the historians' historiographical sensibilities, which prioritize a close, empathetic, and dialectical reading supported by prior scholarship and a longstanding preference for weighty footnotes over the "drive-by" kind of literature review that oversells the authors' hypothesis and undersells the contributions of their competitors. It adheres to the caustic dictum that Giovanni Sartori passed on to us, his graduate students: the easiest way to be innovative is to be ignorant. Social scientists should insist on the right to understand *what* is being tested and not just *how* it is tested; this right is analogous to a new right in the high-tech sector for which there is an increasing demand: the customers' right to repair, which opposes disingenuous corporate claims that the growing complexity of products make closer scrutiny by customers unsustainable.

CHA shares with other methods this attention to the testworthiness of hypotheses. Statistical methods have long emphasized the importance of having good theories to limit p-hacking and to increase confidence that statistically significant co-variations are indeed causal (Achen 2002; Huber 2013; Walt and Mearsheimer 2013). Bayesian analysis does not treat all hypotheses as equal, but establishes the prior probability of their being true through a careful, historically informed vetting process that increases the probability that the results will offer answers later on. We already saw how this Bayesian attention to theorizing worked its way into CHA via process tracing. CHA contributes to these conversations by paying close attention to the construction of theories and concepts and by bringing an insider view of their strengths and limitations.

Inescapability of Heterodoxy. The book repeatedly characterized CHA's methodology as heterodox in order to differentiate it from the orthodox, math-based underpinnings of VBA. It linked this heterodoxy to CHA's effort to bridge the exploratory, descriptive pre-testing stage of the research process with the subsequent stage, which is explanatory and confirmatory. This bridging effort raises the question of how useful the initial differentiation and the more extensive attention to the later confirmatory stage are in the first place. Is VBA not just as heterodox as CHA? VBA, for example, must explore in order to come up with questions, develop concepts in order to measure, theorize in order to construct tests, and pay attention to history and geography in order to specify boundary conditions. This is readily admitted by King, Keohane, and Verba (1994, 13) – the three influential VBA stalwarts. They point out that formulating research questions and theory is part of the research, even though they remain hidden because "investigators take down the scaffolding after putting up their intellectual building, leaving little trace of the agony and uncertainty of its construction." These authors even emphasize the importance of describing before setting out to explain (34). But, like many others, they do not follow up on the full methodological implications of acknowledging the pre-testing elements of social inquiry. They quickly invoke ontological assumptions that all but eliminate historical thinking, and then proceed to expand on the technicalities of causal inference. In the case of King et al. (1994, 91–7), this meant giving advice on how to increase the number of observations. This pattern raises the question whether VBA's acknowledgment of the exploratory stage of research does not end up being more of an empty rhetorical gesture than a full-fledged commitment to give equal treatment to testing and exploration and to think their complementarities through.

This empty gesture and CHA's emphasis on bridging exploration and confirmation invite discussions about the usefulness of this distinction. Let me conclude by looking at history – one very, very last time – to suggest what direction this conversation could take.

The division between exploration and confirmation goes back to the late nineteenth-century dispute on method – *Methodenstreit* – between German and Austrian economists to which referred in Chapter 9 and particularly to the logical positivists' efforts to divide the scientific method into a separate domain of exploration and one of confirmation. Many of these logical positivists lived in interwar Vienna, were Jewish, and belonged to the *haute bourgeoisie*. In part, they devised this distinction as a rhetorical ruse, to respond both to Nazis' efforts to dismiss some theories as being Jewish and to communists' attempts to banish others as being bourgeois. The logical positivists sought to counter such attacks by exiling the early stages – descriptive, theory-generating – of the research process to what they considered to be a pre-scientific, exploratory domain and by limiting actual science to the more formalized, more mathematical, and hence ideologically less readily maligned stage of causal inference (Appleby, Hunt, and Jacob 2011, 167–73). Historically speaking, then, methodological orthodoxy owes its origins to the Nazis' and the communists' epistemological cancel culture rather than being a realistic reflection of the actual scientific process. Logical positivists wagered that it would be more difficult to cancel mathematics than theory. And this rhetorical subterfuge had important consequences, because it not only severed exploration and confirmation but also assigned a very different epistemological prestige to each. I am not about to pin the blame for marginalizing history squarely on Nazis and communists; other factors contributed too. For example, it is easier to teach formalized techniques grounded in mathematics, devoid of different vernaculars, and deployable without requiring attention to the complexities of time (Abbott 2004; Becker 1998; Walt and Mearsheimer 2013). Still, the historical origins of this fundamental division are instructive, because they highlight how the sequencing of epistemology and empirical research shape how the non-CHA traditions conceptualize methodology. The variance-based traditions, which began with the postwar behavioral revolution, followed the orthodox, steam engine version of social science that logical positivists had articulated. It was thus founded on epistemological first principles that were more orthodox and placed methods before questions. By contrast, CHA predates the logical positivists' severing of exploration and confirmation by a good half century, and thus evolved into a more heterodox, language-like fashion. Instead of being guided by first principles, it pragmatically responded to the challenge of finding methodological solutions to answer important macro-historical questions. Ultimately it escaped the logical positivists' effort to sever exploration and confirmation and stuck to its heterodox tradition of bringing the exploratory, descriptive domain of research within the purview of methodology and of encouraging a dialogue with its confirmatory, more technical sibling. CHA lives by the credo (as Barrington Moore might have put it, where he not such a methodological curmudgeon) no heterodoxy, no answers.

Exercises

11.1. CHA scholars often operate in a steam-engine–dominated world that evaluates research according to conventional VBA criteria. They consequently face the challenge of having to talk to the proverbial reviewer or dissertation committee member 2, who raises methodological objections that are unaware of the methodological differences between VBA and CHA projects.[1] Let us assume that you are a young James Morone working on what will eventually become *Republic of Wrath*. You got two "revise and resubmits" and one rejection that raises the following objections: "No clear rationale justifying the case selection. The paper is too descriptive. It lacks a clear causal identification strategy (previously referred to as research design). The findings are not generalizable." How would you respond to such criticisms? Read Morone's (2020, 1–28) introduction in preparation for this exercise. In short, expand on the CHA credo "no heterodoxy, no answer" in rebutting the criticisms of reviewer 2. Or adapt this exercise and draw on your own reviewer 2 experiences. What objections did such reviewers raise and what sort of answers might CHA offer to rebut them?

11.2. CHA's mantra of aligning methods with questions does not come with precise guidelines but requires more informal bricolage-style judgments. Anderson, Ziblatt, Gingerich, and Vogler all use research designs that both do and don't overlap. How appropriate are these designs, *given* the research questions they seek to answer? What exactly are their research questions and what are their ontological properties (i.e., how much do

---

[1] I borrow the term "member 2" from Joe Soss (2021).

they freeze history and geography)? What would Ziblatt, Gingerich, and Vogler have to do to convert their VBA analysis into more of a historical explanation? How would they have to convert their reproduction mechanisms into more generative mechanisms? What would Anderson have to do convert her narrative explanation into a more CHA-like historical explanation? Gingerich and Vogler also use the Black Death as a natural experiment. How central is this natural experiment to increasing your confidence in their results? Contrast their natural experiment with Daron Acemoglu et al.'s (2011) use of the French Revolution to explain variations in Germany's industrialization. Would the French Revolution have been a better natural experiment? Which one provides the better as-if randomization? How important is the temporal proximity of natural experiments to the phenomenon explained to leverage its control functions?

Bibliography

Abbott, Andrew. 1984. "Event Sequence and Event Duration: Colligation and Measurement." *Historical Methods* 17(4): 192–204.

1988. "Transcending General Linear Reality." *Sociological Theory* 6(2): 169–86.

1991. "History and Sociology: The Lost Synthesis." *Social Science History* 15(2): 201–38.

2004. *Methods of Discovery: Heuristics for the Social Sciences.* New York: W. W. Norton.

2016. *Digital Paper: A Manual for Research and Writing with Library and Internet Materials.* Chicago: University of Chicago Press.

Abrams, Philip. 1982. *Historical Sociology.* Ithaca, NY: Cornell University Press.

Acemoglu, Daron, Davide Cantoni, Simon Johnson, and James Robinson. 2011. "From Ancien Régime to Capitalism: The Spread of the French Revolution as a Natural Experiment." In *Natural Experiments of History*, ed. Jared Diamond and James Robinson. Cambridge, MA: Harvard University Press, 224–56.

Acemoglu, Daron, Simon Johnson, and James A. Robinson. 2001. "The Colonial Origins of Comparative Development: An Empirical Investigation." *American Economic Review* 91(5): 1369–401.

Acharya, Avidit, Matthew Blackwell, and Maya Sen. 2016. "The Political Legacy of American Slavery." *Journal of Politics* 78(3): 621–41.

Achen, Christopher H. 2002. "Toward a New Political Methodology: Microfoundations and ART." *Annual Review of Political Science* 5(1): 423–50.

Adams, Julia, Elisabeth S. Clemens, and Ann Shola Orloff, eds. 2005a. *Remaking Modernity: Politics, History, and Sociology.* Durham, NC: Duke University Press.

2005b. "Social Theory, Modernity, and the Three Waves of Historical Sociology." In *Remaking Modernity: Politics, History, and Sociology*, ed. Julia Adams, Elisabeth S. Clemens, and Ann Shola Orloff. Durham, NC: Duke University Press, 1–74.

Adler, Mortimer, and Charles Van Doren. 1972. *How to Read a Book*, rev. ed. New York: Simon & Schuster.

Ahmed, Amel. 2013. *Democracy and the Politics of Electoral System Choice: Engineering Electoral Dominance.* Cambridge: Cambridge University Press.

Ahmed, Amel, and Rudra Sil. 2012. "When Multi-Method Research Subverts Methodological Pluralism: or, Why We Still Need Single-Method Research." *Perspectives on Politics* 10(04): 935–53.

Alesina, Alberto, and Edward L. Glaeser. 2004. *Fighting Poverty in the US and Europe: A World of Difference.* Oxford: Oxford University Press.

Aminzade, Ronald. 1992. "Historical Sociology and Time." *Sociological Methods and Research* 20(4): 456–80.

Anderson, Margaret Lavinia. 1993. "Voter, Junker, Landrat, Priest: The Old Authorities and the New Franchise in Imperial Germany." *American Historical Review* 98(5): 1448–74.

Andeweg, Rudy B. 2000. "Consociational Democracy." *Annual Review of Political Science* 3(1): 509–36.

Andrews, Josephine T., and Robert W. Jackman. 2005. "Strategic Fools: Electoral Rule Choice under Extreme Uncertainty." *Electoral Studies* 24(1): 65–84.

Ankeny, Rachel. 2010. "Using Cases to Establish Novel Diagnoses." In *How Well Do Facts Travel? The Dissemination of Reliable Knowledge*, ed. Peter Howlett and Mary Morgan. Cambridge: Cambridge University Press, 252–72.

Appleby, Joyce, Lynn Hunt, and Margaret Jacob. 2011. *Telling the Truth about History.* New York: W. W. Norton.

Aschwande, Christie. 2015. "Science Isn't Broken." *FiveThirtyEight*, August 19. http://fivethirtyeight.com/features/science-isnt-broken.

Baldwin, Peter. 1990. *The Politics of Social Solidarity: Class Bases of the European Welfare State, 1875–1975.* Cambridge: Cambridge University Press.

Barkey, Karen. 1996. "In Different Times: Scheduling and Social Control in the Ottoman Empire, 1550 to 1650." *Comparative Studies in Society and History* 38 (3): 460–83.

Barry, Brian. 1988. *Sociologists, Economists, and Democracy.* Chicago: University of Chicago Press.

Bartolini, Stefano. 1993. "On Time and Comparative Research." *Journal of Theoretical Politics* 5(2): 131–67.

2000. *The Political Mobilization of the European Left, 1860–1980.* Cambridge: Cambridge University Press.

Barzachka, Nina S. 2014. "When Winning Seats Is Not Everything: Tactical Seat-Loss During Democratization." *Comparative Politics* 46(2): 209–29.

Bates, Robert H. et al. 1998. *Analytic Narratives.* Princeton, NJ: Princeton University Press.

Beach, Derek. 2020. "Multi-Method Research in the Social Sciences: A Review of Recent Frameworks and a Way Forward." *Government and Opposition* 55(1): 163–82.

Beach, Derek, and Rasmus Brun Pedersen. 2013. *Process-Tracing Methods: Foundations and Guidelines.* Ann Arbor: University of Michigan Press.

Beck, Naomi, and Ulrich Witt. 2019. "Austrian Economics and the Evolutionary Paradigm." *Studies in Logic, Grammar and Rhetoric* 57(1): 205–25.

Becker, Howard. 1998. *Tricks of the Trade.* Chicago: University of Chicago Press.

2007. *Telling about Society.* Chicago: University of Chicago Press.

Bennett, Andrew. 2014. "Disciplining Our Conjectures: Systematizing Process Tracing with Bayesian Analysis." In *Process Tracing*, ed. Andrew Bennett and Jeffrey Checkel. New York: Cambridge University Press, 276–98.

Bennett, Andrew, Andrew E. Charman, and Tasha Fairfield. 2021. "Understanding Bayesianism: Fundamentals for Process Tracers." *Political Analysis* 30(2): 1–8.

Bennett, Andrew, and Jeffrey Checkel. 2014. "Process Tracing: From Philosophical Roots to Best Practices." In *Process Tracing*, ed. Andrew Bennett and Jeffrey Checkel. New York: Cambridge University Press, 3–38.

Bernhard, Michael. 2015. "Chronic Instability and the Limits of Path Dependence." *Perspectives on Politics* 13(4): 976–91.

Bernhard, Michael, and Jan Kubik. 2014. *Twenty Years after Communism: The Politics of Memory and Commemoration*. Oxford: Oxford University Press.

Bernstein, Steven, Richard Ned Lebow, Janice Gross Stein, and Steven Weber. 2000. "God Gave Physics the Easy Problems." *European Journal of International Relations* 6(1): 43–76.

Bjornerud, Marcia. 2018. *Timefulness: How Thinking like a Geologist Can Help Save the World*. Princeton, NJ: Princeton University Press.

Blackbourn, David, and Geoff Eley. 1984. *The Peculiarities of German History*. Oxford: Oxford University Press.

Blais, André. 2005. "To Adopt or Not to Adopt Proportional Representation: The Politics of Institutional Choice." *British Journal of Political Science* 35(1): 182–90.

Blyth, Mark. 2006. "Great Punctuations: Prediction, Randomness, and the Evolution of Comparative Political Science." *American Political Science Review* 100(4): 493–8.

Boettke, Peter J., Christopher J. Coyne, and Peter T. Leeson. 2013. "Comparative Historical Political Economy." *Journal of Institutional Economics* 9(3): 285–301.

Boix, Carles. 1999. "Setting the Rules of the Game: The Choice of Electoral Systems in Advanced Democracies." *American Political Science Review* 93(3): 609–24.

2010. "Electoral Markets, Party Strategies, and Proportional Representation." *American Political Science Review* 104(2): 404–13.

Boswell, John, Jack Corbett, and R. A. W. Rhodes. 2019. *The Art and Craft of Comparison*. New York: Cambridge University Press.

Brady, Henry, and David Collier. 2004. *Rethinking Social Inquiry: Diverse Tools, Shared Standards*. Lanham, MD: Rowman & Littlefield.

Braudel, Fernand. 1980. *On History*. Chicago: University of Chicago Press.

Braunias, Karl. 1932. *Das parlamentarische Wahlrecht*. Berlin: De Gruyter.

Brown, Richard H. 1976. "Social Theory as Metaphor: On the Logic of Discovery for the Sciences of Conduct." *Theory and Society* 3(2): 169–97.

Bryant, Joseph M. 1994. "Evidence and Explanation in History and Sociology: Critical Reflections on Goldthorpe's Critique of Historical Sociology." *British Journal of Sociology* 45(1): 3–19.

Butler, David. 1963. *The Electoral System in Britain since 1918*. Oxford: Clarendon.

Butterfield, Herbert. 1965. *The Whig Interpretation of History*. New York: W. W. Norton.

Calvo, Ernesto. 2009. "The Competitive Road to Proportional Representation: Partisan Biases and Electoral Regime Change under Increasing Party Competition." *World Politics* 61(02): 254–95.

Campbell, Peter. 1965. *French Electoral Systems and Elections since 1789*. Hamden, CT: Archon Books.

Capoccia, Giovanni, and R. Daniel Kelemen. 2007. "The Study of Critical Junctures: Theory, Narrative, and Counterfactuals in Historical Institutionalism." *World Politics* 59(03): 341–69.

Capoccia, Giovanni, and Daniel Ziblatt. 2010. "The Historical Turn in Democratization Studies." *Comparative Political Studies* 43(8–9): 931–68.

Caramani, Daniele. 2003. "The End of Silent Elections: The Birth of Electoral Competition, 1832–1915." *Party Politics* 9(4): 411–43.

Carr, Edward Hallett. 1961. *What Is History?* New York: Vintage.

Carr, Nicholas. 2008. "Is Google Making Us Stupid?" *The Atlantic* 107(2): 89–94.

Carstairs, Andrew McLaren. 1980. *A Short History of Electoral Systems in Western Europe.* New York: Routledge.

de Carvalho, Benjamin, Halvard Leira, and John M. Hobson. 2011. "The Big Bangs of IR: The Myths That Your Teachers Still Tell You about 1648 and 1919." *Millennium: Journal of International Studies* 39(3): 735–58.

Chakrabarty, Dipesh. 2008. *Provincializing Europe: Postcolonial Thought and Historical Difference.* Princeton, NJ: Princeton University Press.

Christakis, Nicholas. 2021. *Apollo's Arrow: The Profound and Enduring Impact of Coronavirus on the Way We Live.* New York: Little, Brown Spark.

Cirone, Alexandra, and Thomas B. Pepinsky. 2021. "Historical Persistence." *Annual Review of Political Science* 25: 241–59.

Cohen, Dov, Joseph Vandello, Sylvia Puente, and Adrian Rantilla. 1999. "'When You Call Me That, Smile!' How Norms for Politeness, Interaction Styles, and Aggression Work Together in Southern Culture." *Social Psychology Quarterly* 62(3): 257–75.

Cohen, Elizabeth F. 2018. *The Political Value of Time: Citizenship, Duration, and Democratic Justice.* Cambridge: Cambridge University Press.

Collier, David, and James E. Mahon. 1993. "Conceptual 'Stretching' Revisited: Adapting Categories in Comparative Analysis." *American Political Science Review* 87(4): 845–55.

Collier-Berins, Ruth, and David Collier. 1991. *Shaping the Political Arena.* Princeton, NJ: Princeton University Press.

Colomer, Josep M. 1998. "Electing Popes. Approval Balloting with Qualified-Majority Rule." *Journal of Interdisciplinary History* 29(1): 1–22.

2004. "The Strategy and History of Electoral System Choice." In *Handbook of Electoral System Choice,* ed. Josep Colomer. Houndmills: Palgrave, 3–80.

2005. "It's Parties That Choose Electoral Systems (or, Duverger's Laws Upside Down)." *Political Studies* 53: 1–21.

2007. "On the Origins of Electoral Systems and Political Parties: The Role of Elections in Multi-Member Districts." *Electoral Studies* 26(2): 262–73.

Conrad, Sebastian. 2017. *What Is Global History?* Princeton, NJ: Princeton University Press.

Cook, Earl. 1971. "The Flow of Energy in an Industrial Society." *Scientific American* 225 (3): 134–44.

Cowan, Robin, and Mario J. Rizzo. 1996. "The Genetic–Causal Tradition and Modern Economic Theory." *Kyklos* 49(3): 273–317.

Cox, Gary W., Jon H. Fiva, and Daniel M. Smith. 2019. "Parties, Legislators, and the Origins of Proportional Representation." *Comparative Political Studies* 52(1): 102–33.

Coyle, Diane. 2015. *GDP: A Brief but Affectionate History*. Princeton, NJ: Princeton University Press.

Cummins, Denise. 2012. *Good Thinking. Seven Powerful Ideas That Influence the Way We Think*. New York: Cambridge University Press.

Cusack, Thomas R., Torben Iversen, and David Soskice. 2007. "Economic Interests and the Origins of Electoral Systems." *American Political Science Review* 101(03): 373–91.

2010. "Coevolution of Capitalism and Political Representation: The Choice of Electoral Systems." *American Political Science Review* 104(02): 393–403.

Dahl, Robert. 1971. *Polyarchy*. New Haven, CT: Yale University Press.

1998. *On Democracy*. New Haven, CT: Yale University Press.

Diamond, Jared. 2017. *Guns, Germs, and Steel: The Fates of Human Societies*. New York: W. W. Norton.

Diamond, Jared, and James Robinson, eds. 2011. *Natural Experiments of History*. Cambridge, MA: Harvard University Press.

Dixon, Jennifer M. 2018. *Dark Pasts: Changing the State's Story in Turkey and Japan*. Ithaca, NY: Cornell University Press.

Duffy, Bobby. 2021. *The Generation Myth: Why When You're Born Matters Less Than You Think*. New York: Basic Books.

Eckelberry, Robert Lee. 1964. "The Swedish System of Proportional Representation." PhD, University of Nebraska.

Eliade, Mircea. 1949. *The Myth of the Eternal Return: Cosmos and History*. Princeton, NJ: Princeton University Press.

Elklit, Jorgen. 1992. "The Best of Both Worlds? The Danish Electoral System 1915–20 in a Comparative Perspective." *Electoral Studies* 11(3): 189–205.

Elman, Colin, and Diana Kapiszewski. 2018. "The Qualitative Data Repository's Annotation for Transparent Inquiry (ATI) Initiative." *PS: Political Science & Politics* 51(1): 3–6.

Elman, Colin, and Miriam Fendius Elman. 2001. *Bridges and Boundaries: Historians, Political Scientists, and the Study of International Relations*. Cambridge, MA: MIT Press.

Elster, Jon. 1983. *Explaining Technical Change*. Cambridge: Cambridge University Press.

2000. "Rational Choice History: A Case of Excessive Ambition." *American Political Science Review* 94(3): 685–95.

2015. *Explaining Social Behavior: More Nuts and Bolts for the Social Sciences*. Cambridge: Cambridge University Press.

Emmenegger, Patrick, and André Walter. 2019. "When Dominant Parties Adopt Proportional Representation: The Mysterious Case of Belgium." *European Political Science Review* 11(4): 1–18.

Ermakoff, Ivan. 2015. "The Structure of Contingency." *American Journal of Sociology* 121(1): 64–125.

2019. "Causality and History: Modes of Causal Investigation in Historical Social Sciences." *Annual Review of Sociology* 45(1): 581–606.

Esping-Andersen, Gøsta. 1990. *The Three Worlds of Welfare Capitalism*. Cambridge: Cambridge University Press.

Evans, Richard. 1997. *In Defense of History*. New York: W. W. Norton.

Evera, Stephen Van. 1997. *Guide to Methods for Students of Political Science*. Ithaca, NY: Cornell University Press.

Fairfield, Tasha, and Andrew Charman. 2019. "A Dialogue with the Data: The Bayesian Foundations of Iterative Research in Qualitative Social Science." *Perspectives on Politics* 17(1): 154–67.

Falleti, Tulia. 2005. "A Sequential Theory of Decentralization: Latin American Cases in Comparative Perspective." *American Political Science Review* 99(3): 327–46.

Falleti, Tulia, and James Mahoney. 2015. "The Comparative Sequential Method." In *Advances in Comparative Historical Analysis: Resilience, Diversity, and Change*, ed. James Mahoney and Kathleen Thelen. New York: Cambridge University Press, 211–39.

Ferguson, Niall. 2000. *Virtual History: Alternatives and Counterfactuals*. New York: Basic Books.

Finer, Samuel Edward. 1975. *Adversary Politics and Electoral Reform*. London: Anthony Wigram.

Finnemore, Martha, and Kathryn Sikkink. 2001. "The Constructivist Research Program in International Relations and Comparative Politics." *Annual Review of Political Science* 4(1): 391–416.

Fioretos, Orfeo, Tulia G. Falleti, and Adam Sheingate, eds. 2016. *The Oxford Handbook of Historical Institutionalism*. Oxford: Oxford University Press.

Firestein, Stuart. 2012. *Ignorance: How It Drives Science*. Oxford: Oxford University Press.

2015. *Failure: Why Science Is So Successful*. Oxford: Oxford University Press.

Fischer, David Hackett. 1970. *Historians' Fallacies: Toward a Logic of Historical Thought*. New York: Harper & Row.

Fischhoff, Baruch. 1982. "For Those Condemned to Study the Past: Heuristics and Biases in Hindsight." In *Judgment under Uncertainty: Heuristics and Biases*, ed. Daniel Kahneman, Paul Slovic, and Amos Tversky. Cambridge: Cambridge University Press, 335–51.

Flynn, James. 2009. *What Is Intelligence? Beyond the Flynn Effect*. Cambridge: Cambridge University Press.

Foner, Eric. 2017. "Opinion | Confederate Statues and 'Our' History." *New York Times*, August 20.

Freese, Lee, and Milton Rokeach. 1979. "On the Use of Alternative Interpretations in Contemporary Social Psychology." *Social Psychology Quarterly* 42(3): 195–201.

Friendly, Michael, and Howard Wainer. 2021. *A History of Data Visualization and Graphic Communication*. Cambridge, MA: Harvard University Press.

Gaddis, John Lewis. 2002. *The Landscape of History*. Oxford: Oxford University Press.

Gaikwad, Nikhar, and Veronica Herrera. Forthcoming. "Transparency for Text-Based Sources: From Principles to Practice." *Perspectives on Politics*.

George, Alexander, and Andrew Bennett. 2004. *Case Studies and Theory Development in the Social Sciences*. Cambridge, MA: MIT Press.

Gerring, John. 2003. "APD from a Methodological Point of View." *Studies in American Political Development* 17(01): 82–102.

2012a. "Mere Description." *British Journal of Political Science* 42(04): 721–46.

2012b. *Social Science Methodology* (2nd ed.). New York: Cambridge University Press.

Gerschenkron, Alexander. 1962. *Economic Backwardness in Historical Perspective*. Cambridge, MA: Harvard University Press.

Gibbon, Edward. 1788. *The History of the Decline and Fall of the Roman Empire*. London: A. Strahan and T. Cadell.

Gilovich, Thomas. 1993. *How We Know What Isn't So*. New York: Free Press.

Gingerich, Daniel, and Jan Vogler. 2021. "Pandemics and Political Development: The Electoral Legacy of the Black Death in Germany." *World Politics* 73(3): 393–440.

Gladwell, Malcolm. 2006. *The Tipping Point: How Little Things Can Make a Big Difference*. London: Little, Brown.

2007. "None of the Above: What IQ Doesn't Tell You about Race." *New Yorker*, December 17, pp. 1–8.

2008. *Outliers: The Story of Success*. London: Little, Brown.

2011. "The Order of Things. What College Ranking Really Means." *New Yorker*, February 14, pp. 68–75.

Go, Julian, and George Lawson. 2017. "For a Global Historical Sociology." In *Global Historical Sociology*, ed. Julian Go and George Lawson. Cambridge: Cambridge University Press, 1–34.

Goertz, Gary. 2012. *Social Science Concepts: A User's Guide*. Princeton, NJ: Princeton University Press.

Goldstone, Jack A. 2000. "The Rise of the West – or Not? A Revision to Socio-Economic History." *Sociological Theory* 18(2): 175–94.

Goldthorpe, John. 1991. "The Uses of History in Sociology: Reflections on Some Recent Tendencies." *British Journal of Sociology* 42(2): 211–30.

1994. "The Uses of History in Sociology: A Reply." *British Journal of Sociology* 45(1): 55–77.

2001. "Causation, Statistics, and Sociology." *European Sociological Review* 17(1): 1–20.

Gordon, Robert. 2017. *The Rise and Fall of American Growth*. Princeton, NJ: Princeton University Press.

Gorman, Sara, and Jack Gorman. 2016. *Denying to the Grave: Why We Ignore the Facts That Will Save Us*. Oxford: Oxford University Press.

Gosden, Chris. 2018. *Prehistory: A Very Short Introduction*. (2nd ed.). Oxford: Oxford University Press.

Grafton, Anthony. 1999. *The Footnote: A Curious History*. Cambridge, MA: Harvard University Press.

Grew, Raymond. 1980. "The Case for Comparing Histories." *American Historical Review* 85(4): 763–78.

Griffin, Larry J., and Larry W. Isaac. 1992. "Recursive Regression and the Historical Use of 'Time' in Time-Series Analysis of Historical Process." *Historical Methods* 25(4): 166–79.

Grofman, Bernard, and Arend Lijphart, eds. 2002. *The Evolution of Electoral and Party Systems in the Nordic Countries.* New York: Agathon Press.

Grzymala-Busse, A. 2011. "Time Will Tell? Temporality and the Analysis of Causal Mechanisms and Processes." *Comparative Political Studies* 44(9): 1267–97.

Hacker, Jacob. 2002. *The Divided Welfare State.* Cambridge: Cambridge University Press.

Hagstrom, Robert. 2013. *Investing: The Last Liberal Art.* New York: Columbia University Press.

Hall, Edward Twitchell. 1984. *The Dance of Life: The Other Dimension of Time.* Garden City, NY: Anchor Press/Doubleday.

Hall, Peter. 2003. "Aligning Ontology and Methodology in Comparative Politics." In *Comparative Historical Analysis in the Social Sciences,* ed. James Mahoney and Dietrich Rueschemeyer. Cambridge: Cambridge University Press, 373–406.

   2008. "Systematic Process Analysis: When and How to Use It." *European Political Science* 7(3): 304–17.

Hanson, Stephen E., and Jeffrey S. Kopstein. 2005. "Regime Type and Diffusion in Comparative Politics Methodology." *Canadian Journal of Political Science* 38(1): 69–99.

Hardarson. 2002. "The Icelandic Electoral System, 1844–1999." In *The Evolution of Electoral and Party Systems in the Nordic Countries,* ed. Bernard Grofman and Arend Lijphart. New York: Agathon Press, 101–64.

Hart, Nicky. 1994. "John Goldthorpe and the Relics of Sociology." *British Journal of Sociology* 45(1): 21–30.

Hassner, Ron E. 2007. "The Path to Intractability: Time and the Entrenchment of Territorial Disputes." *International Security* 31(3): 107–38.

   2011. "Sacred Time and Conflict Initiation." *Security Studies* 20(4): 491–520.

Haydu, Jeffrey. 1998. "Making Use of the Past: Time Periods as Cases to Compare and as Sequences of Problem Solving." *American Journal of Sociology* 104(2): 339–71.

Henrich, Joseph. 2020. *The WEIRDest People in the World: How the West Became Psychologically Peculiar and Particularly Prosperous.* New York: Farrar, Straus and Giroux.

Heuer, Richard. 1999. *The Psychology of Intelligence Analysis.* Washington, DC: Center for the Study of Intelligence.

Hobden, Stephen, and John Hobson, eds. 2001. *Historical Sociology of International Relations.* Cambridge: Cambridge University Press.

Huber, John. 2013. "Is Theory Getting Lost in the 'Identification Revolution'?" *The Monkey Cage,* June 14. http://themonkeycage.org/2013/06/is-theory-getting-lost-in-the-identification-revolution.

Hunt, Lynn. 2008. *Measuring Time, Making History.* Budapest: Central European University Press.

   2014. *Writing History in the Global Era.* New York: W. W. Norton.

Iversen, Torben, and David Soskice. 2019. *Democracy and Prosperity: Reinventing Capitalism through a Turbulent Century*. Princeton, NJ: Princeton University Press.

Jacobs, Alan M. 2008. "The Politics of When: Redistribution, Investment and Policy Making for the Long Term." *British Journal of Political Science* 38(2): 193–220.

Jacobs, Alan M., and Tim Büthe. 2021. "The Qualitative Transparency Deliberations: Insights and Implications." *Perspectives on Politics* 19(1): 1–18.

Janoski, Thomas, and Larry W. Isaac. 1994. "The Comparative Political Economy of the Welfare State." In *Introduction to Time Series Analysis*, ed. Thomas Janoski and Alexander Hicks. Cambridge: Cambridge University Press, 31–53.

Jervis, Robert. 1998. *System Effects: Complexity in Political and Social Life*. Princeton, NJ: Princeton University Press.

Kalyvas, Stathis, and Fedorowycz, Daniel. 2022. "The Delphi Syndrome: Using History in the Social Sciences." In *History in the Humanities and the Social Sciences*, ed. Richard Bourke and Quentin Skinner. Cambridge: Cambridge University Press, 116–40.

Karabell, Zachary. 2014. *The Leading Indicators: A Short History of the Numbers That Rule Our World*. New York: Simon & Schuster.

Katz, Richard, and Peter Mair. 1995. "Changing Models of Party Organization and Party Democracy." *Party Politics* 1(1): 1–16.

Katznelson, Ira. 2003. "Periodization and Preferences: Reflections on Purposive Action in Comparative Historical Social Science." In *Comparative Historical Analysis in the Social Sciences*, ed. James Mahoney and Dietrich Rueschemeyer. Cambridge: Cambridge University Press, 270–304.

Kern, Stephen. 1983. *The Culture of Time and Space, 1880–1918*. Cambridge, MA: Harvard University Press.

2004. *A Cultural History of Causality*. Princeton, NJ: Princeton University Press.

Kersh, Rogan. 2005. "Rethinking Periodization? APD and the Macro-History of the United States." *Polity* 37(4): 513–22.

King, Gary, Robert Keohane, and Sidney Verba. 1994. *Designing Social Inquiry: Scientific Inference in Qualitative Research*. Princeton, NJ: Princeton University Press.

Kiser, Edgar, and Michael Hechter. 1991. "The Role of General Theory in Comparative-Historical Sociology." *American Journal of Sociology* 97(1): 1–30.

Kiser, Edward, and Margaret Levi. 1996. "Using Counterfactuals in Historical Analysis." In *Counterfactual Thought Experiments in World Politics*, ed. Philip Tetlock and Aaron Belkin. Princeton, NJ: Princeton University Press, 187–207.

Kocher, Matthew, and Nuno Monteiro. 2016. "Lines of Demarcation: Causation, Design-Based Inference, and Historical Research." *Perspectives on Politics* 14(4): 952–74.

Kosellek, Reinhart. 2002. *The Practice of Conceptual History: Timing History, Spacing Concepts*. Paolo Alto, CA: Stanford University Press.

Krasner, Stephen D. 1984. "Approaches to the State: Alternative Conceptions and Historical Dynamics." *Comparative Politics* 16(2): 223–46.

Kreuzer, Marcus. 2001. *Institutions and Innovation: Voters, Parties, and Interest Groups in the Consolidation of Democracy: France and Germany, 1870–1939*. Ann Arbor: University of Michigan Press.

2003. "Parliamentarization and the Question of German Exceptionalism, 1867–1918." *Central European History* 36(3): 327–59.

2009. "How Party Systems Form: Path Dependency and the Institutionalization of the Post-War German Party System." *British Journal of Political Science* 39(04): 669–97.

2010. "Historical Knowledge and Quantitative Analysis: The Case of the Origins of Proportional Representation." *American Political Science Review* 104(02): 369–92.

2016. "Assessing Causal Inference Problems with Bayesian Process Tracing: The Economic Effects of Proportional Representation and the Problem of Endogeneity." *New Political Economy* 22(5): 473–83.

2019. "The Structure of Description: Evaluating Descriptive Inferences and Conceptualizations." *Perspectives on Politics* 17(1): 122–9.

2022. "Rules of Evidence and the Quality of Description: The Case of the Origins of Proportional Representation." Unpublished ms.

Forthcoming. "The Methodological Legacies of Skocpol's State and Social Revolutions: Locating the Three Pillars of Comparative Historical Analysis." *Politics*.

Kreuzer, Marcus, and Craig Parsons. 2021. "Epistemological and Ontological Priors: Varieties of Openness and Research Integrity." *Perspectives on Politics* 19(1): 186–87 and 1–17 (in Web Appendix).

Leamer, Edward. 1983. "Let's Take the Con out of Econometrics." *American Economic Review* 17(1): 31–43.

Leeman, Lucas, and Isabella Mares. 2014. "The Adoption of Proportional Representation." *Journal of Politics* 76(2): 461–78.

Lepore, Jill. 2011. *The Whites of Their Eyes: The Tea Party's Revolution and the Battle over American History*. Princeton, NJ: Princeton University Press.

Levitt, Steven, and Stephen Dubner. 2005. *Freakeconomics*. New York: Morrow.

Levy, Jack S. 1997. "Too Important to Leave to the Other: History and Political Science in the Study of International Relations." *International Security* 22(1): 22–33.

Lieberman, Evan. 2001. "Causal Inference in Historical Institutional Analysis. A Specification of Periodization Strategies." *Comparative Political Studies* 34(9): 1011–35.

2016. "Can the Biomedical Research Cycle Be a Model for Political Science?" *Perspectives on Politics* 14(4): 1055–68.

Lieberson, Stanley. 1985. *Making It Count: The Improvement of Social Theory and Research*. Berkeley: University of California Press.

Lijphart, Arend. 1968. "Typologies of Democratic Regimes." *Comparative Political Studies* 1(1): 3–44.

1969. "Consociational Democracy." *World Politics* 21(02): 207–25.

1971. "Comparative Politics and the Comparative Method." *American Political Science Review* 65(03): 682–93.

2012. *Patterns of Democracy: Government Forms and Performance in Thirty-Six Countries*. New Haven, CT: Yale University Press.

Lilla, Mark. 2016. *The Shipwrecked Mind: On Political Reaction*. New York: New York Review Books.

Linz, Juan. 1978. "Non-Competitive Elections in Europe." In *Elections without Choice*, ed. Guy Hermet, Richard Rose, and Alain Rouquie. New York: John Wiley, 36–65.

Lippmann, Walter. 1922. *Public Opinion*. New York: Harcourt, Brace.

Lipset, Seymour Martin. 1983. "Radicalism or Reformism: The Sources of Working-Class Politics." *American Political Science Review* 77(1): 1–18.

Little, Daniel. 1991. *Varieties of Social Explanation: An Introduction to the Philosophy of Social Science*. Boulder, CO: Westview Press.

Locke, Richard M., and Kathleen Thelen. 1995. "Apples and Oranges Revisited: Contextualized Comparisons and the Study of Comparative Labor Politics." *Politics & Society* 23(3): 337–67.

Lowenthal, David. 1986. *The Past Is a Foreign Country*. Cambridge: Cambridge University Press.

Lundell, Krister. 2010. *The Origins of Electoral Systems in the Postwar Era: A Worldwide Approach*. London: Routledge.

Lupia, Arthur, and Colin Elman. 2014. "Openness in Political Science: Data Access and Research Transparency." *PS: Political Science & Politics* 47(01): 19–42.

Lustick, Ian. 1996. "Read My Footnotes." *ASPA-CP Newsletter* 7(1): 6 & 10.

Lutz, Georg. 2000. "Der Beschwerliche Weg Zum Allgemeinen (Manner-) Wahlrecht Im 19. Jahrhundert." Unpublished ms., Bern University.

Macdonald, Paul K. 2009. "Those Who Forget Historiography Are Doomed to Republish It: Empire, Imperialism and Contemporary Debates about American Power." *Review of International Studies* 35(1): 45–67.

Mahoney, James. 1999. "Nominal, Ordinal, and Narrative Appraisal in Macrocausal Analysis." *American Journal of Sociology* 104(4): 1154–96.

2000. "Path Dependence in Historical Sociology." *Theory and Society* 29: 507–47.

2004. "Comparative–Historical Methodology." *Annual Review of Sociology* 30(1): 81–101.

Mahoney, James, and Gary Goertz. 2004. "The Possibility Principle: Choosing Negative Cases in Comparative Research." *American Political Science Review* 98 (4): 653–69.

Mahoney, James, and Kathleen Thelen. 2010. "A Theory of Gradual Institutional Change." In their *Explaining Institutional Change: Ambiguity, Agency, and Power*. Cambridge: Cambridge University Press, 1–38.

Mann, Michael. 1994. "In Praise of Macro-Sociology: A Reply to Goldthorpe." *British Journal of Sociology* 45(1): 37–54.

March, James, and Johan Olsen. 1984. "The New Institutionalism: Organizational Factors of Political Life." *American Political Science Review* 78(3): 734–49.

Marks, Gary, Heather A. D. Mbaye, and Hyung Min Kim. 2009. "Radicalism or Reformism? Socialist Parties before World War I." *American Sociological Review* 74(4): 615–35.

Marx, Karl, and Friedrich Engels. 1986. *The Communist Manifesto*. Harmondsworth: Penguin.

Mavrogordatos, George. 1982. *Stillborn Republic: Social Coalitions and Party Strategies in Greece, 1922–1936*. Berkeley: University of California Press.

Menand, Louis. 2021. *The Free World: Art and Thought in the Cold War*. New York: Farrar, Straus and Giroux.

Mettler, Suzanne, and Richard Valelly. 2018. "The Distinctiveness and Necessity of American Political Development." In *Oxford Handbook of American Political Development*, ed. Richard Valelly, Suzanne Mettler, and Robert Lieberman. Oxford: Oxford University Press, 2–29.

Møller, Jørgen. 2016. *State Formation, Regime Change, and Economic Development*. London: Taylor & Francis.

2021. "Reading History Forward." *PS: Political Science & Politics* 54(2): 249–53.

Moore, Barrington. 1966. *The Social Origins of Dictatorship and Democracy*. Boston, NJ: Beacon Hill.

Moravcsik, Andrew. 2010. "Active Citation: A Precondition for Replicable Qualitative Research." *PS: Political Science and Politics* 43(1): 29–35.

Moretti, Franco. 2005. *Graphs, Maps, Trees: Abstract Models for a Literary History*. London: Verso.

Morgan, Edmund Sears. 1988. *Inventing the People: The Rise of Popular Sovereignty in England and America*. New York: W. W. W. Norton.

Morone, James A. 2020. *Republic of Wrath: How American Politics Turned Tribal, From George Washington to Donald Trump*. New York: Basic Books.

Morris, Ian. 2011. *Why the West Rules–for Now: The Patterns of History, and What They Reveal About the Future*. New York: Picador.

2013. *The Measure of Civilization: How Social Development Decides the Fate of Nations*. Princeton, NJ: Princeton University Press.

Mukherjee, Siddhartha. 2016. "The Improvisational Oncologist." *New York Times*, May 12.

Munck, Gerardo L., and Richard Snyder. 2008. *Passion, Craft, and Method in Comparative Politics*. Baltimore, MD: John Hopkins University Press.

Munck, Gerardo L., and Jay Verkuilen. 2002. "Conceptualizing and Measuring Democracy Evaluating Alternative Indices." *Comparative Political Studies* 35(1): 5–34.

North, Douglass C. 1977. "The New Economic History after Twenty Years." *American Behavioral Scientist* 21(2): 187–200.

North, Douglass C., and Robert Paul Thomas. 1976. *The Rise of the Western World: A New Economic History*. Cambridge: Cambridge University Press.

Ogle, Vanessa. 2013. "Whose Time Is It? The Pluralization of Time and the Global Condition, 1870s–1940s." *American Historical Review* 118(5): 1376–1402.

Orren, Karen, and Stephen Skowronek. 2004. *The Search for American Political Development*. Cambridge: Cambridge University Press.

Orwell, George. 1961. *1984*. New York: Signet Classic.

Palagashvili, Liya, Ennio Piano, and David Skarbek. 2017. *The Decline and Rise of Institutions*. 1st ed. Cambridge University Press.

Parsons, Craig. 2007. *How to Map Arguments in Political Science.* Oxford: Oxford University Press.

Paxton, Robert O. 1998. "The Five Stages of Fascism." *Journal of Modern History* 70(1): 1–23.

Penadés, Alberto. 2008. "Choosing Rules for Government: The Institutional Preferences of Early Socialist Parties." In *Controlling Governments. Voters, Institutions, and Accountability*, ed. José Maria Maravall and Ignacio Sanchéz-Cuenca. Cambridge: Cambridge University Press, 202–46.

Pepinsky, Thomas B. 2019. "The Return of the Single-Country Study." *Annual Review of Political Science* 22: 187–203.

Pierson, Paul. 1994. *Dismantling the Welfare State: Reagan, Thatcher and the Politics of Retrenchment.* Cambridge: Cambridge University Press.

  2000a. "Increasing Returns, Path Dependence, and the Study of Politics." *American Political Science Review* 94(2): 251–67.

  2000b. "Not Just What, but When: Timing and Sequence in Political Processes." *Studies in American Political Development* 14(1): 72–92.

  2003. "Big, Slow-Moving and Invisible: Macrosocial Processes in the Study of Comparative Politics." In *Comparative Historical Analysis in the Social Sciences*, ed. James Mahoney and Dietrich Rueschemeyer. Cambridge: Cambridge University Press, 177–207.

  2004. *Politics in Time: History, Institutions, and Social Analysis.* Princeton, NJ: University Press.

Piketty, Thomas. 2017. *Capital in the Twenty-First Century.* Cambridge, MA: Harvard University Press.

Pilon, Dennis. 2013. *Wrestling with Democracy: Voting Systems as Politics in the Twentieth-Century West.* Toronto: University of Toronto Press.

Pink, Daniel H. 2018. *When: The Scientific Secrets of Perfect Timing.* New York: Riverhead Books.

Playfair, William. 1805. An Inquiry into the Permanent Causes of the Decline and Fall of Powerful and Wealthy Nations. London: Greenland & Norris.

Pomeranz, Kenneth. 2001. *The Great Divergence: China, Europe, and the Making of the Modern World Economy.* Princeton, NJ: Princeton University Press.

Przeworski, Adam. 2019. *Crises of Democracy.* Cambridge: Cambridge University Press.

Przeworski, Adam, and Henry Teune. 1970. *The Logic of Comparative Social Inquiry.* New York: John Wiley.

Ragin, Charles. 1987. *The Comparative Method.* Berkeley: University of California Press.

Reese, Michael J., Keven G. Ruby, and Robert A. Pape. 2017. "Days of Action or Restraint? How the Islamic Calendar Impacts Violence." *American Political Science Review* 111(3): 439–59.

Reinhart, Carmen, and Kenneth Rogoff. 2011. *This Time Is Different: Eight Centuries of Financial Folly.* Princeton, NJ: Princeton University Press.

Renwick, Alan. 2010. *The Politics of Electoral Reform: Changing the Rules of Democracy.* Cambridge: Cambridge University Press.

Rokkan, Stein. 1968a. "Elections." In *International Encyclopedia of the Social Sciences*, ed. David Sills. New York: MacMillan, 6–19.

1968b. "The Structuring of Mass Politics in the Smaller European Democracies: A Developmental Typology." *Comparative Studies in Society and History* 10(2): 173–210.

Rosenberg, Daniel, and Anthony Grafton. 2010. *Cartographies of Time: A History of the Timeline*. Princeton, NJ: Princeton Architectural Press.

Rueschemeyer, Dietrich. 2009. *Usable Theory: Analytic Tools for Social and Political Research*. Princeton, NJ: Princeton University Press.

Rustow, Dankwart. 1970. "Transitions to Democracy." *Comparative Politics* 2(2): 337–63.

Sachs, Jonathan. 2012. "1786/1801: William Playfair, Statistical Graphics, and the Meaning of an Event." Branch. www.branchcollective.org/?ps_articles=jonathan-sachs-17861801-william-playfair-statistical-graphics-and-the-meaning-of-an-event.

Samman, Amin. 2019. *History in Financial Times*. Stanford, CA: Stanford University Press.

Santucci, Jack. 2017. "Party Splits, Not Progressives: The Origins of Proportional Representation in American Local Government." *American Politics Research* 45 (3): 494–526.

Sartori, Giovanni. 1970. "Concept Misformation in Comparative Politics." *American Political Science Review* 64(4): 1033–53.

Schaffer, Frederic. 2015. *Elucidating Social Science Concepts: An Interpretivist Guide*. New York: Routledge.

2021. "Two Ways of Comparing." In *Rethinking Comparison: Innovative Methods for Qualitative Political Inquiry*, ed. Erica S. Simmons and Nicholas Rush Smith. Cambridge: Cambridge University Press, 47–63.

Schanbacher, Eberhard. 1982. *Parliamentarische Wahlen und Wahlsystem in der Weimarer Republik*. Düsseldorf: Droste Verlag.

Scheve, Kenneth, and David Stasavage. 2009. "Institutions, Partisanship, and Inequality in the Long Run." *World Politics* 61(2): 215–53.

Schiffman, Zachary Sayre. 2011. *The Birth of the Past*. Baltimore, MD: John Hopkins University Press.

Schröder, Valentin, and Philip Manow. 2014. "Elektorale Koordination, legislative Kohäsion und der Aufstieg der modernen Massenpartei: Die Grenzen des Mehrheitswahlrechts im deutschen Kaiserreich, 1890–1918." *Parlamentarische Vierteljahresschrift* 55(3): 518–54.

Sewell, William. 1996. "Three Temporalities: Toward an Eventful Sociology." In *The Historic Turn in the Human Sciences*, ed. Terrence J. McDonald. Ann Arbor: University of Michigan Press, 245–80.

2009. *Logics of History: Social Theory and Social Transformation*. Chicago: University of Chicago Press.

Silver, Nate. 2012. *The Signal and the Noise*. New York: Penguin.

Simmons, Erica, and Nicholas Smith, eds. 2021. *Rethinking Comparison: Innovative Methods for Qualitative Political Inquiry*. Cambridge: Cambridge University Press.

Simmons, Joseph P., Leif D. Nelson, and Uri Simonsohn. 2011. "False-Positive Psychology Undisclosed Flexibility in Data Collection and Analysis Allows Presenting Anything as Significant." *Psychological Science* 22(11): 1359–66.

Singh Grewal, David. 2014. "The Laws of Capitalism." *Harvard Law Review* 124: 628–67.

Skocpol, Theda. 1979. *States and Social Revolutions: A Comparative Analysis of France, Russia and China.* Cambridge: Cambridge University Press.

1984. *Vision and Method in Historical Sociology.* Cambridge: Cambridge University Press.

Skocpol, Theda, and Eric Schickler. 2019. "A Conversation with Theda Skocpol." *Annual Review of Political Science* 22: 1–16.

Skocpol, Theda, and Margaret Somers. 1980. "The Uses of Comparative History in Macrosocial Inquiry." *Comparative Studies in Society and History* 22(2): 174–97.

Slater, Dan, and Erica Simmons. 2010. "Informative Regress: Critical Antecedents in Comparative Politics." *Comparative Political Studies* 43(7): 886–917.

Smith, Adam. 1977. *An Inquiry into the Nature and Causes of the Wealth of Nations.* Chicago: University of Chicago Press.

Smith, Dennis. 1984. "Discovering Facts and Values: The Historical Sociology of Barrington Moore." In *Vision and Method in Historical Sociology,* ed. Theda Skocpol. Cambridge: Cambridge University Press, 313–55.

Smith, Jason Scott. 1998. "The Strange History of the Decade: Modernity, Nostalgia, and the Perils of Periodization." *Journal of Social History* 32(2): 263–85.

Soga, Masashi, and Kevin J. Gaston. 2018. "Shifting Baseline Syndrome: Causes, Consequences, and Implications." *Frontiers in Ecology and the Environment* 16 (4): 222–30.

Soss, Joe. 2021. "On Casing a Study versus Studying a Case." In *Rethinking Comparison: Innovative Methods for Qualitative Political Inquiry,* ed. Erica S. Simmons and Nicholas Rush Smith. Cambridge: Cambridge University Press, 84–106.

Stasavage, David. 2011. *States of Credit: Size, Power, and the Development of European Polities.* Princeton, NJ: Princeton University Press.

Steinmetz, George. 2008. "The Colonial State as a Social Field: Ethnographic Capital and Native Policy in the German Overseas Empire Before 1914." *American Sociological Review* 73(4): 589–612.

Steinmetz, Willibald, Zoltán B. Simon, and Kirill Postoutenko. 2021. "Temporal Comparisons: Evaluating the World through Historical Time." *Time & Society* 30(4): 1–15.

Sternberger, Dolf, Bernhard Vogel, and Dieter Nohlen. 1969. *Die Wahl der Parlamente: Ein Handbuch.* Berlin: De Gruyter.

Stinchcombe, Arthur L. 1968. *Constructing Social Theories.* Chicago: University of Chicago Press.

Swedberg, Richard. 2014. *The Art of Social Theory.* Princeton, NJ: Princeton University Press.

2018. "On the Near Disappearance of Concepts in Mainstream Sociology." In *Concepts in Action,* eds. H. Leiulfsrud and P. Sohlberg. Leiden: Brill, 23–39.

Taleb, Nassim Nicholas. 2007. *The Black Swan: The Impact of the Highly Improbable.* New York: Random House.

Tannenwald, Nina. 2005. "Stigmatizing the Bomb: Origins of the Nuclear Taboo." *International Security* 29(4): 5–49.

Tarrow, Sidney. 1995. "Bridging the Quantitative–Qualitative Divide in Political Science." *American Political Science Review* 89(2): 471–4.

Tetlock, Philip. 1999. "Theory-Driven Reasoning about Plausible Pasts and Probable Futures in World Politics: Are We Prisoners of Our Preconceptions?" *American Journal of Political Science* 43(2): 335–66.

2005. *Expert Political Judgment: How Good Is It? How Can We Know?* Princeton, NJ: Princeton University Press.

Thelen, Kathleen. 1999. "Historical Institutionalism in Comparative Politics." *Annual Review of Political Science* 2(1): 369–404.

Thompson, Edward P. 1967. "Time, Work-Discipline, and Industrial Capitalism." *Past & Present* (38): 56–97.

Törnudd, Klaus. 1968. *The Electoral System of Finland.* London: Hugh Evelyn.

Toulmin, Stephen, and June Goodfield. 1965. *The Discovery of Time.* Chicago: University of Chicago Press.

Trachtenberg, Marc. 2006. *The Craft of International History: A Guide to Method.* Princeton, NJ: Princeton University Press.

2015. "Transparency in Practice: Using Written Sources." *Qualitative and Multi-Method Research Newsletter* 13(1): 13–17.

Tulis, Jeffrey K., and Nicole Mellow. 2018. *Legacies of Losing in American Politics.* Chicago: University of Chicago Press.

Vallely, Richard, Suzanne Mettler, and Robert Lieberman, eds. 2018. *Oxford Handbook of American Political Development.* Oxford: Oxford University Press.

Verney, Douglas V. 1957. *Parliamentary Reform in Sweden, 1866–1921.* Oxford: Clarendon.

Voigtlaender, Nico, and Hans-Joachim Voth. 2012. "Persecution Perpetuated: The Medieval Origins of Anti-Semitic Violence in Nazi Germany." *Quarterly Journal of Economics* 127(3): 1339–92.

Walt, Stephen, and John J. Mearsheimer. 2013. "Leaving Theory Behind: Why Hypothesis Testing Has Become Bad for IR." *European Journal of International Relations* 19(3): 427–57.

Walter, André, and Patrick Emmenegger. 2019. "Majority Protection: The Origins of Distorted Proportional Representation." *Electoral Studies* 59: 64–77.

Weyland, Kurt. 2016. "Crafting Counterrevolution: How Reactionaries Learned to Combat Change in 1848." *American Political Science Review* 110(2): 215–31.

Wilkerson, Isabel. 2020. *Caste: The Origins of Our Discontents.* New York: Random House.

Wineburg, Sam. 2001. *Historical Thinking and Other Unnatural Acts: Charting the Future of Teaching the Past.* Philadelphia: Temple University Press.

Wittenberg, Jason. 2015. "Conceptualizing Historical Legacies." *East European Politics & Societies* 29(2): 366–78.

Yom, Sean. 2015. "From Methodology to Practice: Inductive Iteration in Comparative Research." *Comparative Political Studies* 48(5): 616–44.

Zaks, Sherry. 2021. "Updating Bayesian(s): A Critical Evaluation of Bayesian Process Tracing." *Political Analysis* 29(1): 58–74.

Zerubavel, Eviatar. 2003. *Time Maps: Collective Memory and the Social Shape of the Past.* Chicago: University of Chicago Press.

Ziblatt, Daniel. 2009. "Shaping Democratic Practice and the Causes of Electoral Fraud: The Case of Nineteenth Century Germany." *American Political Science Review* 103 (1): 1–21.

2017. *Conservative Parties and the Birth of Democracy.* Cambridge: Cambridge University Press.

Ziegler, Donald Jenks. 1956. "Proportional Representation in the Social and Political Conflict in Germany, 1871–1920." PhD, University of Nebraska.

Index

Milton Keynes UK
Ingram Content Group UK Ltd.
UKHW020650070923
428198UK00006B/31